Praise f(
1

MW01094333

"I laughed all through the book until the end, where I became sad to have to say goodbye. I enjoyed myself that much."

- Night Owl Reviews

"...not only well-written and entertaining but downright hilarious. I have not laughed so hard while reading in quite a while. And when I mean laugh, I mean I laughed so hard I was screaming. Warning, do not read this book while on the toilet."

- Indie Eclective

"Tony Slater is very gifted at writing comically, and laughter accompanied every page I read at the account of his daily routine looking after animals, birds and reptiles of all shapes and sizes and degrees of ferocity. Despite the tomfoolery of the writing, Tony never forgets the seriousness of the work carried out by the rescue centre, he never forgets to inform us of the beauty and uniqueness of Ecuador, and more importantly, never forgets to reveal not only how much the animals came to mean to him in the short time he was there, but also how much the whole experience touched him. This is one I will read again if I ever need cheering up. It's a guaranteed tonic."

- Kath 'n' Kindle Book Reviews

"Absolutely brilliant book! I loved every bit of it. Tony has such a fun, absorbing way of writing and you can't help but be swept along on his adventure with him. He might be a self-confessed idiot abroad, but he comes across as an extremely likeable idiot. Definitely the sort of person you would want to go for a beer with, or at least share a bit of fried, cheesy Ecuadorian street-food with. Buy this book! You won't regret it."

– George Mahood, author of Free Country

I bought it on the spot just for the title. It is truly the most hilarious book I have ever read, and I've read some good ones. It was a "In-Starbucks-laughing-so-hard-the-tears-came-and-I was concerned I was going to pee myself" kind of reading experience."

– TravelingCrone.com

Praise for *'That Bear Ate My Pants!'*
by Tony James Slater
(cont.)

"I can completely imagine Tony standing and enthusiastically delivering each chapter to a wide-eyed audience whilst they think inside their heads *This guy is a little bit mental*."

– BookC*nt

"[The] writing captures your imagination immediately and paints a picture of a world I'm unlikely to see that is so vivid, that I feel I have been there with him, every step of the way. I sweated up and down the mountains, I avoided being eaten by the Jaguar, I too chased an unruly teenage bear around an enclosure; I loved every minute of it."

– WomanOnTheEdgeOfReality.com

Fun. Fun fun fun. Did I say fun? It's been so long since I've been able to read a story that I could describe that way. You can pick this up and set it down at will. Read a chapter or two, have a laugh or a gape at the page, then go back to it in a couple of days. An easy read, and an enjoyable one at that.

Intranuovo.com

…it's pee-your-pants funny. It's like a travelogue gone horribly amuck. Brilliant.

– Shéa MacLeod,
author of Kissed by Darkness

DON'T NEED THE WHOLE DOG!

By
Tony James Slater

Various THINGS
@*t* **Different** *Times*

ISBN-13: 978-1512054927
ISBN-10: 1512054925

Although this is a work of non-fiction, some names have been changed by the author.

An e-book edition of this title is also available.

This first paperback edition was printed by CreateSpace.

Cover Design by **Various Things At Different Times**
Formatted for paperback by **Heather Adkins**

Please visit the author's website for a selection of photographs that accompany this book:

www.TonyJamesSlater.com

Author's Note

Before we start, I'd like to thank all of the people mentioned in this book. Some of them were very helpful to me; others were so bloody useless that I got to write lots of funny things about them.

Part of me would like to apologise for this behaviour.

But only part of me.

Most of all, I'd like to thank Linda, for being one of the best friends it's possible to have; my family, for putting up with me writing about them (like they had a choice!) – and Krista, for things I can't tell you about until *at least* Book Three…

Once again, these stories are all true, apart from the occasional name-change.

And in case you were wondering, yes – they were all my fault.

Other books by
Tony James Slater:

That Bear Ate My Pants!
Kamikaze Kangaroos!
Can I Kiss Her Yet?

Yeah, I know! Still quite an empty page.
Well, you're holding Book 2. Books 3 & 4 are out there. And Book 5 is
now en route…
I promise!

DON'T NEED THE WHOLE DOG!

Contents

(Take a deep breath…)

Contents

(cont.)

For Paul

Still in those hearts
You left behind;
Just out of sight
Not out of mind.

Prologue

You know those moments, when you think you'll do something really brave? You convince yourself that you're ready, and screw your courage to the sticking point. You might even say things to yourself, like 'It can't be that bad,' or 'What's the worst that can happen?'

I remember those moments. I don't have many of them any more.

I'm starting to learn my lesson.

The poor dog, sound asleep, was carefully and strategically shaved.

Then a green cloth was draped over the top of him.

The cloth had a small square hole in it, which came to rest precisely over the dog's nut-sack, leaving his balls protruding from the middle of it.

I winced when the nurse gave them a forceful prod with one finger.

That would have woken me up, regardless of the anaesthetic.

But the nurse was just warming up.

Deciding everything was ready, she deftly grasped one testicle between fingers and thumb, and tugged it slightly away from the body.

I nearly dropped to the floor in sympathy when she squeezed the scrotum, tightening the sack to make its delicate contents more prominent.

Then she reached for the scalpel I was holding. She took it, raised it, aimed it and lowered…

And that was as much as I could take. Something about the coldness of the razor-sharp steel, the way it slid through that ball-sack, opening it up like a zipper – affected me *deeply*.

I had no choice.

I dropped my implements on the table, sprinted out of the back door and threw up in the washing machine.

Well, there are worse things to be sick into…

I'd seen a lot since my arrival in Thailand. Some of it beautiful; some, slightly less so. And then there were the things I could never un-see – like my first ever castration. Oh yes, I was living the dream, alright – even though bits of it seemed more like a nightmare.

But all that was nothing compared to what it had taken me to get this far…

The New World

A visit to modern-day America is fraught with danger.

And I'm not talking about gangs, and drugs, and drive-bys and Scientology.

I'm talking, almost before you get off the plane.

I'm talking Customs.

As I queued up to be stamped into the country, I was pulled out of the line and politely informed that I had to join a second, much shorter queue.

In front of me was a seven-foot tall black dude with magnificent dreadlocks all the way down to his arse. And no-one else.

Something told me this was the line for the body cavity search.

Now, I'm plenty scared of drugs and guns and all that other stuff – but there was something much more real, more *immediate*, about this situation.

I could almost hear the *snap!* of a rubber glove from up ahead.

None of the staff were smiling. Maybe they hadn't found their quota of concealments this month, and they were determined to get *something* out...

Or maybe it was just my imagination.

The Rasta-looking guy in front of me held strong in the face of a barrage of questions; he had a relaxed, kind of wearied attitude, as though he'd done this a thousand times before. With hair like that, he probably had.

Or else he was stoned.

Either way, he managed to get through the ordeal unscathed.

Then it was my turn.

The man behind the desk looked like the kind of guy who shaved twice before setting out in the morning. Everything about him was spotless. His crew-cut said he firmly believed he was every bit as vital at keeping America safe as his brothers in the marines. It was a fairly safe bet that he was not wired for comedy. I had to bury that urge, the one that makes me tell stupid jokes when I'm nervous – bury it deep. It was tough. It's a big urge.

"What is your purpose in visiting the United States?"

Damn it! I'd been waiting for him to ask if I was here for business or pleasure, so I could quirk an eyebrow and say 'both, I hope!' like the bad guy always does in spy movies.

That would have been a mistake. I could tell that already.

"I'm here to visit my sister," I said. The truth, and only the truth.

"Where're you from."

"England."

"And what's your sister doing here?"

"Oh, she's working. For Camp America."

"She's working, huh? Is she a US Citizen?"

"Yes, actually, despite the fact I'm British. She goes both ways. She's only my half-sister you see – in fact she used to be my half-brother, until she had the op. We share a daddy, but it's more of a 'who's your daddy?' kind of arrangement. So come to think of it, we might not be related at all…"

No, you're right. I didn't say that. I bit my tongue. Smart-mouthed comments would only make him want to probe my bottom. But oh! My heart still bleeds for that missed opportunity. Instead I told the guy my sister was (unsurprisingly) also English, and braced myself for the next inevitable question.

"So how come she's working here?"

"She has a J-1 Working Holiday Visa." I was ready for it. After all, I'd done the paperwork for her. Hell, I'd even applied for and accepted the job for her! Sort of like a 'Get-Off-Your-Arse-And-Go-Travel' present. She'd been so happy when she found out. Tears of joy, I recall. And those less-commonly reported strangling-sounds of joy, too.

The Customs Officer was glaring at me.

"And do you intend to work here?"

"Oh, no." Then, "No, sir!" I added. I felt sure he'd like that.

"Do you have a visa?"

"Erm? Visa? I thought… don't you give them here, on arrival? I'm just here as a tourist."

"Uh-huh. How long are you planning on staying in America?"

"Ah… about two weeks."

"Uh-huh. And how much money do you have?"

Money?

Shit!

Why the hell did that matter? I felt a small bead of sweat

gathering speed down my chest. I dug in my pockets. "I've got… uh… about fifty dollars…"

"FIFTY dollars! That's not going to get you very far in this country. I'm going to ask you again, *sir* – are you planning on looking for work in the US?"

"No! No, not at all. It's my mum. She's got all the money. When I meet up with her I'll have plenty. We didn't want to split it up, that's all."

The man eyeballed me for a good few seconds.

"I thought you said you were going to meet your sister." It was an accusation, not a question. This was turning ugly. Some fast explanation was required.

"My mum is already here," I told him. "She's also coming to meet my sister, then we'll travel around together. Mum has all the money because she flew in yesterday —"

"I'm going to ask you this once: how many members of your family have already entered this country?"

"Oh, just us. The three of us, I mean. Well, they've entered. I'm, ah, hoping to."

"And you all entered separately." He was accusing us again. Of what, I had no idea.

"Well, my mum and I were supposed to be on the same flight, but I had to delay mine because I lost my passport…"

"You LOST your PASSPORT?!" The guy's eyes positively bulged with the scale of this revelation.

Oh shit, I thought.

"So what's this?" he gave a sarcastic shake of the little brown book he was holding.

"Ah yes, well I had an emergency passport issued in 24 hours. They do it in Newport, in Wales."

"Oh yeah? 'Wales' huh? They do that here, too. Only they go to Mexico. How much did you pay for this?"

"No, no, it's real! Wales is a real place, honest! It's a country. They have the closest passport office to me because I live in Cardiff, which is *in* Wales."

He was not impressed.

"You know, a minute ago I could have sworn you told me you were English…"

It was a long time before they let me through. I remained unviolated by the narrowest of margins. I'd love to say my honesty won out in the end – but this was, after all, the Land of the Free… market. Eventually

I'd dug out my wallet and spread a stack of credit cards across the desk. They give them to you so easily as a student and I'd always known they would come in handy one day. Two of them were even gold and silver coloured, which whilst it means nothing at all in England (the third one had a horse on it), apparently makes a difference over there. Satisfied that I wasn't going to steal jobs from hard-working Americans to fund my adventures, they'd eventually let me go with a stern warning to 'get my passport sorted out'. I resisted the urge to point out (again) that it was perfectly fine – or to mention that I'd never done a hard day's paid work in my life.

Finally my mouth had gotten the message.

Sweaty and trembling, I grabbed my rucksack from its lonely perch on the long-vacant carousel and walked from the airport, glancing nervously around me.

Two armed police officers stood underneath a giant 'Welcome to Arizona!' sign. I kept my head down and tried not to look at them.

I looked far more like a drug smuggler than I had when I'd arrived.

The bus was clean and safe and mercifully free of weirdoes. I know that sounds harsh (and a bit hypocritical, coming from someone as weird as me), but wherever nutters roam, they always seem to seek me out. Seriously – if you're missing a nutter, come and look next to me. I collect the damn things. A friend once told me it's because I smile at people. This is not generally accepted behaviour in the western world, where most of us are too concerned with being robbed and/or stabbed to death to risk exchanging smiles with a stranger. In fact, one of the things that sets nutters apart from the rest of civilization is exactly this; they smile at people. I guess it's hardly surprising that most of them see me as a kindred spirit. And then gravitate towards me like flies on a fresh cow pat.

A giant concrete highway carried me out of the city of Phoenix, into a landscape of small green hills – which were quickly replaced by mostly-yellow hills covered with scrubby patches. Before long we were driving between sand dunes, which looked to be held together by the tenacious vegetation.

I saw my first ever full-size cactus, and that really made me feel like I was on holiday. Which, just for a change, I was.

Following the same massive road for almost three hours, we passed through several different weather systems, and geographies too – experiencing perfect blue skies over flatlands filled with wheat, then torrential rain over the rocky, broken desert. By the end of the trip we were in the forest, which I took as a good sign. I love trees. I find them sheltering and nurturing. Sadly, I don't think the feeling is mutual, on account of me having spent the last three months in Ecuador conducting the tree equivalent of genocide.

In a first for me in foreign bus journeys, I arrived on time and in the right place, more relaxed than when I started and still nutter-free. I reclaimed my rucksack from the bowels of the bus and turned to survey Flagstaff, Arizona. It was… quaint. And kind of brown. Well, they do call it 'The Copper State'. I could think of some less poetic descriptions, but then that's probably why I don't work for the local tourist board.

Four dusty figures, arranged in size order from miniature to giant, approached me as the bus pulled away. *Here we go*, I thought, *here come the crazies.*

And I was right.

The smallest silhouette was my mum – at four-foot-bugger-all, wearing bright blue shorts, an orange top and a floppy hat, she was one fishing rod short of being a garden gnome. My sister Gillian, standing next to her, was longer, leaner, and looked substantially less like a gnome. Next to her and longer, leaner still, was her new best friend – a particularly pretty Australian girl called Krista, who had predictably adopted the nick-name 'Roo'. And next to Roo loomed her new boyfriend, Richie – a towering slab of muscle, blonde haired and blue-eyed, he looked like the kind of all-American boy that even customs officials wouldn't doubt. Except that he was from New Zealand – and he was grinning madly at *everything*. I could tell straight away that we were going to get along.

That night we drank, in the lounge of cheerful little backpackers' hostel, and I did my best to punish those foolish officials who had let me into their precious country. I flouted the laws of the land and bought booze for my new friends, despite the fact that only my mum and I were old enough to drink there. It's bizarre; most Americans can drive at sixteen, and are allowed to own a gun at eighteen, yet almost none of them can legally drink until they turn twenty-one.

Madness!

Or maybe it's for the best. Seeing as how they all have guns. I have no desire to get shot for eyeing up some drunken teenager's girlfriend.

I told Gill about my narrow brush with US Customs.

She was fascinated by the tale. "And… did they?"

"No."

"Whew! So you nearly had your arse —"

"Shhh! Keep your voice down, will you!"

Then Gill did something I did not expect. She stood up. "Ladies and Gentlemen," she announced to the room, "this is my brother! And his anal cavity has not been violated recently!"

Then she sat down. There were a couple of sniggers from the far corner. Mum was staring at Gill in shock.

"You've changed," I told her.

It was true. She'd left home a scared, self-conscious, quiet little sister.

And she'd been cursing me most inventively for making her go.

All that was different now. I could tell by the way she spoke, the way she stood; Gill was becoming more and more… like me.

Poor girl.

Dealing With Loss

How did I lose my passport?

Easy.

One minute it was there, the next… gone.

I'd taken it out with me to get it photocopied, in case I lost it – and as a direct result of that precaution, the little bugger had vanished. Straight after, I'd gone shopping for stuff to take to America, because most of my clothes had been torn apart by wild animals. I'd arrived back from Ecuador with a gigantic (and very colourful) woolly hammock, and not much else but the clothes I was standing up in. And even they had blood stains on them.

It just didn't seem right to take them on holiday.

So I hit the town. Somewhere on my shopping spree, most likely in the changing rooms where I'd experienced the sensation of *new* jeans (defined as jeans that didn't have holes my balls would hang out of) – my passport and I had parted company.

This is not something you want to discover five hours before you're due to board an international flight.

My temper was the next thing due to be lost.

"Bastard, bastard, BASTARD! What the hell am I going to do?"

"Call the shop," Mum demanded. "Call every shop you went to. Check the car, check your coat, check your old jeans… what's left of them." She was on the case, understandably nervous as she was now facing the prospect of a solo trip to America.

It had been her idea (and her treat, since I was broke) that we fly together to the States, to meet my sister and bring her home after her three-month stint as a summer camp counsellor. Mum had made all the plans and arrangements on her own, which by itself was cause for concern – most days she struggled to place an order at McDonalds.

Seriously, this is an actual example of her conversation with the counter assistant:

Mum: "Can I have a Big Mac meal and… another Big Mac Meal.

Two Big Mac meals.

Assistant: "So, is that four meals?"

Mum: "No! Two meals. But one of them without the drink."

Ass*: "So, one meal, and one burger and fries."

Mum: "Yes. Two Big Mac meals…"

Ass: "Another two?"

Mum: "No! The same ones. And I'll have a cup of tea with one of them."

Ass: "The one with the drink?"

Mum: "No, the other one. Actually, with both. And…"

Ass: (sighing) "So, two Big Mac meals."

Mum: "Yes please! Two big mac meals. But no drinks."

Ass: "Ahhh? Is that with the drinks, or without?"

Mum: "Without, thank-you."

Ass: "Okay. So altogether that's two Big Macs?"

Mum: "No! Four! But the last ones without drinks."

Ass: "Ah! Okay. That's… two meals, and…"

Mum: "Actually I'll have a cup of tea with one of them."

Ass: (frantically pressing buttons) "Okay,"

Mum: "In fact, I'll have tea with both."

Ass: "Right…"

Mum: "Oh, but you know that first Big Mac?"

Ass: "Ah, yes?"

Mum: "Can that one be coffee instead?"

Ass: "I think so…"

Mum: "And can you take the pickle off that one?"

Ass: "Um… I think so."

Mum: "Actually, don't worry about it. I'll have that one. Take the pickle off one of the others."

It's only because McDonalds employ the finest university graduates in the UK that we manage to get any food at all. And the best thing about it? We order the exact same thing every time we go there!

(*I'd like to apologise to McDonalds employees worldwide about how this abbreviation turned out. If it's any consolation, I know exactly who was being the ass in that little episode!)

Ah, Mum!

We love to let her do it.

And we *love* to take the piss out of her afterwards – it's like a family tradition.

However, it highlights a trait in her that she is well aware of.

She's not the most organised person in the world – and she flaps like a pissed-off penguin.

She really, really didn't want to go it alone.

But she was going to have to.

As the afternoon progressed I narrowed the loss down to one shop – Debenhams in the high street – but no-one there had seen the thing. Staff had been questioned and I'd tried to get word to the cleaners, all to no avail. There was only one thing for it – I was going to have to get a new passport.

So we packed poor mum off on the bus to the airport, and I called the airline to beg.

The staff at Delta Airlines were awesome. They said they could delay my flight for 24 hours at no extra cost. I went for it, because the price of delaying it any longer was astronomical. I knew it was possible to get a passport in 24 hours – I'd heard of it before. But how? I leapt from the phone to my computer…

And that was when I discovered that our nearest passport office was in Newport, South Wales – not far from my flat in Cardiff. A bloody long way from Somerset, where I was currently staying with my parents though. But closer than London. Just. Dad scanned the rules while I printed out the necessary paperwork.

'If the application is submitted by midday,' the website said, 'the passport can be processed the same day.'

It was Thursday evening. We could leave early in the morning for the passport office, but we had to be sure we'd make it – they were closed all weekend.

It was nearly 8am. A soggy Friday morning in September. Newport was a good two hours' drive away. Things had been looking good – until, filling in the application form, I'd realized that it had to be countersigned by someone who knew me. Someone who could testify that I was real. But not family. And that person also had to be a doctor, lawyer, or management-level professional of some kind…

This was a bit of a bind. Sadly, my friends are not highly placed. What can I say? I studied acting, and then became a professional vagabond. Neither of these things led to my social circle being populated by over-achievers…

Either of my parents could have signed it – if they weren't my parents. And if one of them wasn't already on her way to America.

Dad came up with the only answer; Bob, his best friend at work, was also management-grade. And a jolly nice chap to boot. So instead of Newport, our first stop was his office in Taunton; a little over half an hour in the opposite direction.

Bob was a big bloke, larger than life and eternally cheerful. He loved computers and he loved his job, which was with computers. He didn't love bureaucracy – who does? – but he was happy enough to help me with my predicament.

Until he finished signing the form. That's when he noticed that it asked for his passport number, presumably to prove that my Dad and I hadn't invented him. He didn't have his passport at work – who does? Unfortunately Bob loved his work so much that he commuted for well over an hour just to get there. There was no way we could drive to his house and get back in time.

But Bob wasn't defeated. Not yet. He called his wife at work and explained the situation. She was a teacher at a school just down the road from their house. If she could find an excuse to nip home, say, in the next ten minutes, we would be in with a chance… and that is when our bad luck began to break.

It was an INSET Teacher Training day, and all the children were off. God, I used to love those days! I was even more grateful for them now.

She drove straight home and rooted around for the passport – for a scarily long time. Eventually she discovered it hidden in a sock drawer. She called back with the number, good old Bob put pen to paper once more, and we were gone in a flash – gunning my Dad's old Vauxhall Senator down the M5 towards Newport.

There was traffic. Oh, was there ever traffic! But I won't get into that.

We arrived in time – barely.

Dad had to drop me off outside while he went looking for a place to park; that's how tight the time was.

Inside there was a queue, but I didn't care. As far as I was concerned we'd made it! The clerk who took my form waved me towards the photo booth in the corner and told me to hurry. Asshole! Like it really mattered to him. I looked at the booth. It took coins only. Pound coins.

Eight of them.

Eight pounds?

The shock stole my breath for a moment. It was double what I'd expected to pay, and double what I'd brought. Dad arrived and had almost enough to make up the difference… almost. But not quite.

"Any shops nearby?" I asked him. I already knew the answer.

He shook his head.

There was only one thing for it.

"Has anyone got a pound they can lend me?" I threw my plea out to the crowd. Surely in the queue there was some kind-hearted person… ideally one who spoke English. Hm. That ruled out most of them, by the look of things.

Then it happened; a kind old lady shuffled forward with a single pound coin for me. Actually, she could have been an axe-murdering old lady, but I didn't care; at that point I could have kissed her.

I put the cash in the booth, sat in it for my photos, and joined the queue again.

It was all working out perfectly. Or it would have been, had the photos been acceptable.

But they weren't.

"You're smiling here, you see," the clerk pointed out. "Guidelines call for a neutral expression. And also… you have your sunglasses on your head."

WHAT? Shit! It was true. In my panicked rush, I hadn't even noticed.

"But… I…"

"You'll have to get another set, I'm afraid."

"You've got to be *shitting* me!"

His expression didn't budge an inch.

He was probably used to being sworn at.

The clock ticked down. Less than five minutes to the cut-off.

I glanced around the room and saw nothing that could help me.

Desperation was setting in.

I had only one option left.

"PLEASE," I yelled into the queue behind me, "has ANYONE got EIGHT POUND COINS to lend me?"

In the car on the way to the airport, I sat looking at the document that would identify me on my travels for the next ten years. The eyes in the photo glared back at me in hatred. It looked like I was about to reach through the frame and strangle someone. It was the kind of face that would grace the cover of a psychotic horror novel. By the time the passport office customers had had a whip round and collected enough coins for my second set of photos, I was seething with frustration and rage. I'd managed to maintain a neutral expression by massive effort of will, but nothing could control my eyes. 'I will fucking stab every one of you,' said those eyes. Even the clerk had recoiled slightly, but couldn't find an excuse to refuse it – probably because he thought he'd get stabbed. I'd been looking at him with those exact same eyes.

13

It's hardly surprising, in hindsight, that they didn't want to let me into America.

A Great Big Hole

I stood on the very brink of the Grand Canyon and looked down. "Deep, man." It was the wittiest thing I could think of to say – guaranteed by the time we got to the next hostel I'd have thought of a dozen better quips, and no-one would care. Such is my curse.

I had to admit though, it was impressive. In the heat-haze of the perfectly clear day, the opposite rim of the canyon was blurred; slightly muted like an old faded photo. I was only looking through fresh air, but quite a lot of it. It gave the impression that the other side was a painting, a giant piece of stage scenery that looked great from far away, but up close you'd be able to see all the brush strokes.

A huge condor drifted lazily below us, which was quite surreal.

Behind us, a newly arrived tour group gathered around their guide as he started his spiel. We sneakily drifted closer, so we could hear his droning, nasal voice. He could reel off the numbers alright, as though visitors to the biggest geological feature on the continent didn't already have a guidebook featuring it. I instantly attributed to him three qualities: deadly bored, deathly boring and intensely annoying. The risk of being stuck on a bus for a week with someone like him is exactly why we'd decided to rent a car. Yes, it meant the occasional hair-raising near-miss, when Mum suddenly remembered which side of the road to take a roundabout on – and navigation being none of our specialities, we must have been the only people this century to 'lose' the Grand Canyon for over an hour.

Still. I felt we were ahead of the curve on this one.

"Two-hundred and seventy-seven miles long, eighteen miles wide and over six thousand feet deep…"

Whenever I hear guides reel off these kinds of numbers, it always reminds me of C-3PO telling Han Solo that the odds of successfully navigating an asteroid field are approximately 3720 to 1. Is it true? Who knows? Who cares? It's just arbitrary numbers. They might as well say

"Over a quarter of the contents of a hundred-thousand domestic laundry carts would fill less than ten percent of the bottom two-thirds of this canyon." Or "It would take five million grannies six centuries to knit enough embarrassing jumpers to fill it."

We have no frame of reference.

He could have told us you could drop Belgium into the Grand Canyon without touching the sides, and everyone would have believed him. (I would. And I've been to Belgium; it wouldn't be much of a loss).

But I wanted to know more exciting facts. Actually I just wanted to upset his monotone drawl.

"If I jumped off, how long would it take for me to hit the bottom?" I asked, putting my hand up like I was in school.

"I'm afraid you can't do that," was his reply.

See, that's the trouble with these western nations. It's health-and-safety gone mad, I tell you.

We left them to it.

More than anything, Mum wanted a donkey ride to the bottom.

I don't think she's ever gotten over our trip to Blackpool beach.

(In fact neither have the donkeys, but that's a different story).

The rides here went down into the canyon by the narrowest, crumbliest of paths. It was a trip for the adrenaline junkie, with ten extra points for anyone who made it down with clean underwear. We were all super-keen, until Mum asked about the price.

"$500? Bloody hell! For a ride on a donkey?"

"We don't have donkeys we have mules," explained the woman behind the booking desk.

"But still... would donkeys be cheaper?"

"Do we get to keep the donkey afterwards?" I quipped.

"It's quite a long ride," she pointed out. Patiently. She must have gotten this reaction a lot.

Mum was crestfallen. "We only wanted to go for a couple of hours..."

"The ride takes two days."

"Oh! Really. Ah. Well then. It still seems rather expensive."

"It includes accommodation and meals in the hotel at the bottom."

"I see..."

"And it's fully booked a year in advance."

"Oh. Aren't there any shorter rides we could do?"

"Yes, there are —"

"Great!" Mum cut her off. "We'll do one of those!"

"—but they go from the other side of the canyon."

There was a pause while we digested that nugget of information.

All of us naturally turned towards the window and its view over the edge, as though looking would make it easier to gauge the possibilities of getting there.

"Well, it's only eighteen miles away," I reminded them.

No-one found this particularly funny.

"I don't suppose there's a bridge around here?" I tried.

The woman gave me a flat 'don't push it' look.

And that was the end of our donkey ride.

Instead we wandered along the edge, taking photos, standing as close as we dared to the drop-off (whilst ignoring mum's pleas to 'come away from there!') and daring each other to look over the precipice.

For some reason, Mum always gets extra nervous when I stand near the edge of high things.

Perhaps because I once confessed to her that I get this overwhelming urge to jump, just to see what it feels like…

Or perhaps because she knows how good my balance is.

(It isn't.)

Apparently there are various religious groups so impressed by the spiritual significance of the area that they travel from all over the US to hold ceremonies right on the edge of the Canyon.

I know this because I found the place where they do it; it is marked with a large sign which simply says 'Site of Rim Worship'.

Yes, I know. I fell about laughing, as did the rest of the group when they saw this – except Mum, bless her, who stared at the sign with a confused expression, before looking around her for something she'd missed.

"I don't get it," she complained.

Poor, innocent woman.

I just had to enlighten her. "Well Mum, what must happen is that people of a religious persuasion from all over the US come here to hold their ceremonies on the edge of the canyon."

"That's what I thought it meant."

"And while they're here, they take it in turns to stick their tongues up each other's arseholes."

That night I slept in the car.

It wasn't entirely my fault.

We'd arrived at a motel, the only one we could find, only to be told by the owner that reception was closed for the night. We begged for a bit but she was having none of it. This pissed me off a little; I generally go out of my way to help other people if I can, and to make them feel welcome at very least. She just couldn't be bothered, as though helping a clueless group of weary travellers wasn't worth her effort.

"We could have checked ourselves in," I complained to the others. "In fact I think I'm going to."

It took me less than five minutes to break in to the motel through a back window. Sometimes I felt the need to demonstrate my more esoteric skills, and this was one of them; if only to prove that obnoxious woman wrong. This room was now most definitely open. I lay on the bed for a bit, but couldn't convince the others to join me. They were afraid 'inside' would take on a different meaning if the owner saw us and called the cops, so we made do with a tiny strip of gravel-and-grass verge down the road. The girls pitched their tent and froze in it, while Richie, Mum and I curled up uncomfortably in the car seats.

It wasn't the best night's sleep for any of us, but we had a tube of Pringles awaiting us for breakfast.

Sometimes, you have to be grateful for the little things.

"I still don't get it," Mum confided in me as I was about to drift off.

But I was too tired to draw her a diagram, so I let it pass.

Dressage

The thing that Gill and Roo had been most looking forward to since leaving Camp America was an experience they had agreed upon and booked whilst still living under canvas. It was the whole reason we were even in this part of the country, instead of chilling out in – I don't know – say, California? Ah well. The pair of them were in super-high spirits as our huge rental car rolled up outside the Monument Valley Visitors Centre. We were going on an overnight excursion; horse-riding into the desert, amongst the massive rock formations that gave the valley its name.

We had a quick look at the souvenir kitsch in the visitors centre, including a range of authentic Native American handicrafts that had tiny 'Made in China' stickers on them. Then we got back in the car and waited. And waited. We'd arrived ridiculously early, as we wanted to get the hell out of the place we'd spent the night, and now we were stuck in the Monument Valley car park, wondering why there were so many people about. Their tanned silhouettes lined the road running past the visitors centre, some with chairs and picnic blankets. It was an odd sight, because there was nothing else to see; we'd recently driven down that road. It was very, very long, otherwise completely empty, and went absolutely nowhere.

We didn't have to meet our guides until noon, so we ate our Pringles and sorted out what we needed to take with us on the ride. We'd be staying in a traditional dwelling of some kind, so we needed sleeping bags and jumpers; everyone knows it gets cold in the desert at night. Hats and long sleeves for the ride, to ward off the sun, and of course long trousers…

It wasn't until now that we'd actually bothered to talk about this. And as we did, we discovered that Richie had a problem. I'd never seen him in anything other than thin surfing shorts, and now the reason became apparent; thin surfing shorts were all he had. Fine to cope with the baking heat whilst strolling through canyons, but less than ideal for long horse-back rides. Roo had some spare jeans – but Roo was built like a twig. Nothing she had would fit anyone who'd eaten a full meal in the last few months. Both Gill and Mum had jeans – but as I might have mentioned, they are both somewhat vertically challenged. Mum's eyes, for example, were about level with Richie's navel. I, on the other hand, take after my Dad. I'm a gnat's tadger short of six feet, and I definitely had jeans. But I was wearing them. So, fumbling around in my rucksack, I discovered the only other clean item I had left; a pair of thin cotton pyjama pants. Richie reluctantly pulled them on over his shorts, revealing in the process that not only was he a slab of solid muscle, he was also a rather tall one; my pyjama bottoms ended at shin-height, allowing his ankles to protrude in a most immodest fashion. *Goodness*, I thought, *whatever will the ladies of the house think?*

And so, suitably bedecked, we went to meet our Navajo guides.

There were four of them, looking like unkempt cowboys, and they didn't feel the need to bother with introductions. We were whisked away by a ramshackle Jeep, driven deep into the flat red wilderness to meet with our mighty steeds. The corral stood alone in the desert, with not even a tent for shelter let alone a stable block. The small ring of wooden fencing held half a dozen flea-bitten horses, and looked decidedly temporary.

Roo was wide-eyed immediately, though what about was hard to tell.

"Are these the mustangs?" she asked.

"Yes, yes!" our guide enthused. "The best! Desert mustangs. Very beautiful!"

"They are beautiful. Do you breed them?"

"No. We catch. Yesterday."

Roo seemed to choke a little at that. "These are *wild* mustangs?"

"Desert mustangs!" The man beamed with pride at her. "We bring here for the ride, then after we release. Catch again next time. It is our way. Come! Choose horses!"

As we approached the fence I saw the look on Roo's face.

"So, have these horses been ridden before?" I asked her.

"I… probably. Surely? Or not… I can't tell." I got the feeling she was a bit less happy than she'd been five minutes ago. I decided to cheer her up.

"We'll be alright though. How bad can it be?"

The look on her face said it was best not to ask.

I was delighted with my horse. A scrappy-looking brown thing, it outweighed me so marginally that I immediately lost any fear of it. It had tufted and matted spots all over its coat, plus bald patches and scars – it was clearly feral, but not in the 'I'll bite yer face off' kind of way. I sort of had the feeling that if it tried to get away I could dig my heels into the ground on both sides and that would be the end of it.

Gill had a scrawny piebald, black and white in blotches all over it, like a real Indian stallion. It had proved tricky to get a rope around at first, charging up and down the fence, kicking out and jumping. Gill was a little concerned about this. Mum and Richie knew no better, and were mounted (with a stool and a struggle) onto a medium-sized pair of roans. Roo had been picked out for a 'special horse' on account of her admitting to having ridden before. "Expert rider!" our guide had pronounced her, and led her to the biggest of the wild beasts, a gigantic filthy black. Luckily she was doing a remarkable impression of being an expert; her horse seemed to be waiting patiently beneath her.

No helmets were passed around because apparently helmets weren't required.

Or provided.

"Not in the desert!" our guide explained, scuffing the ground with his shoe. "See? Only sand!"

I figured I could survive without a helmet, as I've never been a big fan of following health and safety guidelines. Gill and Roo, who'd spent most of the last three months trying to stop ten-year-old girls from killing themselves on horseback, had somewhat different opinions on this.

But the problem was easily solved, as there weren't any.

It looked like we were about to go. Richie clung nervously to the front of his saddle, grinning around at us as though to prove he wasn't really scared. My horse pranced a few steps. Then Gill's snarling piebald bucked. It was a huge move, kicking out viciously with both back legs, as the spine arched up and over, and the horse's whole body thrashed from side to side. The accompanying noise was the scream of a demon-beast giving birth.

When the horse came down, amazingly – miraculously – Gill was still on top. It had happened so fast she hadn't even had time to react. Now, sitting calmly once more, I watched the blood drain from her face. I don't think even she knew how she'd held on.

One of the guides, who was still on foot, walked over to the head of the animal and levelled a finger at its nose. "No," he told it.

Which seemed to settle the matter.

And then we waited some more. It was late in the afternoon when we finally set off, because our chief guide hadn't shown up when expected – or for quite some time after that. It turned out he'd been part of the crowds of people lining the road. There was a fun-run going on and his daughter was taking part. Watching out for her so he could wave when she went past was far more important than leading some paying idiots on a horseback tour. When Mum, ever anxious, asked how long the ride would take, we were told it was usually four hours – but with such confident riders as us (!) – maybe only three…

"How much further?" Mum was getting worried. It had been a longer ride than any of us anticipated. We'd been plodding along for well over four hours, following a series of vague indentations in the dirt. At first exciting, then less so; now vaguely monotonous and verging on the painful for those of us not used to riding. The reassurances of our guides were keeping my doubts in check, but less so for Mum. She wasn't used to relinquishing control to the Gods of fate and was already way outside her comfort zone. With dusk falling in the desert, surrounded by strangers, astride a beast she didn't trust as far as she could throw it, she was understandably concerned.

"Don't worry Mum," I told her, "these guys do this all the time. It's probably part of it, a night ride. Exciting!"

"I'm not sure riding at night is a good idea," she replied.

One of the guides nudged his mustang a little closer. "Night ride? No, not a good idea. Horses can't see where they go. You fall real easy."

"So we don't ride at night? At all?" Mum asked, sounding doubtful.

"No, no! Not at night."

"So how far away are we from the camp? It's starting to get dark…"

The man glanced around, standing up in his stirrups to get a look at the land ahead – and, disconcertingly, turning in the saddle for a glance behind us. "Not long now," he said, and nudged his horse towards the front.

"I hope he knows where he's going," Mum said. "I don't want to be out here after dark."

Darkness fell. We plodded along, the horses taking the occasional misstep which would cause their rider to cry out and grip the saddle a little tighter. All other conversation had long since ceased. I heard something wailing in the night, in the distance, and wondered what kind of creatures roamed this desert at night. Snakes for sure, which was another bad reason to be out there on a horse. But did they have coyotes? Or was I just remembering that from *Road Runner*?

The wail grew, coming closer, revealing a deep rumbling component that had been out of earshot before. Then we saw the lights, and reined in our horses as an old Jeep bounced along the trail towards us. The mechanized cavalry had arrived to lead us to our destination.

The guy in the Jeep had some good news and some bad. The good was, Mum was free to travel with him the rest of the way; she was not in the best of moods by this point and took no convincing at all. He helped her off the horse and into the car with equal difficulty; after four hours sat astride, her legs weren't much good for anything else. The bad news was that this Jeep was the wrong Jeep; he'd packed all our belongings into the other car, then rather cleverly driven this one to the camp. Hence, it would be a sleeping-bag-less night for all concerned. Though at this point we were far more interested in getting there and getting fed. I was starting to develop a deep ache in parts of my anatomy where one generally prefers not to develop a deep ache. To elaborate; I had squashed my love-spuds more than once against the solid saddle peak, and was beginning to doubt my own abilities to stand once we finally got the chance.

As the Jeep rumbled off, we turned and headed after it, leading me to believe (privately, of course) that we'd been heading completely the wrong way anyway, and could have passed the camp miles ago.

"Hey, sorry about your bags," the guide said as my horse came abreast of his. "That guy, he's a bit crazy. Always making mistakes."

That's great, I thought. Nice, professional outfit.

"So, can he just drive back to the start, you know, and bring the bags? Or the other car?"

"Oh, no. Too dangerous to drive in the desert at night. Too easy to get lost." And with that nugget of information imparted, he trotted off, to play at leading from the front once more.

When we arrived at the camp site an hour later, the stars were spectacular. The moon was giant and full, hanging low over the shadowy mountains in the distance. With my eyes adjusted I could almost believe it was as bright as daylight, but of course anything in shadow was pitch black and impossible to see. I dismounted with legs like rubber, holding onto the saddle as I experimented with how much weight they'd take. Poor Richie, I thought. If I was feeling this sore… oh, that poor bugger! I desperately wanted to massage my testicles, to get some sense of the damage done to them; they'd been numb for the last leg of the ride, which was a new and deeply unsettling experience for me. There are some things, though, you just can't do in public, even in the semi-dark wilderness of the desert at night. Whipping my crown jewels out and examining them gingerly by the moonlight was probably one of them.

Supper was subdued. It was also freezing frigging cold, a fact we hadn't noticed whilst riding – probably because we were all rigid with fear, expecting to be pitched forward into the ground with a horse on top of us at any minute. Now the chill desert winds stole every sliver of warmth, penetrating our shirts and jeans in spite of the fire's glow. Again I thought of Richie, sitting there in a t-shirt and my pyjama pants – poor, poor bugger! He never moaned once. He had Roo to keep him a bit warm – though she had less body fat than the last steak I'd eaten, and looked about as insulative as a HB pencil. I never did find out if Richie was putting on a brave face for her, or if he honestly was as tough as Chuck Norris.

Another thing I never discovered was the identity of the food we ate that night. The guys made a delicious flat bread, cooked up on the spot from a plastic bag full of a flour mixture. Then they hauled out a battered old pan and made some kind of stew that was so heavily spiced none of us could manage more than a few bites. After a glance around the fire at our watering eyes, one of them muttered something under his breath and reached for the bag of bread mix again...

The hut, called a 'Hogan', was made of logs stacked waist high, then getting narrower with each subsequent course rather like an igloo. It was simple and effective, and from the inside quite beautiful; the wood was untreated, showing exactly how it had been put together, like an architect's Lego set. From the outside, roughly plastered in mud to keep the wind from getting in, it looked like it had been squeezed from the bowels of a constipated T-rex.

Spending the night in it was even colder than sitting around the fire next to it.

Sometime around dawn, Richie and Roo snuck off into the desert for a little time to themselves. About four minutes later they slunk back, looking defeated. I don't care who you are, or what your needs are; no-one, but no-one, is going to take their clothes off in that temperature.

Instead of watching the dawn, we steadfastly ignored it in favour of trying to get some sleep. I don't think any of us had managed it up until that point. Then, as the sun began to warm the world around us, one by one we dozed off – only to be prodded awake in time for breakfast.

For which we had bread.

Mum elected to ride the Jeep home. I couldn't blame her; my arse felt like it had been raped by a rhinoceros, and putting it back into the same saddle for the same ride only in reverse, seemed like adding insult to injury.

I did it anyway of course, but no-one has ever accused me of being overly clever.

The first part of the trip was relatively sedate, once the pain in my bum cheeks had settled down to a constant throb. The striking red desert, now revealed in all its glory, was magnificent. Impossibly vast outcrops of rock flung themselves vertically, creating the immense red monuments that gave the valley its name. They looked out of place, as though dropped from a spaceship. Hm. Maybe it was an ancient obstacle course? A place to take your flying-saucer driving test?

An hour out from the camp we paused on a slight ridge to fully appreciate the vista. Funny how one of the most natural, unspoilt locations in the world looks so… unnatural. I loved it.

As we trotted off in a cloud of red dust, the spirit of adventure took a hold of me. The wind whipping through my hair, the endless, boundless desert on all sides – it was more than I could resist. I kicked my horse in the flanks and squeezed my thighs – about the only part of my childhood horse-riding lessons I can remember. The horse lumbered off, gaining speed slowly at first, but soon caught on that I wasn't about to stop him. His gait changed suddenly to a mad gallop, bouncing me around like an apple in a tumble dryer.

We shot ahead of the pack, pounding along the hard red dirt as I gripped the reins and the saddle peak for all my worth. Then I heard a shout that was more than half a scream – and Richie surged past me, barely clinging on to his own thundering mount. His horse had decided it was a race, and not to be outdone, had pulled out all the stops. Mine countered, racing on, overtaking Richie who looked about ready to yell "HEEEELLLP!"

His horse took the bait again, and struggled to pass mine, barrelling along with Richie slamming up and down on his back like a sack of oats. Plumes of fine red dust rose, streaming out behind our hooves, clouding our view of the others – not that either of us dared to look back.

We on-off galloped the whole way back. During our slightly

calmer periods, the others – trotting along in a much more controlled manner – would catch up, which I think offended my horse's sense of superiority. Off we'd go again at full tilt, closely pursued by Richie, the pair of us hanging on for grim death. My arse must have been black and blue by now; there was no finesse in my riding style, just a desperate desire to stay on and live through it. Richie, having never ridden before in his life – well, I can't speak for him, other than to say he looked utterly terrified the entire time. I think there were moments, on that ride, that I came close to seeing him cry.

By the time we got back to the corral, the horses were as knackered as we were. The exhilaration of flying across the desert was fading, to be replaced by a weariness of body and soul that made collecting my bags seem like an epic undertaking. I honestly just wanted to fall to the ground and lie still on the dirt. I didn't think that would have gone down too well with our guides though. We Brits are a strange lot. The sudden desire to imitate a collapse was immediately followed with the thought that I couldn't possibly let our hosts know how uncomfortable I'd been with their excursion. Perish the thought! I was determined to keep up the pretence of satisfaction. Surely it's only the English that do this; smile and say thank-you after a horrible experience, to avoid hurting the perpetrator's feelings. The worse the experience, the more profound our gratitude, almost as though to compensate for the extra effort involved in causing us so much discomfort! It's not even a rational process, it's just so ingrained that we do it without thinking.

Mum practically fell from the Jeep and hobbled over to claim her things from the second car. "I should have remembered from last night," she said. "There's no seat padding. No suspension. Being in that thing is worse than being on a horse!"

Then she turned to the driver and thanked him profusely for the lift.

Shaking, exhausted, filthy and variously injured, we shook hands with our guides and headed back to the rental car. I was already having fantasies of sleeping all the way to wherever we were going next. Richie had just one fantasy though – getting out of my pyjamas! On both days, whilst riding they had ridden up his legs, eventually ballooning out around his thighs like the pyjama version of Marilyn Monroe's white dress. He looked ridiculous of course, but he'd been terrified beyond the point of being able to pull them down again. Instead he had endured – and endured was the right word. Demonstrating yet again his amazing capacity to handle stuff that would make me vomit, he pulled the pyjama legs up one at a time to show off the damage. He had long, shiny wet patches running the length of both calf muscles. Knees almost to ankles, the battle between rough horse-hide and delicate human skin had been lost; he had a pair of red-raw burst blisters, almost a foot long apiece. And they were full of dust, horsehair, woollen blanket fibres and lint; all the nastiness of our desert experience, distilled into two weeping wounds the size of tennis shoes.

"Yeah, they're sore *as*, bro," he said, when pressed.

We dusted ourselves down as best we could and collapsed into the car. With the doors shut to block out the ever-present wind, at last I could hear my own thoughts again.

It was around this time that it struck me; those were just a handful of ordinary blokes that could ride. They didn't own a business. They didn't own any horses. They had just enough horse gear to manage, most of which looked like it had been thrown away ten years ago by a proper outfit. If they needed a license of some kind, they obviously didn't have one. They didn't own any land; they'd just built a nice hut out in the desert, where they hoped no-one else would find it. I had a feeling they lived in it. Their tour was just a case of following the tyre tracks to their house and back, and knocking up a few extra servings of whatever psychotically spiced dinner they were planning on eating that night. Their sole claim to legitimacy as tour operators was their Native American ancestry, and the fact that they owned a pair of knackered trucks between them. I never dared visit the website Gill had booked with, for fear of finding it shut down for credit card fraud.

But we'd had fun. That's what counts. And at least one of us still has the scars to prove it.

Hunger Pains

Roo and Richie left early the next morning, taking with them the rest of the glamour – suddenly, instead of being a community of fun-loving young travellers with Mum tagging along for the ride, we were three-quarters of my family on holiday without my dad.

It also signalled the end of our adventure. After dropping off the rental car and taking the same epic bus journey I'd done on arrival, only in reverse, we turned up at a motel on the outskirts of Phoenix. We needed a shower and we needed food, both quite badly.

And Gill still needed to book her flight home…

For tomorrow night.

I think her organisational skills – along with her stature – were inherited from my mum.

The motel was nicer than expected, given the dives we'd been staying in. It had some ornamental pools in the middle of an enclosed courtyard, which I *really* wanted to go swimming in. It took the combined efforts of both family members, neither of whom fancied spending their last night in a prison cell, to convince me not to.

So we showered. We dressed in our least travel-stained clothes. Then Gill spent an hour cursing the ancient pc in reception, which didn't respond too well to such treatment. Sensing trouble, Mum went over to offer some assistance.

For this reason I stayed clear, operating on a principle a good friend had once explained to me.

She'd described it as the Rule of Slaters: the more of us that get involved in any given situation, the more complicated it becomes.

After much analysis, I can confirm that the Rule of Slaters is frighteningly accurate.

So I sat and watched, as the drama unfolded.

Mum: "Have you managed to book anything yet?"

Gill: "I don't know! The bloody page won't load. Piece of shit old computer!"

Mum: "Will you need your passport?"

Gill: "Shit! It's in the room. But I daren't leave the computer!"

Mum: "I'll get it. How are you going to pay?"

Gill: "Shit! I need my purse. It's in the room too. But you'll never find it."

Mum: "How much is the flight?"

Gill: "I don't know."

Mum: "Have you got enough money?"

Gill: "I don't know!"

Mum: "Did you at least book the bus yet?"

Gill: "Shit! What's that bus website again?"

Under a hail of abuse, the computer finally crashed halfway through the confirmation process. The result; we still didn't know if she'd booked a flight or not.

So, somewhat cheesed off, we approached the motel bar to order food – only to be told they'd just shut for the night.

Nothing we said could convince them to give us anything, and when I asked for directions to the nearest restaurant, the only advice forthcoming was to get a taxi into town.

Now, being cheap is second nature to my family, as we've never had much money. That's why we were all staying in one room. Taking a taxi both ways, into and back out of town, would cost more than the food we planned on buying – but this was America! Surely there was at least a dozen fast-food outlets within a five minute walk.

So, *sod them*, I thought. *Useless buggers.*

And we set off into the great outdoors in search of sustenance. The others begged me to be less picky than usual, as not only were we all starving, we had a lot to get done that night.

"I promise," I said. "The first place we find, we will eat in."

Or… not. We strolled along the highway, bordered at this point by what looked like light industrial-type buildings. Occasionally we passed a shop of some kind, closed up and tightly shuttered. Street lights were scarce, but the moon was high and we were hungry enough to stride doggedly onward.

After half an hour, with no sign of wakeful civilization, both the women were ready to give up. I wasn't; if we didn't find something to eat now we had one bag of crisps between us for the whole night – and that was only left because someone had sat on it. I knew in my bones that there was food around the corner – if not this one, then the next! Or the next…

There came a point where there weren't any more corners. The road stretched off into the distance, straight and wide, still lined with closed down warehouses and garages. We'd passed a couple of takeaways in our odyssey, but unbelievably they'd all been shut. It was like the zombie apocalypse had come to Phoenix while we were in the shower – nothing moved on the streets bar the occasional car, powering past at top speed, headlights blazing. We were starting to despair. It had been a much, much longer trip than any of us anticipated, as I'd kept pushing the others onwards in search of something – anything. Now we had the long walk back to contemplate, alone in the dark, dead centre in what appeared to be America's fast food black hole. And we were still bloody hungry.

Unless…

Suddenly, there it was! Shining brightly in a deserted car park, set well back from the road, the glowing beacon of a KFC. We were saved!

The doors were locked and the restaurant was shut but the Drive Thru was still doing business. Or it would be, if there was any business. We hadn't seen another soul since leaving the motel, and even the few cars that passed seemed to be avoiding this place. Never mind. I think I'd have eaten out of a bin, if I'd have seen one first.

We trudged wearily up to the speaker and started to make our order – and that's when we hit a snag. It turns out, they won't sell Drive Thru food to people on foot.

"But that's ridiculous," I told the disembodied voice. "We need food now. We're starving! I've got cash right here…"

"Customers Without Vehicles are Not Allowed in the Drive Thru," he said, capitalizing each word as though talking to an idiot.

I am not an idiot. Okay, so I am an idiot – but *he* didn't know that! How dare he…

"Look, just serve us some food, mate – there's no-one around who even cares."

"I'm afraid I can't do that sir."

"Listen, you bloody well give us some food or I'll come in there and get it myself!"

"I'm afraid I can't do that sir."

"ARGH!" I booted the metal pole supporting the speaker in frustration.

Instantly Mum and Gill were beside me, pulling me back. They knew my temper from long before I became a sophisticated world traveller. They could tell I was about to do something really stupid.

And then we heard that sound, the one villains dread – a single, lazy 'WEERP' of a police siren. Just enough to say 'I'm here, watching you.'

We collectively shit ourselves.

Silently, the cop car slid up to us and the driver's window rolled down.

"What seems to be the problem Ma'am?" The officer was talking to Mum, for which I was grateful. I'd already discovered that my sense of humour doesn't go down well with people in authority.

Mum, bless her, was up to the task. Gnome like she may be, but she is utterly fearless. And has no sense of the ridiculous, which is what makes it so much fun to be around her.

"Excuse me Officer," she said, "we're looking for some food. Is there a McDonalds round here?"

The cop looked like he'd been slapped. "Are you English?"

"Yes we are. This is my son and my daughter."

"So what are you doing out here so late at night?"

"We're just looking for some food. The hotel shut its bar and there doesn't seem to be much round here."

The driver glanced over at his partner. "I think you guys had better get in."

"No!" I jumped to our defence. "Honestly, we're just looking for food. We nearly found some, only they won't serve us because we don't have a car. We'll go straight back to our hotel afterwards, I promise!"

"You'd better jump in," he repeated. His partner had already gotten out and opened the door for us. "It's not safe," he added.

Not safe...? That struck a chord.

We piled into the back seat and sat staring at the wire grill that screened off the rest of the car. The door shut behind us and the second officer climbed back in.

"This is, ah, not a real nice neighbourhood you picked," the driver said. "Walking around here after dark, well it's likely to get you mugged, or worse."

"Probably much worse," his partner added. "What hotel you staying at?"

Mum told him.

"Holy sh...! Wow, that's quite a walk! I can't believe you made it this far. You sure you didn't see anyone?"

"No sir."

"Wow... okay. Well, we're gonna have to take you back. Can't let you walk around here any more. There's no chance you'll make it that far twice, without running into trouble. You guys are lucky!"

"Not that lucky," I quipped. "We still didn't find any food!"

The driver craned his neck to look at me. "England, huh?"

And he shook his head, put the car in gear and drew up to the Drive Thru speaker. "So, whaddaya want?"

Lost and Found

We all made it home safely of course, although we still didn't know if Gill had gotten on a flight until she got off it. She landed not long after Mum and I did, and we all made the gruelling bus journey from London to my parent's house in Somerset.

We got back to find I'd had a phone call just after I left.

They'd found my passport.

The phone call was by way of an apology. It had been discovered by the cleaners, less than an hour after I'd dropped it in the changing rooms at Debenhams.

Because all cleaners are famously clever types (I should know; currently I am one), they'd done exactly the right thing. They'd taken it straight over to the Post Office and had it sent directly to the Department of Immigration. Once there, it had been safely and immediately destroyed. No fear of my identity being used to smuggle in a foreign national! The country was once again made safe from illegal aliens. Well, apart from the ones that nip in on tourist visas. And those ones that sneak on board trucks that come through Eurotunnel. And the boat people…

So I was of course very proud of the swift and appropriate action the cleaners had taken with my passport. Although a little part of me would still prefer they'd, you know, just dropped the bloody thing into Lost Property.

Damn it.

My Dad had another surprise for us; he'd bought something special while we were away, and was very much hoping we'd be as excited about it as he was.

Now, my Dad has been known to buy strange things on occasion. By way of example, we own a six-foot cuddly meerkat toy, which takes up so much room in the house it's like living with a whole other person. It just arrived one day and started occupying half the sofa, with no explanation beyond Dad's cry of 'Hey, look what I've got!'

Mum's expression at the time – horror, tempered almost immediately by resignation – said it all, and it was this same expression she adopted as we gathered in the lounge and collectively braced ourselves for the news.

My Dad, alone every night for two weeks, with new shopping channels springing up daily... It was a frightening scenario. What crazy-assed gadget had he been suckered into buying? Laser-based microdermabrasion? Bioflavonoids? Electric Penguin Cleaner?

No, he assured us, it was nothing like that. Nothing crazy at all.

He'd given up his hobby of buying stupid things.

He'd bought a house.

Wales. Again.

So. Dad had bought a house.

Now that we'd had a couple of weeks to get used to the idea, we were starting to get excited about it – although Mum was convinced he was taking the piss until he drove us all the way up there to have a look at the place.

I'd decided to give up my flat in Cardiff in order to save money for travelling, but we still had a perfectly good house to live in – a charming, four bedroom cottage, surrounded by fields in the heart of the Somerset countryside. The new house was none of these things. It was in a town called Treorchy, front-on-the-street, a tiny terraced house sandwiched between dozens of identical grey boxes. Also, it was surrounded by industrial estates at the bottom of a valley in South Wales.

Now, I've nothing against Wales, but it's not exactly Barbados.

What had happened is this: while we were away, Dad had decided to enter the property market. He dreamed of doing what all those folks on TV programmes did, which is buy a knackered old place, fix it up and sell it on for a whopping great profit. He wasn't motivated by greed – just an honest desire to pay off the mortgage on our 'proper' house.

He's quite a clever fellow, my Dad (as is my Granddad – proving that genetic traits really can skip generations). He'd done his figures and decided we could buy and do up the property, borrowing enough money to cover the costs, in the hope that by the time we were done house prices would have risen enough to make it all worth while.

The timing wasn't great. The property bubble had already burst and everyone who had enough money to buy and renovate old houses had already done it. We came into it at a time and level of cash-flow where South Wales was the only area we could afford to buy even a knackered house. Times had been hard in the Welsh valleys since the closure of the last coal mines; there were some 'minor' unemployment problems and consequently, property prices were the pits.

Sorry!

I couldn't resist it.

What I meant to say was, they'd hit rock bottom.

Treorchy was a hot-bed of angst and unemployment; people who'd been born there had a tendency to die there, though probably not as frequently as when the mines had been in operation.

It's always nice to know, when you're buying something, that you're getting good value. Dad knew he was getting a shit-hole, because it said on the estate agents' specs; 'This house is a shit-hole.'

Okay, it didn't, but it should have.

'In need of modernisation' is the stock phrase these days. It can mean anything from 'the décor is a bit dated' to 'the toilet is still in a shed at the bottom of the garden'.

What it meant for us was a hundred-year-old house which was clearly getting ready to do what hundred year-olds do best: collapse and die.

To say the house was a mess would be an injustice to the entire concept of 'mess'. We'd give it a bad name. No, this house was derelict.

The carpets were mouldy – so much so that to walk on them sent spores pluming into the air with every footfall. The walls were damp and stained, covered in filthy Anaglypta wallpaper.

If I had to guess, I'd say it was last decorated in the mid fifties – by an eighty year old blind man with dementia.

As we progressed through the house, we discovered that this was disturbingly close to the truth. Past the two ground floor reception rooms, the narrow hallway turned back on itself… and then plunged into the depths! A staircase so steep it was verging on death-trap, descended into impenetrable gloom. We groped our way down, not trusting the ancient electrics, and slowly our eyes began to adjust. Ahead of us in the dank basement was a room that would once have been the coal hole. Sacks tipped down a chute from the street above would have piled up in here, filling the place with thick black dust. But not any more – no, buried beneath the house in the farthest corner from any kind of natural light – is where the last owner had decided to live.

The walls of the coal cellar were crudely boarded and papered over in bright blue speckles. The paper hung limp now, and the room stank of mildew. A dark brown rug as thick as a bear's pelt covered the cramped footprint of the room – about the same size as an average bathroom. On that nasty, doubtless infested carpet, rested two items of furniture; a disintegrating armchair, well-chewed, and a Formica coffee table with a telly on it.

The TV had a rabbit ears antenna on top and a dial to tune in the channels.

It was one of the saddest things I'd seen.

Some ancient fellow, reclusive and alone, must have spent his last days in that armchair, trying to make out something through the static on a TV he'd probably owned since they were invented.

There was a good chance he'd died in that chair, lonely and forgotten beneath the house that had become his prison.

Or maybe he was sitting on a beach in the Caribbean, sipping cocktails and sniggering at the people dumb enough to pay him almost sixty thousand pounds for his old crap-shack.

But for now, the place felt like a mausoleum.

The 'kitchen' was next-door. I use the word lightly, because there were few of the conventions one would expect from a kitchen. Cupboards, for example. Appliances. It had a rusty gas cooker in one corner and a rusty sink in the other.

It had a floor of flagstones – bizarrely enough, with weeds growing through them. I lifted one up out of curiosity and lowered it again quickly.

There was nothing but soil underneath it.

The magnitude of this discovery made me feel slightly sick.

I had to tell someone.

"Dad, I've a horrible feeling that this house doesn't have any foundations."

"Don't be daft! What on earth makes you say that?"

"Well, I've looked at the foundations, and there aren't any."

"Rubbish!"

I showed him.

He went a bit pale.

"Oh. Um… maybe that's normal?"

"I don't think it's normal, Dad."

"Maybe it is? I mean, we are in Wales…"

The basement was so dark because at some time in the distant past an ill-advised extension had been built right across what would otherwise have been a back door to the garden. The house was three stories high at the back, and the ground floor's external door and windows had ended up inside this bare concrete addition. I think it was designed to be a 'sun room' – which, if you know anything of the weather in South Wales, was a joke in itself. It probably got less use than fifth gear on the Popemobile.

Unfortunately, what little sunlight they do get was now totally blocked from the rest of the basement level. The sun room, with its corrugated sheet metal roof, would have to go – it was item 104 on a rapidly growing list of jobs, and looked to be about as difficult a task as I could imagine. It was built like a World War II gun emplacement; I had no doubt it was the strongest part of the house. What we really needed there was one of those rectangular blocks of C4 that super-villains seem to have an unlimited supply of.

However we managed it, the bunker had to go.

I just hoped the three-storey back wall wasn't relying on it for support.

Dad was upstairs with a tape measure. It didn't seem the most likely of tools, given the state of things. A sledgehammer perhaps, or a jackhammer. At least *something* with the word 'hammer' in it.

My dad's approach to DIY has come under fire in the past for being a bit – how do I put this tactfully? A bit shit.

Sorry Dad.

He's what a polite person would call 'an enthusiastic amateur', and what an experienced tradesman would call 'Get-tha-fugg-off-ma-site-ya-pillock'.

He gives it his best go, but lacking quality tools (he tends to buy his at Poundland) and with most of his desire focussed on getting it done as quickly as possible, he does lean towards the 'well, it'll do for now' school of home improvement.

However, amongst his many redeeming features is an utterly unfazeable optimism. If you told him a meteor was about to strike the planet tomorrow and extinguish all life forever, he'd tell you what a nice day it was for it – and how he'd always wanted to see one up close. It's one of the things we all love most about him – depend on even, for our own stability and sanity.

Except for now.

When optimism meets inadequacy, it makes for a very cheerful, very upbeat, complete-and-total-disaster.

"It's not too bad," he said. Optimistically. "We'll just put a bit of wallpaper up…"

Oh. My. God.

"You're not serious…? Are you?"

"Now there's nothing wrong with wallpaper, I don't know why you make such a song and dance about it. It'll have to be wallpaper to cover up these walls. You can't paint them in that state."

"Can't… can't paint…?" I was already starting to hyperventilate. "Dad! What the hell are you on about? Can't *paint* them? Dad you can't do bloody anything to them! They'll have to be ripped out and re-plastered. Everything! Every single surface in the house! It's got bumps and cracks and holes, and… you can't *possibly* just cover all that up with wallpaper! The bloody house is falling down!"

"Oh, well the holes we'll have to fill. We'll get some Polyfiller, don't worry."

"Polyfiller? Are you kidding me? Dad, we need a bulldozer and a cement mixer! And a shitload of bricks – about a house's worth… at very least we need a full team of plasterers."

"It'll be fine! Don't get so excited."

And he got that glazed look in his eyes. I could tell he was calculating the required number of wallpaper rolls. (Seriously – he has a special look reserved just for that.)

I took a deep, calming breath.

There was no need to create an epic row.

Not over wallpaper.

Not on day one of a project which looked like it could last a lifetime.

After a last scout around to take in the details we'd been too shocked to appreciate at first, we held our council of war.

Dad firmly believed that a quick sweep up of the debris, liberal application of Polyfiller, papering over the cracks and slapping down a carpet in every room was the best solution.

We differed somewhat in our opinion.

The only reason I wasn't advocating out-and-out demolition of the property was because it was a terraced house; its walls were shared by the houses on either side, so knocking it down would most likely bring them down too. There was a fair chance it would bring the whole row of fifty-odd down, like a row of dominoes collapsing all the way down the valley back to Cardiff.

The quality of turn-of-the-century Welsh construction left a lot to be desired.

At the very least, I thought the interior needed gutting. Hell, half of that job had been done for us by the passage of time. The walls had to come down. The ceilings had to come down. The flooring had to come up – and all of it had to be replaced.

"We can keep the skirting boards though," Dad suggested. "They're in very good condition."

"You know what? You're right," I told him, "let's keep those skirting boards. They're very nice. It's just the rest of the house that needs to be gutted."

Gill agreed with me about the necessary modernisation works.

Mum struggled, caught cautiously between her husband's blatant optimism and her children's over-dramatics.

She wasn't quite ready to call in the wrecking ball, but she could tell we were way beyond the scope of what we'd started calling the 'tosh and splosh' approach.

For now though, we had to agree to differ.

Clear-up began straight away. We had shovels, gloves, and had accepted that our clothes might get a bit dirty. An hour after we started, we nipped out to the B&Q (DIY superstore) in Cardiff and bought masks, belatedly wishing we'd worn overalls. The atmosphere in the house was less than wholesome; a decade's worth of dust and grime, newly disturbed, flooded the airspace, reducing visibility to about six feet.

We were caked in the stuff from head to toe.

Still, we made progress.

We ripped out the boards lining the old man's coal hole to find bare, rough rocks behind them; it was another worrying clue as to the structural quality of the property we'd purchased. Building regulations have come a long way in the last century – they came into existence, in fact. Previous to that I'm pretty sure you could do anything you wanted, and the mining company that built these terraces to house it's poorer workers seemed to have done just that. They obviously hadn't felt the basement needed 'proper' walls. After all, who was going to see them underground? So they'd built them out of rubble, and saved the bricks for the two floors above ground – where presumably people would appreciate them.

We tore up the carpets. They were full of insects.

Beneath them were more carpets. These were full of dead insects.

Beneath them was something that may once have been carpet, back when they were knitted by hand from grass and donkey hair. This last stuff was clearly decomposing and came up in strips that resembled mummified skin.

It made me think of the dirt floor under the kitchen.

Not a bad place to bury a body, that.

Better get it concreted over, just in case.

Amidst groans and gagging sounds, Gill and I rolled up the most fetid of the carpets and manhandled it down the absurdly steep steps to the basement. It was heavy and it was disgusting, and we had to stop frequently while Gill adjusted her load.

She'd offered to take the front end, which meant she was now carrying it backwards down the stairs. It also meant that, because of her semi-gnomic stature, every time I took a step down I was poking her in the face with it.

"Ack! It won't stop.. BLEGH! Touching my... Ptah... fucking mouth!" she moaned.

"Sorry Gill!" I called. And thrust onwards.

While I tore huge holes in the filthy 1960's wallpaper (quickly, before Dad could decide to keep it), the others made a start on pulling up a last layer of glued-down vinyl floor tiles.

They were also decomposing, which was a true testament to how bad the conditions were in the house; I was under the impression that most oil-based products take centuries to bio-degrade.

Mum was chipping at them with a butter-knife, whilst delicately pinching her nose with the other hand. Black squidgy crumbs were scattering out from the coin-sized hole she'd made. She seemed to be enjoying herself though, with her tongue sticking out the corner of her mouth in concentration, so I chose not to comment on the efficiency of her methods.

"Got one!" she said eventually, holding up most of a perished tile.

Then she looked around her at the hundred-odd tiles still attached, and scowled.

And picked up the butter-knife again.

When we decided to call it a day, the place looked worse than when we'd arrived, which I considered quite an achievement.

You know those moments when you look at a gargantuan task, in the new light cast by all your efforts have achieved, and suddenly it doesn't seem so impossible after all?

This was not one of those moments.

"It's going to take a century," I said.

"It does look like a long job," Mum agreed.

"We're gonna die in this house," said Gill.

I couldn't dispute that. It had the ring of prophecy about it.
"Oh, don't be so dramatic!" Dad scoffed. "It'll be alright."
But you know what?
He was wrong.

The Property Ladder

"It's a great idea!" I told Dad. "Really! Honestly, it's the best idea ever," I enthused.

Now it was my turn to be wrong.

Applying to be on a reality TV show was most definitely NOT a good idea.

It was in fact a very, very bad idea, the ramifications of which would be felt throughout my family for more than a decade.

True enough, there have been worse ideas in history – building the Millennium Dome in London for example, and that bloke that burned Rome to the ground just for a laugh. Oh, and did I mention the Millennium Dome?

But little did I know, as I strove to allay Dad's fears, just what I was letting us all in for.

"Being on TV while we renovate the house will help us sell it when it's done," I explained.

This was possibly the worst advice I have ever given him, and more than makes up for a lifetime of being told there's 'nothing wrong' with train-spotting.

There is *everything* wrong with train-spotting.

But that's beside the point.

Reality TV is evil incarnate.

I'd like to say I got into it with the best of intentions, but that would be a lie.

I did it because I wanted to be on TV.

It was the frustrated actor within me, the one that was too crap at acting to get on telly on its own, that made me apply. It surely wasn't a coincidence that a top property renovation show was looking for projects to film at precisely the same time I was starting a project and looking to be filmed? It had to be fate.

This could be my time… I thought.

It was bound to be a bit inconvenient with cameras around and time spent being interviewed, but that was a small price to pay for fame and fortune.

And anyway, my family would be paying it.

I could thank them with the first million I made as an A-list movie star.

Rachel, a researcher for the show, called me back straight away. They'd had a project fall through on them, and were desperate to find something else that would be finished before their deadline. Could we do it in time?

Of course we could.

Well, that's what I told her. I decided to let her break the news to my parents, as they couldn't hit her – not while they were being filmed, anyway.

There was one other problem. The show followed renovations from start to finish, so it was very important that we not start any work on the house until a decision had been made about using us.

"We won't touch a thing," I told her.

So she agreed to bring the crew to Treorchy for a test shoot on Monday.

Which meant we had a weekend to hide all evidence of the work we'd already done.

I suddenly wished we'd been less enthusiastic in our demolition.

With mixed feelings about the whole thing, the four of us made the two-hour trip to Treorchy, where our house sat waiting for us with two of its three floors ankle deep in rubbish and rubble.

Whatever else I may say about my family, they are all hard workers.

One wheelbarrow at a time we scooped up the shredded wallpaper, splintered wood and mounds of plaster, and carried it down the steep, narrow stairs, through the basement, through the concrete bunker, out of the back door, down the garden – and bunged it all in the shed.

The shed was already a nightmare we didn't want to contemplate; from the outside it looked like a place where murders were committed. Tiny windows, so grimy they were opaque, peered out from a slimy, moss-covered hut. It was clad all over with what looked disturbingly like asbestos.

Inside it was much, much worse. It was full – chock a block with rusting tools, metal bars, giant cogwheels, chains, more tools and enough jagged scrap metal to build an entire Mad Max style fortress.

More than anything it resembled the den of a medieval torturer.

Into it we cast the previous contents of the house – including several large pieces of its walls. Then we jumped out, wedged the door shut, and pretended it had never happened.

The disgusting carpets, cast out to rot in the jungle of the back garden, would be rather more difficult to disguise.

"I can't believe we're doing this," Mum moaned, as she struggled to sweep up the millions of sticky rubber crumbs she'd chipped out of the floor.

We spent two whole days cleaning up a mess that had taken one afternoon to create.

No-one thought to mention that it was all my fault, so I wisely kept quiet.

I could already tell this filming lark was going to complicate matters.

On Monday morning we were at the house early to meet the crew.

They weren't happy that the carpets were gone, but they could hardly believe their eyes as they looked around. I felt I could read their minds, so obvious was their synchronised reaction: *you actually bought this place? It looks like a bunch of maniacs broke in here and tore it apart!*

The test-interview could have gone better.

Each member of my family have their own delightful quirks, all of which came to the fore simultaneously. In case you haven't noticed, I'm partial to a joke or two. While my sister shares this trait, she at least is wise enough to save it for those who appreciate it. My Mum doesn't do jokes well because she doesn't get jokes, but she makes up for it by doing four times as much regular talking as anyone I know. And my Dad, bless him, turns out to be camera-shy.

So when Rachel asked an innocuous question like, "What do you hope to get out of this project?"

Our joint response went something like this:

Gill: "We're hoping that by developing here we'll make enough money to…"

Mum (cutting in): "Yes, we'll make money because the price was so low, even if it isn't worth a lot when it's finished it's bound to make a profit, because we got it so cheaply, well, not too cheaply when you see what a mess it's in, but still cheaply enough for a three bedroom house, compared to the rest of the country anyway, so all we need is to keep our costs down and find some decent tradesmen, which we're struggling with at the moment, but I'm sure it will all work out, because although we've never done anything like this before, we all do a lot of DIY and we're all very creative, I do quite a lot of handy crafts like sewing and wood carving and the kids used to love painting little models, and we do have some experience because we've had to decorate every house we've ever lived in, which is quite a few over the years, and we built an extension on our last house, well, we had it built, but we helped out with the digging and everything…" at which point she had to breathe or risk passing out, so her diatribe would trail off.

Taking advantage of the air gap, I would add something like, "I just want to make enough cash to keep me in crack and whores!"

My Dad would just stare at the camera throughout, with a slightly goofy grin on his face, and say nothing.

By the time they left, the film crew had been subjected to about 500 words from Gill; mostly the start of sentences and no endings; 500 words from me, almost entirely in tasteless jokes; about 15,000 words from my mother, during which she had enumerated our pets, our hobbies, our past few holidays, our hopes, dreams, previous jobs, future travel plans, flaws and foibles, and I'm fairly sure taught at least one of the crew to decoupage. My Dad, when asked why he'd spent the entire day stood behind us grinning like a lunatic, said he was just trying not to look stupid.

It was a failure of epic proportions.

'We have absolutely no chance of getting on the show,' I wrote in my journal that night, 'because we came across as a family of morons.'

And what could be further from the truth?

Ahem.

When I got the call from Rachel saying that Dave, her director, would love to film our renovation, I was so relieved I didn't dare ask her why. I wondered if she'd noticed something in us, a hidden quality – maybe in me, even? Could it be she'd seen through the nervous joke-telling reflex, and decided that I was worthy of a shot at the big time?

Obviously not a question I could ask her directly.

And anyway, I doubt she'd have given me a straight answer. She'd have come up with something clever and entirely believable about how interesting it would be to watch a family co-operate on such an enormous challenge.

Whereas the truth of the matter was this: morons make good telly.

She would have told me anything I wanted to hear to get us on that show, because as far as she was concerned, she'd struck gold.

The First Week

It wasn't the first week. We'd been sneaking in to work on the house every weekend for a month – but the film crew didn't know that.

It was an indication of just how bad the place was, that after days and days of hard labour by the entire family, it still looked as though nothing had been done.

So, this officially became Week One – and the beginning of what was known as 'the strip out'.

Director Dave informed us he would be back quite often during this period, as filming the demolition work was a high priority.

"Once you start rebuilding, it all gets terribly dull," he explained, which cheered us up no end. He wanted the maximum bang for his buck, and it goes without saying that the most exciting footage would be of us beating the crap out of stuff with hammers.

But being filmed for a documentary is all about rules – most of which are in direct contradiction to your natural instincts. Such as:

Taking it in turns to speak.

Keeping quiet whilst off-camera.

Standing still on your mark.

Not looking at the camera.

Some rules are even harder to adhere to than others:

Not making silly faces at the camera.

Not being sarcastic.

Not telling jokes.

Not pantomiming light-sabre duels…

And then occasionally there came a rule that threatened to compromise the integrity of the entire project.

Like having to say what we were told to say.

Which I thought kind of defeated the purpose. But hey, what did I know?

The atmosphere couldn't have been more different from our laid back family visits. There was no strolling through the property, pointing out jobs as we spotted them and discussing what to tackle first with a vague air of disinterest.

Because there was so much to do, it didn't look like we would ever get it all done. It made each task seem at once daunting and inconsequential. How could any one job matter when there were so very, very many of them? It was hard to create any sense of urgency.

Not so with the TV crew.

Theirs was a world of high stress and constant pressure. They moved fast, and as efficiently as they could given the fact that they were working in a ruin. Cables snaked everywhere; after discovering on their first visit that all the plug sockets in the house had holes for three round pins, they were taking no chances. Ranks of battery packs lined the walls, plugged into lights and monitors and each other. The crew's breaks were orchestrated into the gaps when other people were working; it meant there was always something going on, often several things at once, usually at high speed and quite often right on top of me. I've never been particularly agile; 'bloody clumsy' would be a more accurate description of me. In tight confines, with several industrious individuals and thousands of pounds of delicate equipment, 'disastrous' became an even more accurate description.

I was quickly banned from any room in which my presence was not immediately required on camera. I hadn't actually *broken* anything – well apart from a folding reflector, which only cost about £50 – but the potential waxed strong, and the crew could tell. They'd had experience of people like me.

The presenter, when she was ferried in by minivan, turned out to be very down-to-earth. She was friendly and approachable, although she didn't have much time for us; every minute of her day was mapped out well in advance, and not a moment of it was wasted.

To the crew she was intense and commanding, like a military officer dictating the deployment of people and gear as they set up the shots she envisaged.

Then the camera flicked on, and instantly she transformed. Calm and confident, she addressed her audience with an air of authority that couldn't be challenged. Not by us, at any rate.

She had a vague grasp of our plans of course, but knew very little about the hours of reasoning that had gone into our decisions. She pursued our choices aggressively, which I understand as it was the point of the programme. The trouble came when we were forced onto the defensive and found ourselves hamstrung by the rules.

"I think you're mad to even consider building a new bathroom," the presenter said. "You can't possibly get it done on your budget."

"Ah, well we've already got a builder who's agreed to do it," Mum replied.

"CUT!"

"I'm so sorry *dahling*, you can't say that," Dave informed her. His aristocratic drawl bordered on self-parody. "This is our first visit. Officially, no work has been done yet you see, and nothing agreed upon. We're still in the 'planning stage', before you've engaged builders and so forth. So, could we try that again please? And remember, don't mention the builder."

"ACTION!"

Presenter: "You can't possibly get it done on your budget."

Mum: "Erm… we, err… *we* think we can."

It was already starting to sound like we didn't have a clue.

When the TV company had agreed to film us, we'd had to promise them faithfully that we would finish on time. We were filling a gap left in their schedule by another project that had stopped completely when one of the renovators died. It had shocked and saddened them all, and left them with a major headache; they still needed one more episode to complete their series. They were running short on time and getting desperate when my request had arrived – and now the burden of that time pressure had been shifted onto us.

The programme would air in March. It was now November, giving us less than four months to complete it.

We'd planned on taking six – roughly, and with no realistic expectation of achieving it. There was no padding in our meagre budget for hiring extra help. This new deadline meant one thing, if nothing else;. we would all have to work a lot harder.

On top of that, we'd signed up for a total of eighteen filming days. Six more would be designated 'Presenter Days', when the star of the show herself would be here to advise and criticize. We'd already figured out that nothing much would get done on those days; when we weren't repeating ourselves on camera we'd be hiding silently in the basement while the presenter was filmed pretending to paint a square foot of wall.

I found it most amusing that she did so whilst wearing a tailored leather jacket worth more than our entire decorating budget. The rest of us, naturally, were dressed in the oldest, crappiest clothes we could dig out of our wardrobes – and they were already ruined. We looked like a bunch of homeless fashion victims who'd been sleeping in a landfill site. And that was how we would be appearing on the TV screens of the nation.

It was quite a relief when the presenter left, whisked back to London to visit another project. The crew were also more relaxed once they were left in peace. The next morning they arrived early to film us as we began the mammoth task of making the house liveable again.

They didn't have to wait long for drama; our first major problem was in the bag by 10am. The builder called to have a chat with Mum. He'd have been perfectly happy to do the job as originally planned, he said, but there was no way he could meet our ambitious new timescale. Like everyone else in his trade he was booked up for months in advance, and couldn't simply move us up in front of his other jobs. Sadly, this meant he was out, and we would have to start looking for a builder all over again – one who could not only do the work for our fun-sized budget, but could also do it *right now*. That presenter was bang on the money; the new bathroom had become an impossibility overnight.

Either she was eerily prescient, or she knew something that we didn't.

Yep, you guessed it.

It was the latter.

With hundreds of similar programmes under her belt, she knew far more than we could ever hope to about the nature of this industry. But she knew something else, too. She knew TV.

The crew told the story and they controlled all the strings. And she was the star of their show. Anything she said became a self-fulfilling prophecy; this slight hiccup was to be the first of many. The crew didn't need to wait for us to have problems to film – they were already creating them for us.

For now though, we had far more mundane concerns.

Structural concerns.

"I'm worried about the floor boards," Gill confessed to me, over a well-earned cup of tea. "I know we wanted to polish them up, but they might not be strong enough anymore. Every time the film crew start moving their equipment around I hear this squeaking… I don't think anyone else has noticed though. I hope the floor doesn't cave in."

"If the whole house collapses, it would solve all our problems," I pointed out.

"There it is again! Listen!"

I strained my ears towards the other room. "Sorry dude, I can't hear anything."

"It's just occasionally, a really sharp squeak like something working loose."

"Ah well. Let's focus on the stuff we know about for now."

So we focussed on demolition.

Not all of it intentional.

Shortly after the tea break ended, we heard a crash and a shriek from upstairs. We pounded up to the top floor to find Mum choking on a cloud of black dust.

In one hand she trailed a long strip of wallpaper.

"I thought I'd see if it would come off," she explained. "I only gave it a pull…"

Peeling away a strip of limp wallpaper, she'd met a little resistance and tugged harder. Instead of freeing the paper, a big chunk of plaster had succumbed, crumbling to the floor in pieces and billowing back up into the air as dust.

Together, we peered into the hole. The ancient black plaster had been applied over skinny wooden strips (called laths, I found out later), which were nailed in turn to the studs (the larger bits of wood that made up the wall frame).

Time had petrified the plaster, turning it brittle, and Mum's enthusiasm had dislodged it, turning it to powder – a large portion of which she had subsequently inhaled.

There were at least four layers of wallpaper, each more hideous than the one below it; between them they made up a thick skin, which must have been holding the wall together for the last fifty years.

But no longer.

Now cracks radiated out from the hole like a kid's drawing of a spider's web.

"Looks like we'll be re-plastering one wall after all," Dad said.

Mum was still spluttering in the corner, plumes of black dust rising from her hair every time she coughed. Her eyes were squeezed shut and streaming.

"Is there… any water?" she rasped.

But with a squeak of protest from the floorboards, Dave arrived, squinting through the haze whilst holding a handkerchief over his mouth and nose. He quickly appraised the damage and turned to congratulate Mum.

"That's splendid work, *dahling!*" he told her, beaming. "Could you possibly do that one more time – for the camera?"

Lenny

Lenny was a short, stocky Welshman in his mid-fifties, with gigantic grey eyebrows and a nose to match (gigantic I mean, not grey). He had a cheeky twinkle in his eye, which I liked; I got the impression that he was a loveable old rogue, which, as it turned out, was half right.

Lenny was our new builder.

He came to give us a quote, and left with a firm handshake from my Dad. Lenny's price was right; his availability was immediate. That was all that mattered at this point, and we really had no choice, but Lenny put us all at ease with his casual appraisal of the job in hand. He had knowledge of this kind of house, knowledge of frugal budgets (he was Welsh) and enough experience to tackle all the stuff that we didn't have a clue about.

"We'll be in and out of here in under a month," he told us.

We even got him on camera saying it.

Lenny's three-man crew set to work the next day, pulling down the ceiling of the basement with ruthless efficiency. I was horrified by the violence they unleashed, attacking with crowbars and pick-axes and, from the look of things, sheer rage.

What made it worse was that we'd never intended to remove this ceiling; alone of all the rooms, this one had been refinished quite recently, with smooth, skimmed walls and a ceiling of modern plasterboard.

When I approached Lenny with my concerns, he said that the ceiling had to come down anyway because of the lights we wanted to put in, and that it was all included in his cost.

Which was fair enough, I guess. Not true, as it happened, on either account, but it did seem to make sense at the time.

Of course, it would have been nice if they'd told us about it first.

Or, you know, *asked* us.

Still, with a full team of builders and a plumber on site, it was starting to feel like we were making progress. Gill and I moved into an upstairs bedroom, so that we could be on site to supervise full-time. For the foreseeable future we would be sharing an inflatable double bed on a square of cheap carpet in the least-filthy room we could find.

Our parents had to keep working at their day-jobs, or the money would dry up rapidly – this meant they had to spend their weeks at home in Somerset, and make the trip up to Treorchy every weekend.

By way of compensation (and prompted no doubt by guilt about leaving us in a building site), they bought us rather a lot of booze.

It is still to be decided whether or not this was a good idea.

The plumber and his apprentice capped off the water to the house and installed a single temporary tap – in the basement.

This meant two things; firstly, drinking anything with water in it after 4pm meant negotiating the deadly basement stairs in complete blackness, which came with a high probability of death – thus, the alcoholic beverages came in quite handy; and secondly, the toilet no longer worked. Which meant that, even after staggering down the stairs blind-drunk, we still had to grope our way out in total darkness, through the concrete bunker, and pee in the back garden.

Oh yes, life was grand.

Until the plumber quit on us.

This was quite a blow. It didn't take long to establish that every listed plumber within a hundred miles was booked solid for the next three months – something to do with us being in South Wales, in the depths of a typically unpleasant winter.

I couldn't understand what had gone wrong with the first guy – he'd seemed like a decent bloke – so I gave him another call.

This time, to beg.

"I'm sorry to leave you in the lurch," he said, "but it's your builders, you see. We can't work with them."

The sound of that made my blood run cold.

"Ah. Why is that? Are they bothering you in some way?"

"It's not so much for me, as it is for my apprentice. He's only fifteen, you see."

"And the builders have been bothering him?"

"It's not all of them. It's just one. You know Dai, the idiot with the leering look?"

I knew the one.

"You mean the one who can hardly speak?"

"Yes, that's him. Well, I don't know how to tell you this, but he's… *known*. Locally, like."

"Known? Locally? Known as what?"
"As a paedophile."

But the builders had already started work. Money had exchanged hands, in cash so as to secure a slightly better (presumably tax-free) deal; unfortunately, we were stuck with them.

It cast a new, slightly more sinister light on all of Lenny's assurances. Just who was working on our house for these bargain-basement prices? Was he so cheap and so readily available because no other bugger would be stupid enough to employ him? What kind of people were we trusting to re-build our house?

Was the rest of his workforce also 'known locally'...

As serial killers, perhaps?

It was a worry, to be sure. I added it to the list.

That list was getting longer by the minute.

The shed was my other major problem.

Squatting evilly at the bottom of the garden, that shed looked older than time itself. It exuded a menace, a brooding presence that was biding its time, allowing us to become complacent. Then, when we least expected it, we would wake to find ourselves locked in that nightmare chamber, saw blades and steel spikes and rusty chains wrapped around us...

Okay, so perhaps my imagination was getting the better of me.

But only because I had to empty the thing and then knock it down – and I could tell it wouldn't be going without a fight. I was going to chuck all the metal in the skip and burn the massive wooden frame – but one thing I definitely did not plan to do, was dig up the floor underneath it. Because... well, you never know.

First things first, though.

I hired an asbestos removal contractor to come and have a look at the thing.

"What do you think?" I asked him. I was afraid his answer would mean more bad news for our budget.

"Oh aye, it's asbestos, that is."

"The roof?"

"The whole thing, I reckon."

"Ah. So. What do we do? Or rather, what do you do?"

He was rather small, this man, and had a lovely lyrical voice which went up at the end of everything he said, as though it was a question.

"What were you going to do with it? Before you knew it was

asbestos?" he asked.

"We were going to chuck it in the skip."

He considered this for a moment.

"Right, now there's two things you can do. One is, I can price it up for you to get my team in here to remove it all, and dispose of it all safely."

That did sound expensive. I was all ears for option two.

"Or two, you can wait until your next skip comes, put these in the very bottom, and cover them over with building rubble. That way no-one will ever know, see?"

This seemed to me like the better of the two options. The most cost-effective, if you like. This has gone on record as the first time in history that a tradesman tried to screw *someone else* over to help *me*. I quite liked it.

"I thought you'd be wanting the job to be honest, trying to convince me to get your team in."

"Well normally I would, see, but I have to say, I don't like the look o' that place."

"Too big a job?"

"No, not really. But it gives me the creeps, like."

The shed's powers were growing. Its mildewed walls were the colour of fear. I decided not to tell the bloke that I believed it was possessed, and that I waited nightly for it to try to murder me in my sleep.

"You think we'd get away with it?"

"With chucking it in the bottom of a skip?"

"Yeah…?"

"Oh, I reckon you will," he said. "I mean, that's what we do."

The Must-Have Moments

Rachel had given me a list of the things they wanted to film, and a much shorter list of the ones they absolutely *had* to.

Missing any one of these was a potential deal breaker – although I had to wonder, just who would lose the most if they did decide to stop filming us.

For reasons known only to them, removing the bathroom fixtures was on the second list. Thus, with a fresh skip ordered (our sixth, which was a pity as we'd only budgeted for two), and the bathroom next on the list of jobs, I placed a call to Rachel to organise a visit. It had to be set up far enough in advance that they could make their travel arrangements – but not too far in advance, or something was guaranteed to go wrong and force us to change the date. What resulted was a more or less constant dialogue between Rachel and myself, sending my mobile phone bill through the roof. I was talking to Mum and Dad every night too, to give progress reports, but more often than not they phoned me – usually while I was having a wee in the back garden, or biting into a steaming hot pizza – and all of those calls happened in the evenings.

At our first meeting, Rachel had signed a cheque to me for £50, to cover extra expenses incurred by being part of their programme.

It was the only thing we ever got from the crew – they even casually forgot to send us a copy of the finished programme, when it aired. We had to tape it ourselves from Channel 4.

£50 eh! They spared no expense. Literally.

My phone bill for the first three months of the project was over £600. In the fourth month I dropped the phone down the toilet, so it ceased to be a problem.

Right now though, wedged against the side of that toilet, in possibly the least pleasant place in the whole house, Gill was chipping off wall tiles. It was her own fault; she got that position because she's so damn short.

To get us both in shot at the same time, the crew had asked Gill to crouch down, and then positioned me stooping over her. It looked good on camera, so they said, but was a very unnatural position to work in. The first tile I prised from the wall pinged off straight onto Gill's back, then bounced off onto the floor. "Sorry dude," I said.

Then I chipped off another one. It, too, landed smack on her back before falling to the floor. Her back twitched in annoyance, but she daren't complain. "Sorry, dude," I said again.

The next tile I dropped landed slightly further up her back.

"Sorry dude!"

I couldn't resist it – I'd discovered a new game. See how much abuse Gill could take, whilst being filmed – because she was trying to ignore me so as to avoid ruining a take.

Normally she'd have attacked me with her rubber mallet by now.

Another tile bounced off her shoulders into the bath.

"Sorry dude!" I said, cheerfully.

This type of humour did not sit well with the TV crew.

"You've got to stop being funny," Rachel told me. "Stop clowning around and start giving us straight answers, so we have something we can use."

She was grumpy today, and I had a feeling it was mostly my fault. In preparation for our second visit from the presenter, she'd been looking at the footage from the first one.

On that day the whole family had been marched from room to room, with the presenter asking each of us in turn what we had planned in there.

After doing this in every room – and there were a lot of rooms in that house – I was struggling to come up with new things to say, and was a bit bored of repeating myself. So when we reached the top floor, I'd tried a new tack.

"So, this is the master bedroom," the presenter had reminded me. "What are your plans in here?"

It struck me as a pretty dumb question. Unsurprisingly we were going to put a bed in there. I honestly couldn't think of anything else to say about it, so my 'say something stupid' reflex had kicked in. The result:

"Because this is the master bedroom, we're going to import a ton of sand, spread it around about ankle deep and set up a couple of deck-chairs. Get a kind of beachy theme going on. Maybe invest in a paddling pool."

The crew had not been impressed.

And the presenter hadn't asked me any more questions that day.

Now Rachel was making me promise to behave. It was one more nail in the coffin for my dream of stardom; if I didn't have the chance to say crazy things, how would my personality ever shine through? How would the TV execs, watching the edits in a posh studio in London, ever recognise my potential? It was starting to look like we'd be making a very ordinary kind of programme, bereft of all the elements I'd hoped would set it apart.

For the first time I had the thought; *this might not have been a good idea.*

After the excitement of chipping off a wall full of tiles, we came to the main event: removal of the bath. The film crew were adamant that Gill and I be the ones to lift it out and cart it off to the skip. We'd have done it anyway of course, because that's what we were there for, but it did strike me as a little daft; four members of the crew plus a whole team of burly builders stood around and watched as Gill, all five feet of her, strained beneath the weight of the huge steel enamel bath.

The fact that it was half-full of tiles probably didn't help.

"How much further?" she groaned.

"Not far," I lied.

The back garden never seemed longer than at that moment, as we struggled down the broken path towards the gate. Manoeuvring the bath through the narrow gate without tripping on debris from the shed was no mean feat. I fantasized about ditching the bath as soon as we were beyond the garden wall, but then the camera man followed us out through the back gate. Thinking we'd hear "CUT!" at any moment, we staggered down the alleyway behind the neighbours' houses, all the way to the end of the alley where the skip was waiting. My arms felt about three inches longer; poor Gill could hardly breathe.

I daren't risk a glance back to see if we were still being filmed – it's a catch 22 situation, in that as soon as you look at the camera to see if it's on, you've ruined the take and have to start all over again. But always in the back of my mind was a niggling worry: maybe I'd missed 'cut' being called? Were the rest of the crew really still there behind us, recording our every move? Or back in the house, taking a tea break, and wondering where the hell we'd got to?

Gill slipped on a fresh turd. This alley was prime dog-walking territory for most of the neighbourhood, and wasn't exactly an area of outstanding natural beauty.

She managed to hold onto the bath though, and I could see her fighting with the desire to say something nasty about the parentage of people who don't clean up after their animals.

Fear won out. We couldn't risk ruining this take; there was no way we'd manage this a second time.

We arrived at the skip, and there was nothing else to do but heft the bath over the side. My muscles shrieked in protest; Gill was gritting her teeth and shaking visibly with the effort as we hauled it up, up, and over – and then we lowered the thing very gingerly onto the floor of the skip.

And at last, we heard 'cut'.

"That's great," said Dave, who had been sneaking along at a safe distance behind the camera.

"Did you want it in the skip?" I gasped. "We didn't know what to do, so we just carried on."

"Ah, yes, that was great. We'll get some close-ups of you lifting it into the skip later. For now though, we'd just like to get that again please, exactly the same, from the bathroom."

"What? You want us to take it back in again?"

"Yes, just to give us some options. We'll stay a bit wider this time."

"But…" Gill wheezed. "But we… oh, bugger it."

I asked if we could tip the tiles out into the skip.

We couldn't. For continuity reasons.

So we hauled the bath out again and carried the damn thing all the way back into the house, to the bemusement of the builders.

"Don't it fit, eh?" Dai asked.

I ignored him.

On our second attempt, walking backwards through a doorway carrying half a ton of bath-tub, Gill crashed into Dave and stomped heavily on his foot.

Needless to say, that take ended there; very nearly with Gill flat on her face in the bath, and Dave underneath it.

"I'm so sorry," Gill said. "Are you okay?"

"Oh I'm fine *dahling!*" said Dave, brushing away her concerns with an effeminate wave. "Didn't hurt a bit." And he rapped his knuckles against his kneecap. "It's false."

"Oh, that's good!" said Gill. "Well not good obviously, I mean, good that I didn't hurt you. Because…"

And she was wise enough to leave it there.

Gill has that ability – to stop talking before she digs herself in any deeper – something I never manage to achieve.

"I'm not hurt at all," said Dave, generously ignoring the fact that Gill could barely stand by this point. "Okay, why don't we take it once more, from the top?"

Three times we removed that bloody bath. As a direct result, Gill developed the ability to touch her toes without bending over. I don't think she'll ever forgive me for getting the TV people involved.

Hitting The Wall

Later that night, something occurred to Gill. She sat up in bed, damn near catapulting me off the other side. "Of course!" she exclaimed to no-one in particular.

"What? I was sleeping, damn it."

"Dave has a wooden leg!"

"Yes Gill, I know. Only it's probably metal and plastic. He's not a pirate."

"But don't you see – that's where it's coming from."

"What? Where what's coming from?"

"The squeaking! It's not the floorboards – it's Dave's leg!"

"Oh?"

"You know, every time the crew moves around, we can hear that high-pitched creaking?"

"I see. Well, that's a relief."

"So the floor isn't going to fall in. Old Dave just needs an oil change."

"Great. You can tell him tomorrow. After we get some sleep."

"I'm not telling him! How embarrassing. I already stood on him once. You'll have to tell him."

"I'm not telling him! No way!"

"Why not? He seems to like you."

"I know! Gill, that man is constantly calling me 'dahling'. There is no way in the world I'm asking him if he'd like to borrow some lubricant."

On the list of 'Must Be Filmed' moments, there was one in particular that our legless director had been adamant about.

"As soon as you know when you're bringing that living room wall down, make sure you give us a call," he'd said.

The next day I gave him a call.

"Hi Dave! I know when we're bringing the lounge wall down!"

"Oh, splendid! When is it?"

"In about an hour."

"WHAT? But that's impossible! Why didn't you call me sooner?"

"I only just found out myself. Because I caught Lenny hitting it with a sledgehammer."

"But you can't do it yet. You have to wait for us!"

"Well, that's what I tried to tell Lenny, but he didn't seem too keen."

"Just stop him, please, at least for a couple of days."

Lenny looked doubtful. "It's holding the whole job up now," he complained.

"Surely there's something else you can do?"

"The longer it takes, the more expensive it'll get, you see."

It was a standard response. And one I couldn't ignore.

I called Dave again.

"Look, these guys are really keen to get that wall down. I don't want to delay them too much – they'll only find a way to charge us for it."

"I'll see if I can have a crew out to you tomorrow," Dave told me. "A cameraman on his own, perhaps. I know a fellow in Cardiff. Leave it with me."

"Okay, but let me know as soon as you decide. I don't have a lot of control over these guys you know – they sort of take what I tell them under advisement, and carry on doing whatever they want."

"Just don't let them knock that wall down. We simply must get that on tape! It's essential to the programme."

I sprinted downstairs into the lounge, to find Lenny marshalling his troops. Now all of them were carrying sledgehammers.

"No! No, no. Don't do it," I told them.

"But this wall see, is gotta come down, innet?" said Dai. Incoherent – presumably illiterate – and a sexual deviant. Dai was quite a catch.

"Look, we've got a man coming to film it tomorrow. Don't do anything else in here 'til then, okay?"

Behind me there was a dull thud, as the third member of Lenny's team swung his hammer into the wall.

"Oi! What the hell are you doing?"

He looked at me, brow furrowed in confusion, as though wondering who I was and when I'd materialized in front of him.

"Don't. Hit. The wall," I explained.

"But is gotta come down now innet," Dai said.

This was not going well.

"Look, DO NOT hit ANYTHING 'til I get back!"

I ran upstairs and called Dave again.

"We have a bit of a problem. They aren't really listening to me I'm afraid."

I could feel his anger and frustration radiating out of the phone. I felt exactly the same way – although, the more I thought about it, it was Dave that was causing my frustration. If not for him, why would I give a shit when the builders knocked something down? So long as I wasn't underneath it at the time?

"It is absolutely vital that we get that on camera. Look, I'll get our man to drop what he's doing and get straight out to you. He'll be there in a couple of hours. You can stall them until then."

"Um… I'll try…"

"Right."

He hung up.

I let fly a good few swear-words, aimed at Dave for demanding the impossible, and at Lenny, for stubbornly doing the opposite of whatever I asked him.

I was caught between a dick and a head-case.

I couldn't help but wonder, how the hell I had gotten myself into this mess?

Oh, that's right. World Fame.

"If you keep this wall up until the camera gets here," I prayed to whatever deity was listening, "I promise I will never try to get famous again."

As if in response, I heard a *crunch!*

Shit! There was a definite thudding coming from the room below, almost as though a bunch of idiots with hammers were beating the crap out of a forbidden wall.

"Oh, the useless bastards!"

I ran to the stairs, the rhythmic ringing of steel-on-stone getting louder as I approached. There was a clatter which sounded suspiciously like a falling brick.

"Stop, stop, STOP!" I yelled.

I was about halfway down when a gigantic CRASH! shook the whole building. A cloud of dust billowed from the doorway at the bottom of the stairs. I fought my way through it, arms up to protect my face, one eye open just a crack. Inside the room the dust was already settling.

"Oh for fuck's sake! I told you NOT to do that!"

"S'alright," Dai told me, grinning like an idiot. "We done it already, see!"

I opened my mouth to… what? Scream? Curse? Demand they put the bloody thing back up again?

I closed my mouth. It tasted like hundred year-old plaster. I left the room, went back upstairs and picked up the phone.

I really, really wasn't looking forward to making this call.

It hadn't occurred to me until then, quite how much Lenny's crew didn't want to be on TV. Anytime I mentioned something that had to be filmed, they did their level-best to balls it up for me on purpose. It should have been a warning, really, that they were so worried about having their work documented. I just assumed they were camera shy – well, that two of them were shy and one was a child molester. In the long run this assumption probably cost us about £5,000, which is why they say that to ASSUME makes an ASS out of U and ME. This one made an ass out of all of us – with the film crew right there to record the whole lot.

And it still didn't make me famous.

Blaze of Glory

Later that week we had the first of many bonfires in the back garden.

Actually it was more like one bonfire, piled so high it burned all through the night, only to be rekindled in the morning with yet more chunks of shed and wheelbarrow after wheelbarrow of skinny wooden laths. It carried on like this for quite some time.

By the middle of the third day, Gill and I had become quite adept at piling up debris for the fire. We'd burnt almost every piece of wood in the house – apart from the skirting boards, which we'd decided we couldn't afford to replace.

We were taking a break to admire our creation when Gill was struck with an idea.

"It seems a shame to waste such a nice fire," she said. "Why don't we get something to cook on it tonight?"

We'd been eating exclusively from the three takeaways on our road, rotating between them on a nightly basis. I never would have thought it possible, but I was finally getting sick of pizza.

"That is a bloody brilliant idea!" I said. Gill always did have a streak of evil genius.

"We'll go to the shop before it closes and get, what? Sausages? Burgers? Bread rolls? Onions?"

"Onions might be going a bit far," I said, eyeing the towering inferno in front of me.

"Okay. We'll let it die down a bit then, and cook some stuff afterwards."

So that is what we did.

It was already freezing outside by the time we stopped working, so we took a big bottle of cider out with us to ward off the cold.

Suitably fortified, we faced the task at hand.

"How the hell do we cook on this thing?" I asked.

Gill had more experience with this than me – I was in the shittiest troop of Boy Scouts that ever dobbed and dibbed. While better equipped, more motivated groups were off canoeing or climbing mountains, our lot played football outside the Scout hut – as though they didn't do enough of that at school – and sod all else. As the lone voice of geek-lust, I only ever managed to achieve two things in the Scouts (unless you count getting stuffed into a wheelie bin more times than I care to remember). I got my reading badge, for proving not only that I owned a book, but that I'd actually *read it*. I even prepared a report on it, but the mood in the Scout hut had been ugly that night; the leader knew if he let me read it out, I'd be going home in a bin again.

My second proudest (and only other) achievement during the two years I belonged to the troop was this: I got my Camp Cook badge. For making sandwiches.

Thus, I was relying on Gill to provide the culinary expertise.

The same summer I'd spent getting mauled by wild animals in Ecuador, Gill had spent getting mauled by ten year old girls at summer camp. Consequently she had acquired a terrifying repertoire of nonsensical songs about hippopotami, and extensive experience of campfire cooking.

Allegedly.

But her fires had been rather more sedate affairs. Even burning low, this monster was far too hot to sit next to. We began with long sticks, skewering the burgers and standing there holding them until our jeans began to smoke.

"We're doing great at cooking trousers," Gill pointed out, "but my burger is still frozen. Maybe I should Sellotape it to my legs."

Instead we tried using longer sticks, but they burned through quickly, depositing a pair of half-cooked burgers in the midst of the blaze.

"We could wrap them in foil…" she suggested, trailing off as she realised the obvious. "If we had foil."

"We need some kind of griddle," I told her.

This garden had bequeathed us a vast quantity of unexpected metal items, but most of them had ended up in the skip. There were still piles of crap amongst the rubble of the shed, but that wasn't the kind of ground one crossed in the dead of night.

"Windscreen!" Gill said.

You could be forgiven for wondering why she'd had that thought.

In fact, the previous owner had planted a large number of car windscreens all around the garden. We never figured out why. Maybe they were booby traps. Or maybe he was trying to grow them.

So we chose the cleanest, and manoeuvred it delicately onto the fire. Now we were in business!

We just had time to dig out another couple of beef burgers from the packet when the glass exploded outwards, showering us in tiny, glittering cubes.

We both sat there, too stunned to react, as the shards rattled to rest all around us.

Gill was the first to recover. She brushed a few lumps of glass off the burger in her hand and looked over at the fence where we'd stacked the rest of the windscreens. It was thick with frost.

"I think that windscreen was a bit cold," she said.

"Yes. I think so too."

But what to do? We couldn't be defeated. Not when victory was a sausage sandwich away...

"I've GOT IT!" I leapt up and headed for the ladder leaning against the back of the house. Jutting out from the window ledge at first-floor height was a busted-up TV aerial. I'd been meaning to pull it down for days. I honestly thought it would have fallen off on its own, as the brick it was attached to had eroded completely. As I yanked on the thing it seemed reluctant to surrender, clinging on to the side of the house for all it was worth. Finally I wrenched the thing up and down, and was rewarded with a snap. After that it came away easily – trailing a long wire that led back into the house. I pulled on this wire and it kept coming, until one last violent yank seemed to free up the other end. And the aerial was ours!

"What took you so long?" Gill asked.

"Um, well it was still connected. A bit."

"Oh. Shit."

"Well, we probably needed a new one anyway..."

"We *definitely* need a new one now. You'd better add it to the list."

"Yeah. Oops."

Nevertheless, it worked a treat. The double row of sticky-out spines could almost have been made to balance burgers and sausages on. Gill cooked up a storm, though she still couldn't sit close enough to tend them regularly because clouds of noxious black smoke would erupt without warning from the fire, engulfing our food.

"I'm a bit worried about that," Gill admitted, as we tucked into our dinner. "God only knows what we've put onto this bonfire. Plaster, plastic, glass, chemicals..."

"Yeah, and paint, and carpet, and foam from that old armchair... and some of that shit from the shed roof!" I reminded her.

"What I'm thinking is, these fumes are probably quite toxic. And we're cooking on them. We might just have poisoned our burgers."

"It's a good point," I conceded, pausing before taking another bite.

"But they look alright, eh?"

"Yeah." Gill shrugged. "And I'm seriously sick of pizza."

So we ate the lot.

Then, in celebration of our successful meal, and possibly under the influence of assorted dangerous chemicals, we decided to create the mother of all bonfires. It was Gill's idea, of course. "If it burns all night, and is gone by morning, we'll be nearly done with burning stuff."

It felt good to combine a strong work ethic with a strong play ethic, so we piled everything we could find onto the fire and coaxed the flames higher and higher. We had to sit further and further away, with freezing cold backs and burning hot faces.

At one point I stood up to fetch more cider and was garrotted by an unseen assailant. Gill creased with laughter as I collapsed back to earth making strangled noises. "What the fuck is that?" I demanded.

I fumbled around with the torch, shining it into the impenetrable darkness above us, and finally managed to focus on my attacker. It was a long length of black cable, strung clear across the garden at head height. "What the hell? No way that was there before!"

It was some minutes before we figured it out, stumbling towards the back of the garden, tracing the wire with our hands.

"It loops up to the telegraph pole," Gill said.

"So it's the phone line? But why didn't we notice it before?"

And that's when it hit us, at exactly the same moment.

"It runs directly over the fire," I said.

"We melted it," Gill finished.

"Maybe we can tighten it up again?"

Gill gestured towards the raging inferno between us and the house. "It's still over the fire. And we can't really turn the fire off."

Of course, there was nothing we could do. The line, passing right over the hottest part of the blaze, was going to hang lower and lower until it was consumed.

"Well, there is one thing we can do," I corrected myself.

That night, by the glow of our one dangly light-bulb, I dug around for a pen and made a note on my 'Jobs To Do' list.

No.287: Get new phone line fitted.

Our One Dangly Light-bulb

There is a reason we only had one.

The dangly light-bulb was the height of innovation.

It had been made by Dad for our caravan holidays, and consisted of a length of electrical cable with a light fitting at one end and a plug at the other. The cable passed through a large plastic bulldog clip, allowing us to attach the lamp to any convenient surface – so long as that surface could cope with the heat generated by a 240 volt light fitting. It had to be kept well away from clothes, and curtains – basically any kind of textile – and anything made of plastic. And when the dust settled on it at night, it made a smell like burning insects.

I dunno. Maybe it was burning insects.

I think you can buy purpose-built, somewhat safer versions of this lamp, for about £3, but Dad had made this one out of spare parts – ten years ago – so it was free.

The dangly light-bulb was a vital part of our encampment, which was currently set up in what would eventually become the Master Bedroom.

We'd started out in the front bedroom, where Mum had accidentally pulled half the wall down. The unbelievable amount of dust stirred up by this, and then by ripping all the lath-and-plaster out, had forced us to retreat to the lounge – and now the same problem, caused in part by the wall coming down, had prompted us to move back upstairs.

Wherever we were, the set-up was the same. A square of black carpet that had been clean at the start of the project (it had originally been beige).

A pair of folding camp chairs, which we used to keep our work clothes off the floor at night. This was a natural impulse, though a fairly pointless one; after wearing the same outfits for up to a week at a time, there was every chance that placing them on the floor would only make the floor dirtier.

And we had a desk, covered in tools, paperwork, and a fine

coating of the ubiquitous black powder.

To ensure our comfort, Mum and Dad had left our camp festooned with electrical devices. We had a toaster. A microwave. A kettle. A fan heater, a CD player, our one dangly light-bulb – and a vacuum cleaner.

No prize for guessing what we used least.

But the electrics were in a delicate state. We had one 'live' socket working downstairs – the only one that didn't have round pin holes – and everything else daisy-chained off it. Several 4-way socket adaptors were plugged into each other, looking remarkably like that picture you get on the instruction sheet, under the warning 'DO NOT PLUG ADAPTORS INTO EACH OTHER!'. This little sculpture hummed ominously. Extension leads looped away in all directions, towards the lounge, the bedrooms, and downstairs to the basement; it was like living in the lair of a mad engineer.

We could plug in up to four things at a time in the bedroom. Most of the time we only needed three. Unfortunately only two would work at once, or there would be a colossal 'BANG!' from the fuse box and we'd lose the lot. We discovered this soon after dark on our first night – along with the fact that we didn't have any replacement fuses.

That was a long, cold, dark night.

And more importantly, we couldn't have a cup of tea.

From then on we had a two-device limit. During the day we could listen to the radio, or blast out our favourite tunes on the CD player – as long as we remembered to turn it off before we started making lunch. Then the beans were heated first, followed by the toast, and when all the other appliances were safely switched off, we could risk using the kettle.

During the day we relied on our own activity and the sun to heat us up. If nothing else, it encouraged us to work harder; as I might have mentioned, they don't get a lot of sun in Wales. If it shines for more than two days in a row, the locals get suspicious and start firing arrows at it. But in the evenings, when the dark closed in, the bitter winter's cold came with it.

Then it was decision time.

Evenings were not about what we wanted, but what we wanted *most*.

Light and heat were the first priorities.

It was like playing chess; fan heater takes stereo.

But after soldiering on for a few hours, clearing up debris by the light of the dangly bulb, sooner or later we would flat out *need* a cup of tea.

This was our number one dilemma.

The little heater struggled to maintain a civilized temperature as it was, due in no small part to the size of the house and the number of holes in it. We could just about keep our bedroom habitable by running it full-bore and keeping the door closed at all times. Turning it off, even for ten minutes, was a betrayal of all it stood for; it rarely forgave us, and seemed to take a perverse pleasure in blowing only cold air for the first half-hour after we started it up again.

Which meant that, after a hard day's toil in the garden, we could have light and heat – but not the cup of tea we so desperately deserved. Or we could see what we were doing while we froze our asses off, and have a cup of tea in the cold – or we could stay nice and warm and cosy – and brew up in the dark.

It's a testament to our tenacity (and our Britishness) that we finished off a box of teabags every other week.

Going to bed was an altogether more pleasant experience. We looked forward to it all day, every day. Like one of those dubious old sitcoms where the whole family slept in one bed, Gill and I became quite pragmatic about our shared living arrangements.

She'd brought her laptop and we were slowly working our way through a stack of sci-fi series we'd bought on DVD. We could bed down in the warmth of our sleeping bags, turn the light off and watch an old episode of *Dark Angel* quite comfortably – until one of us needed the loo. This of course meant a three-floor climb through the pitch black house, down to the basement and out of the back door. So the light would have to go on while we scrabbled to find the torch, which meant the heater had to go off. We became remarkably efficient at synchronising our bladders for this reason.

Drinking all that tea probably didn't help.

There was one other aspect of this particular living arrangement that never ceased to amuse me. Our air mattress, despite being brand new, was knackered right from the start, leading to a nightly ordeal of re-inflating it with a tiny electric pump. It sounded like we were running a diesel generator at maximum power, which must have delighted the neighbours (as we typically knocked off work at around 1am). Within minutes of unplugging the pump – long before the heater had managed to restore warmth to the room – the bed was sinking. At that moment, as Gill lay there relaxing – reading by the dangly light-bulb perhaps – I could 'fall' purposefully onto the mattress, which would catapult Gill off the other side with alarming ferocity – usually into a small pile of tools. To this day, I don't think she realised I was doing it on purpose. Even though I did it every night. I would always apologise profusely, complain that we'd only just inflated the damn bed – and then go to sleep with a smirk. Well, once the dangly light-bulb was turned off.

But I hated waking up in those days.

The air mattress predictably deflated over the course of each night so that in the morning we woke up as stiff as the floorboards we were lying on. Once I even woke up from dreams of drowning under a swimming pool cover to find the thing on top of me, dripping with condensation.

It was cold, so bitterly cold in those mornings, and our lone fan-heater had been struggling all night to keep us cosy. The air was thick with dust still, and the first thing I did on waking was wipe my face – turning my hand black in the process. The damn stuff got everywhere, but it seemed to love it up my nose. I could dig around in there for several minutes before I got it all out - yet another delightful daily occurrence.

But the real reason I hated waking up early was not the fact that I was sneezing hundred year-old plaster, freezing my balls off and lying on a plank; it was because I needed a shit.

And I couldn't have a shit.

As the search for a replacement plumber was still on-going, we'd been without a toilet for rather longer than we'd anticipated. Weeing in the garden, whilst not particularly sanitary, was a necessary evil – and I could at least be grateful that I was born a man. Gill suffered considerably more than me in this regard.

But for the last month, our only opportunity to lay cable was to leg it to Carpanini's Café down the road, and buy a cup of coffee. It was a regular part of our day; we generally took only two breaks – one for lunch, and one for a cup of coffee and a shit.

The café staff knew this, knew us in fact, and were always amused by our visits – until the morning after those possibly-poisoned beef burgers, when Gill got desperate all of a sudden, ran full-tilt down the road to the café and sprinted past the counter without stopping.

"A coffee and a shit please!" she yelled as she passed.

Even in Wales they consider that bad manners.

Alas, the café didn't open until 9am. Sometimes, just to torture us, they'd wait until 10am. None of that mattered though, on the mornings I woke at six with that clenching feeling in my stomach... I'd struggle up, fumbling for shoes and clothes in the pre-dawn gloom. With no lights in the rest of the house, I'd stumble downstairs into the basement, falling over at least three unfortunately positioned tools or piles of rubble as I went, and make it to the garden just in time. In sub-zero temperatures I'd whip my tackle out and pray that no-one else in the long line of terraces was looking out of their back window at that moment. My wee steamed in the frigid air like it was sending smoke signals to a distant observer, while I shook with cold and concentrated on three things;

1) Steadiness – I had to ignore my chattering teeth and shivering arms and wee in a straight line, rather than all over my feet.

2) Stability – because footing in the garden was uncertain at best, and it wouldn't do to fall face-first into a puddle of my own piss.

But most of all:

3) Pressure regulation. Because if I lost control for even a split-second, and peed too enthusiastically, there was every chance that I would shit myself.

Pied Piper

Mum was having an impossible time locating another plumber. Not only were they all busy, none of them were keen to pick up where someone else had left off. Something about not being able to guarantee their work when it had been started by somebody else.

Finally she'd resorted to begging each of the tradesmen that came to site, in the hope that one of them would know someone who could help out.

I think it was an electrician who finally uttered the fateful words: "I might know a guy. If you're desperate."

It was not the most auspicious of introductions.

But there were several overriding factors here:

We still had no heating. It was now December.

We still had only one tap for water – and it was leaking.

We were going weeks at a time without a shower – whilst being filmed in close-up for TV.

The café had put the price of their coffee up (which I think they did solely for our benefit – the buggers).

And we were still pissing in the garden – despite the fact that we were also now working in it on a daily basis.

We were very desperate indeed.

James the plumber was very nearly the answer to our prayers.

He was young. He was friendly. He was available, and amazingly enough we could almost afford him… Yes I know, I'm making him sound like a male prostitute.

Sorry! My mistake.

James the plumber was most definitely not a male prostitute.

James the plumber was a drug dealer.

He would rock up quite cheerfully, at about 10:15am. His first order of the day was to roll a giant spliff, and share it with his mate who was here to help him out. Presumably by consuming enough of the drugs himself, the friend would keep James standing, and thus able to work.

Not that he did much work; 10:30am was knock-off time, and James and his mate would disappear for a much needed breakfast at a café further down the valley.

It usually took them about an hour.

After that work did commence, and they alternated cutting holes in the floor and soldering copper pipes with smoking until around 1pm, which was lunch.

They took an hour for lunch, worked until 3pm, and then it was home-time.

It meant that progress was painfully slow; for days at a time nothing seemed to change, especially on the days they knocked off early 'to go to another job', which I assumed to be plumber code for 'let's go get baked back at my place'.

I couldn't really say anything, because we were fresh out of plumbers. They don't grow on trees apparently – although this one was doing his level-best to become a vegetable.

After he'd been there for a week, chopping chunks out of our floorboards seemingly at random, James surprised me by asking if I'd like to come for breakfast with him. I thought, why not? Maybe in an unguarded moment he'd let me in on his plans for the plumbing, so I would finally have a clue as to what he was doing. Perhaps I'd get a chance to ask him about some of his more dubious decisions, including the hole he'd cut at the top of the stairs. It was the very top step, the edge of the landing if you like – or rather, it should have been. James had removed the floorboard entirely at this point, lopping it off just shy of the joist. It didn't seem easily repairable, not with enough strength to survive being in such a high-traffic area, and for now it meant that anyone coming up the stairs had a 50/50 chance of putting their foot right through the ceiling. I'd almost done it at least once a day since the hole arrived, and was only saved by my habit of running up the stairs so fast I skipped the top step entirely. Dad, his mind preoccupied with matters of finance, hadn't been so lucky. He'd put his foot right in it, and had been saved from falling through the ceiling below by the existence of a copper pipe under the floor, which had taken his weight long enough for him to pull his foot back out. Consequently, this pipe was no longer attached to anything.

We hoped it was nothing important.

Gill agreed to stay behind and make sure the builders didn't destroy anything vital while I was gone. And anyway, she wasn't invited.

Supposedly, 'chicks don't dig this place'.

James drove his car at frightening speed, down the narrow main road with cars parked on both sides. His driver's seat was reclined almost to the horizontal, and his mannerisms were as laid back as his position. At one point I was convinced he was asleep, until a lightening-fast gear change and a sudden squeal of brakes signalled our arrival at...

A closed-down industrial estate.

Huge steel gates barred the way, chains dangling from the latches. The enclosing fence was formidable, topped with coils of rusty barbed wire. There were no gun towers that I could see, but I couldn't be sure they weren't there somewhere. Beyond the fence lurked a huddle of abandoned warehouses, huge, sheet-metal sided monstrosities with their bottom halves covered in graffiti. Junk lay here and there, in the alleys between derelict brick buildings, cars that were slowly disintegrating sat on concrete forecourts with weeds growing through the cracks. It was a scene from our post-apocalyptic future, brought to life (or lack thereof) somewhere in the middle of the Welsh valleys.

In fact it struck me as the kind of place you'd take someone if you were going to rape them and murder them. James motioned me to get out and haul the gates open while he drove in; they swung ominously closed behind us when I let them go.

I suddenly wished Gill was here.

James crawled the car through the maze of industrial buildings, following a route he knew well. Grass grew in the middle of the first alleyway he took us down, and I had the feeling it hadn't seen much traffic in the last decade.

What the hell was going on here?

Then he pointed out a tiny sign nailed onto the corner of a warehouse in front of us.

'BREAKFASTS' it said, in flaking brown letters.

A row of slightly newer cars filled the gap between it and the burnt-out brick building next door.

"You've got to be kidding me!"

But he wasn't.

Sectioned off from the main part of the warehouse was a small, bustling café. It was invisible from the outside; the door we entered by was a featureless sheet of metal. Inside, the array of paint-stained overalls and work boots on display confirmed my suspicions; this was a tradesman's café, undiscovered by John Q. Public, and those present were obviously keen to keep it that way.

That way, they didn't have to worry about pesky things like insurance and taxes. And health inspections.

The place was full of huge, bearded, tattooed men, grimly shovelling food into their gobs at high speed. There was a sullen buzz of conversation, but most of the patrons were concentrating on eating. It reminded me of a prison canteen, only dirtier and less cheerful.

The meal they served up was as deadly as a cyanide milkshake.

Fried sausages, fried beans, fried eggs, fried bread. Black pudding. Fried. And chips. Two, three or four of everything was the only variation on offer; both my erstwhile plumbers ordered the latter, and were presented with a pile of food dripping enough grease to keep a battleship oiled. It was so big it came on two plates. I opted for a slightly smaller version, as I hadn't partaken of the spliff they'd shared on the drive here; hence, my need for munchies was proportionately less.

Now I knew why they needed an hour for breakfast. It took me half that time just to figure out where to start!

But it was worth every minute.

As we ate, James regaled me with stories of how ridiculous the training to be a plumber was. The final exam was apparently multiple choice, and so hard to fail you could let your dog take it for you and still have a reasonable chance of success.

I asked him if floor carpentry was on the syllabus, and was relieved to hear that it was. Although he didn't hold his training in high regard, I was glad to know that he wasn't just making it up as he went along – because to the unqualified observer, it sure did look that way.

Back at the house, he did me a good turn when I got The Fear, clinging on to the top of a very, very tall ladder whilst trying to paint above a window. It was a top floor window, which meant the third floor as we were outside the back of the house. The ladder, long and spindly, reached all the way up from a distinctly dubious footing in the garden, and ran out of rungs a good thirty feet from the ground. Right at the top, I'd been painting around a window frame, but having to stretch up to reach the top of the lintel made it impossible to hold on. Suddenly I was at the effect of the wind; every buffet of the ladder translated along its length, shaking me just enough to make me wet myself. One gust too much and I could take no more; I slipped the paint bucket handle over my elbow and fled downwards. By the time I reached the bottom I was trembling with equal parts fear and embarrassment. I couldn't believe I'd been defeated by such a simple job, yet the thought of going back up the ladder to finish it off made me break out in a cold sweat.

James had seen me through the window and come out to see what I was up to. I took the opportunity to rant about the circumstances which saw me dicing with death just to paint a sodding window ledge.

"Ah, give it here then," James said. He didn't sound too worried.

He took the brush and bucket off me, slowly climbed the ladder right the way to the top, then dared a rung or two even further than I had (because he was a fair bit shorter than me) and deftly painted the last patch. It didn't seem to bother him at all; he climbed back down in the same relaxed manner, placed the bucket and brush by the bottom rung, and strolled back into the house without a word.

I'd thought I had no fear any more – now I knew otherwise.

This was a man with no fear.

"Although in hindsight," Dad said later, "he was probably stoned out of his mind the whole time."

Hammer Time

My mother operating a jackhammer is a sight to be seen.

For starters, she's not considerably taller than the jackhammer we'd chosen to rent.

She probably outweighed it – but not by much.

So we'd each taken a turn, showcasing our unique reactions for the camera.

It was pain for me; I'd been far more concerned with looking strong for the viewing public that I had been about my technique. Consequently, I'd managed to jackhammer my foot on all three takes, and had to go and sit down for a while.

After grim determination from Dad, and maniacal glee from Gill (she practically rode the thing around the garden) – it came down to Mum.

To her credit, she barely hesitated, grunting with the effort of holding the thing upright when Gill passed it over.

She gripped the handles, waited until everyone else was clear, and then squeezed.

Mum became a blur. The vibrations of such a tool, normally directed into the ground, instead travelled upwards and enveloped her completely. The point of the tool tracked forwards, pulling her with it – then it skittered off sideways, spinning her around like a top. One moment she was headed back to the house, leaving a trail of chipped concrete, the next she'd spun again and was being pulled towards the fence. The whole time, her concentration was absolute; this could be told by the tip of her tongue, protruding from the side of her mouth in a way that apparently helps her focus. It was vibrating too, so that to look directly at her face was to think she was blowing a dark pink bubble.

Then the hard hat she'd been given – far too big, even at its smallest setting, for her pin-sized head – slid forwards over her eyes. It was vibrating too.

First Gill, then me, then Dad, rushed to her aid.

No? Don't believe me? Well that's good then, because it was a lie.

In fact we fell about laughing, so hard that some of the crew joined in.

By the time Dave called 'cut!', even he was cracking a smile.

Mum had to be extracted from the jackhammer, which she had managed to lock into the 'on' position. She wobbled over, still trembling, to sit on a chunk of the smashed conservatory.

"I did it," she croaked.

"Yes! Congratulations! Although I think *it* did *you*, more than the other way around."

"Yeah," said Gill, "we should get you a badge that says 'I've been Jackhammered!'"

Dave squeaked over with a request.

"That was magnificent *dahling!* Could we do it one more time? This time —" he paused to fix the rest of us with a dark look "— without the laughter?"

Mum sighed. "Okay. But can you wait until the ground stops shaking?"

The 'sun room' floor was wrecked that day, and proved to be made of poured concrete almost a foot thick. It was staggering, and almost certainly the strongest part of the whole house. The big chunks had to be broken down into smaller chunks just so we could lift them into the wheelbarrow.

But just when we thought we were winning, Gill and I started to work on the path.

Whoever built that path, built it to survive Armageddon. Seriously. After the bombs have gone off, when mankind is extinct and cockroaches have inherited the earth, this thing will be their super-highway.

There was a thin layer of concrete on top of a thicker, much darker layer of concrete. My hammer bounced off both of them with little noticeable effect.

Below the thicker concrete was a layer of stones and gravel, which presumably had been put down as a base for the pour. What had been put down as a base for the gravel though, was a double-layer of house-bricks – all mortared together as though they were the wall of some long-buried building. Cursing and swearing in disbelief, Gill and I also unearthed dozens of iron bars from beneath the bricks. I don't think they'd been added to the mix intentionally to strengthen the path, but they did a bloody good job of it. It was a bit short for a 747 runway, but I'm sure it could have taken the weight.

It took us longer to destroy that path than it did to dig up and re-turf the entire garden.

I did love using my hammer though. I'd carefully weighed up the cost-to-destructive-potential ratio of all the hammers on offer in B&Q – and then thought *bollocks to that*, and bought the biggest. Its handle came up to my waist, which allowed me to strike a suitably heroic pose while I summoned up the strength to lift the thing – and never, not for one minute, did I regret buying it. I don't care what you've heard.

A similarly-proportioned axe – which was easily big enough to decapitate a brontosaurus – had been vetoed by Mum for budgetary reasons.

"And we're not exactly overrun with brontosaurus at the moment," she'd pointed out.

Ah well.

At least I had the hammer.

There was something very satisfying about it. It made me feel like a *man*. Like I was back in Ecuador, chopping down trees with a rusty machete the size of a bread knife. I'd been using it a lot whenever the TV crew were around. In my head my muscles rippled, golden in the sun as I wrenched the hammer from the crater I'd created, swung it high overhead, and released it for another titanic impact.

In reality, nothing was golden – not my pale, scrawny frame and certainly not the drizzly Welsh weather. The sky was as grey as the concrete, and my oversized hammer was making about the same amount of difference to both.

Even Gill was doing better at it than me.

She was using a much smaller version of the same tool, which I had labelled a 'Gill-sized' hammer. She took turns with the big one just as I took turns with the smaller, but as far as I was concerned there was no issue of whose was whose.

Unfortunately.

With considerably less theatrics than I was putting in, Gill was chipping away at the path, flaking fragments off the uppermost layer that seemed to be defeating my best efforts.

All that was set to change though.

Dai had arrived in the back garden, carrying a pile of splintered planks which look suspiciously like our skirting boards.

His eyes lit up as he watched the hammer raise, fall, and ricochet off the concrete with a dull thud.

"Gis 'ere," he said, striding forward with hand outstretched.

Chagrined, I surrendered the hammer. Okay so I wasn't having much success, but the last thing I wanted was tips from this dick-head.

What can you do though? Can't argue with someone you can't understand.

Dai smacked the hammer into the ground a few times, then brought it up in front of us, pointed to the corner of the head and said, "See! It's the breakin' edge this, the breakin' edge!"

He smashed the ground, another three strokes, eliciting nothing more dramatic than the familiar dull thud. This concrete could absorb a blow better than a lorry-load of Kleenex.

Dai wasn't bothered at all by his less-than-spectacular results.

"You gotta use the breakin' edge, the breaking edge, innet." he told us - and he swung the hammer again, three brutal stokes into the concrete path. As before they had about the same effect as we had been achieving on our own.

"See?" said Dai, as though this proved something. "You gotta use the breakin' edge, see!"

Again he attacked the path three times.

"See?"

Gill and I exchanged confused glances.

"Use the breakin' edge, innet!"

Up came the hammer. Down came the hammer. Three more savage strokes.

I had a feeling I knew what was coming next.

"Dai!" I caught his attention before he could speak. "We use the… 'breakin' edge', do we?"

"Yeah, that's it, see, the breakin' edge, this here's the breakin', edge, see?"

And he swung for the path with a vengeance.

I felt like I was in Groundhog day. Gill looked at me, amused and perplexed in equal measure. The man was clearly an idiot; anyone spending more than ten minutes in his company would figure that out. But now he seemed stuck in some compulsive loop, attacking the path, extolling the virtue of the tool in barely discernable English, then some chip misfired in his brain and he felt compelled to do it all again. It was like his reset button was stuck down.

Another round of instruction followed by demonstration occurred.

I had to say something to Gill. To check this wasn't something going wrong in my own mind. Was I standing there in the middle of the path, comatose, seeing the same images over and over while my family frantically phoned the paramedics?

But no. Gill was looking as bemused as I must have been.

Further down the path Dai continued his demonstration, bobbing up-down, up-down, up-down, pausing only to bawl something incoherent about the 'breakin' edge'.

Gill and I watched his violent retreat down the garden.

"We have a problem," I said to her. "I think we broke our idiot."

Goo-d Intentions

The decision to re-plaster only the walls that couldn't be saved was a nightmare disguised as a blessing. Well to be honest, I always thought it was a nightmare, but the pressure on the budget had to be alleviated somehow, and a whole-house plastering was never really on the cards.

Instead, Gill and I became masters in the rarely-seen art of Goo-ing.

We would pick a wall. Then we would identify the flaws in it. Then we would fill said flaws with a small quantity of a substance rather like Polyfiller (but of a substantially cheaper and less-known brand). According to the instructions on the tub, this was the time when we would wait anything up to an hour for the stuff to set – but in reality it was when we turned our attentions to the next bit of wall and reached for the tub of goo again. We got through a lot of that stuff. Tubs and tubs and tubs of it.

And once the goo-ing was finished, there came the sanding.

Except, the goo-ing never did finish. There were occasional cries of triumph when one or the other of us thought they had filled all the cracks in a particular wall, but this joy was short-lived. Closer inspection always revealed more imperfections, as the better we made the finish, the more perfectionist we became about it.

Gill and I, in hindsight, were not the right people for a job like this.

I know people who write three or four books a year. My first book took me six years. Why? Because I just couldn't leave the damn thing alone...

So we goo'ed each wall again, and again, and *again* – each time raising the bar a little higher in terms of the standard we were trying to achieve.

Add to that the monstrous size of the house, spread across three stories, and the sheer quantity of walls – the Victorians not being overly fond of open-plan living – and the task was literally endless.

Every so often an overly enthusiastic bit of sanding precipitated a crumbling, and a previously goo'ed section of plaster would fall away leaving us to start again.

We got through packet after packet of sandpaper.

When we both developed a cough, we tried wearing masks, but it just wasn't practical. Hot breath blowing up past your nose makes your whole face sweat in seconds – which, combined with an atmosphere composed mostly of plaster dust, gave rise to special effects worthy of a Hollywood zombie movie.

With our clothes and hair caked in solid white, strings of a paste-like substance hanging off our faces and the only visible flesh colour coming from stripes where our frown-lines were, it was no wonder we drew attention when we trekked down to the café for a cup of coffee and a shit.

It was around this time that the TV crew returned for another day of interviews – and this time they wanted to catch us in bed.

"What time do you get up?" asked Rachel.

"About six am. Sometimes seven on the weekend." Dust billowed in the disturbed air between my mouth and the phone.

"Oh! Six am! Ah, we can get out to you by, say, nine o' clock?"

"Okay... do we just wait for you?"

"Yes, yes! Don't do anything! Stay in bed! Take the morning off!!"

That did give me cause for a chuckle. When she got to see our living arrangements... perhaps then she'd understand our work ethic.

Gill was instantly suspicious when I broke the news to her.

"We've got a morning off!"

"Oh? Why?"

"Well, they want to film us in bed."

"In *bed*? Doing what?"

"Being bloody uncomfortable, presumably. I think they want to interview us on what it's like to live on site while the building is going on."

"Ah. Right. Do you think we should tidy up?"

I glanced around. A layer of fine white powder lay over everything. It looked like it had been snowing. I was suddenly reminded of the first month of the project, when everything had been coated in black from the demolition of the ancient lath-and-plaster. "Well, you know what'll happen if we do."

"Yeah. When we wake up it'll look exactly the same."

So we decided not to bother.

But when you've gone to sleep on a bouncy castle and woken up on a double-bed-sized used condom, a lie-in loses a lot of its appeal.

We lay there for a bit, breathing dust from the floor, feeling guilty, and then we undertook our second cunning deception of the film crew; we worked. After a quick bowl of Cornflakes we managed to put in a good couple of hours' sanding before they arrived.

We got a bit carried away actually. When the knock on the door came, I was balanced on the landing bannister, straining to reach a crack in the wall directly above the foot of the stairs. Gill was underneath me, wearing most of the plaster my exertions had dislodged.

"Shit! They're here!" she said. "Look at the state of the place!"

I ran downstairs to let the crew in, brushing the worst of the plaster off me as I went. I passed Gill, who just shook herself like a dog; a great cloud of white dust billowed out from her clothes, hanging in the air as she retreated back to the bedroom. I could sense some fast talking would be required.

I opened the door to Rachel.

"Hello there!" she said. "Sorry to wake you." She took two steps inside, and squinted through the haze. "God, this is terrible! Is it normally this dusty?"

"Dusty?" I asked her. "Where? In here?"

"What, you mean you don't notice it?"

"Notice what? I don't know what you're talking about."

"This dust! It's so thick in here, I can hardly see!"

"Oh, really? That is strange. I must just be used to it."

It was bizarre to crawl back into my sleeping bag and lie there while the crew clambered around us with tripods and sound recording equipment. They stirred up dust and sneezed, forgot things and swore, and generally made a right old racket. Gill and I lay there, trying to keep warm; the fan heater no longer took priority over our meagre electrical supply.

When the interviews started, we both found ourselves complaining more than usual. The invasion of our privacy didn't really bother us, but it brought home to the crew exactly what kind of a mess we were living in. I don't think they'd fully realised it until then.

"We don't mind the basic conditions," Gill explained, "it's the filth! Last week I went to run my hand through my hair and... it stuck!"

"The dust is the worst part," I added. "It's chalky. Not crunchy, like the last stuff. It's in everything we eat you see, and everything we drink. There are places on my body where the light of day never shines – and I bet all of them are clogged with plaster!"

"When I sneeze, I make a cloud!" Gill said.

"You don't want to know what happens when she farts!" I quipped.

None of that made it into the programme.

But I think the crew gained a new level of respect for us from that point on. And it goes without saying that they started to feel sorry for us.

They'd had to leave early to get to us while it was still morning. They'd made the whole journey from London without a single coffee break, and none of them were happy about it.

I started to offer them a brew, but all eyes turned to where the mugs sat on our desk, coated in dust.

"I could go down to the tap and wash them for you," I offered, but I could tell they weren't impressed. "Trouble is, by the time the coffee was ready, they'd be in the same state... We've sort of gotten used to it."

But Rachel was on the ball, ever eager to solve a problem before it arose.

"I'll go out for coffees. There's a café down the street." She pulled out her notebook and pen. "Ready?"

Dave placed his order first. "A Mocha, today I think, with the usual. Thanks terribly, *dahling.*"

"Just a skinny latte," one of the others piped up.

"Same for me, but full-fat with cream."

There was a bit of light-hearted ribbing of the guy who'd made the calorific choice. Finally the cameraman spoke up. "I'll take a chai latte. With soy milk, of course."

Rachel scribbled in her notebook, the very picture of efficiency. I had to smile.

"And what would you guys like?"

Gill and I exchanged glances. Mischievous glances.

"I'll have a coffee please," I told Rachel.

"Just a... coffee...?"

"Yes thanks!"

"Any particular type?"

"It's the one on the menu, right under 'tea'."

"And above 'orange juice'," Gill chipped in. "I'll have the same, thanks."

Rachel was gone a good bit longer than I expected her to be. I got to wondering how far down her list of demands they'd let her get, before dropping a reality check on her. She was so obviously not from around here that she made us feel like locals. Unfortunately for Rachel, reality in the Welsh Valleys was somewhat grimmer than she was used to.

I could imagine her going through her entire spiel to the letter, years of experience honing her to forget nothing lest she risk upsetting some important TV executive.

And I could imagine the amused reply by one of the ladies who ran the café.

"Right you are love, seven coffees coming up. Sugar's in them packets just by there."

Rachel returned with polystyrene cups of generic 'coffee', with biro scrawled on the sides to identify the contents. There weren't many variations.

The crew were appalled by this inadequacy, shaking their heads in disbelief and muttering words like 'quaint'.

The women in that café had a sarcastic streak.

It was most amusing to watch Dave scowl over a steaming white cup with S&M written on it.

Me and Gill weren't used to morning coffee. It was a luxury, so we hoarded it. The lids remained firmly in place at all times, and we would peel them off only occasionally for a quick slurp.

The crew were less cautious. Lids were discarded and coffees left to cool while the day's shots were discussed. The result of this, after five minutes or so, was a thin white film on the surface of the liquid, which didn't endear it to its intended recipients.

"Bloody hell!" someone moaned, "It's covered in scum!"

"Yeah." I touched my crusty-coated hair. "That happens."

That was the first and last time they bought coffee from Carpanini's.

It was another day of gruelling interviews, following the now familiar format: ("Are you happy with the work the builders are doing?" "Yes." "How much, a little or a lot?" "A little." "So, not very happy then?" "No." "Okay, say that in a sentence! Start with 'I'm not very happy with the work the builders are doing, because…'").

It got old very quickly, as Gill and I were ever more conscious of the amount of work we still had to do. None of it got done while filming was taking place.

But very occasionally, there were benefits.

As they were leaving that evening, Rachel came to us and offered to take us back to their hotel for dinner.

We jumped at the chance! It meant more than just real food – it meant that ultimate luxury, the one we longed for on a daily basis for weeks at a time – a shower!

We grabbed some clean clothes (we had plenty of them tucked away in our rucksacks, as there never seemed much point in changing clothes during the week) and left with the crew.

It was good to get out of the house for a bit – though we made damn sure we left the heater on for when we got back.

Sitting in the dining room of a posh hotel in Cardiff, we couldn't have felt more out of place. Even our 'clean' clothes were only clean by comparison; they were still splattered with old paint and oil, and, in my case, blood. Luckily, it was quite late and the room was deserted.

We talked about the project of course, but I was trying to avoid saying anything I'd regret later. One thing I could be sure of was that any unguarded remark made off-camera would come back to haunt me as soon as filming recommenced.

Instead I tried to talk about life beyond Treorchy; I was sitting next to Dave, so I thought I'd try to impress him with a few of my exploits.

When I told him about my time in Ecuador, his eyes lit up. He quizzed me relentlessly for the next half-hour, and I proudly informed him that I was hoping to write a book about it. I told him that, much as he did, I faithfully recorded everything that happened around me.

"So, is that what's in this journal of yours, then?" he asked.

Oh-oh. I should have known it was a mistake to bring it.

All five crew members stared hungrily at the small leather-bound book in my lap.

"Read us something from it!" said Dave.

"Um… no. No, it's not like that. It's all…"

And then I realized what kind of a bind I was in. The book was full of the kind of details they'd love to hear – along with plenty they wouldn't. Every time they'd pissed me off, thrown our schedule into chaos with their demands or given me a stern talking to about my sense of humour, I'd written it in there. And not very politely. There was absolutely no way I could let them look at that book. I had to say something to divert them… even at great cost to myself.

"This is just poetry," I said with a sigh. "I… I write poems about how I feel…"

I looked up to see interest dying in some of their eyes. Some, but not all.

There was only one thing I could do.

"…and vampires," I added, cringing inwardly.

That did the trick.

I'd written vampire poetry when I was about fourteen, and had never dared tell anyone about it since. But now that adolescent awkwardness paid off, allowing me to paint myself as… an awkward adolescent.

If the crew had gained any respect for me over the last few weeks, I could be sure it was gone now. They'd be poking each other and laughing about it in the bar after we left.

"And he lies there at night – in bed with his sister – and writes *poetry* about *vampires!* Oh, you couldn't make this shit up! Yeah, that guy is never getting laid."

We left soon afterwards.

As Rachel escorted us out, Dave called the others to attention and began an informal meeting. "Okay, so how are we coming along with the story?" he asked.

It was the last thing I heard before leaving the room, and I remember wondering what on earth he meant by it. There was no 'story' in what we were doing, at least not in the conventional sense. It was all developing day by day, in real time. What on earth did *story* have to do with what we were filming?

We didn't find out that night.

And the next morning – joy of joys – it was back to sanding. We still had all the woodwork in the entire house to do – barring the skirting boards, which Dai had enthusiastically ripped out without asking us about.

To make the job easier on our hands, we made a series of trips back up the valley to B&Q. One by one over successive days and weeks, we bought half a dozen different power sanders – and every one of them was a clear violation of the Trade Descriptions Act. Oh, they could sand – just about – but where the hell was the power?

Even leaning on them with all my weight (an inadvisable thing, by the way, when halfway up a ladder over an open staircase), I still couldn't get them to work any harder. They buzzed (or screeched) and vibrated – but that was about all. That's why we ended up with six of the bloody things. I kept thinking that maybe Dad's habit of buying the cheaper brands was to blame, but as we worked our way up the hierarchy of sanding machines I came to the conclusion that all of them (at least the ones in our price bracket) were powerless.

So I just called them sanders – or occasionally 'piece of shit-arse-bastard-fucking-sander!' – usually when one slipped from my grasp, smacked me in the face and caused me to fall backwards off my ladder. And then down two flights of stairs.

Bloody sanders.

I did a much better job with my own two hands and a phonebook-sized packet of extra-coarse sandpaper, which would have been fine, if time consuming – except that, of all the jobs on the project, I absolutely hated sanding.

You know what?

Let me tell you a story about me and sanding.

A Story About Me And Sanding

As some of you might know, I went to France once.

I didn't enjoy it.

Not because of France – I can't really blame a country for the weirdness that ensued within its borders now, can I?

What's that? I can?

Oh, goody!

Friggin' France.

What you don't know, is what I got up to while I was there.

After escaping from the gypsy-killing farmer, I spent the last of my cash on a train ticket to Moûtiers, a small town on the edge of the French Alps. From there I was hoping to hitch a ride to the tiny ski resort of Méribel, where I planned on spending the whole winter working in a chalet while I learned to snowboard.

I felt my whole life had pointed me towards this moment; I'd never even seen a snowboard before, but I knew that this was something I just *had* to do. If I became a snowboarder, people were *bound* to like me. I think it's the law.

After half an hour hiking along the main road to the mountains with my cardboard sign, I got lucky – a crummy little Lada pulled over with a wrinkly old French bloke at the wheel.

At first he patted my shoulder as he spoke, as though to emphasise his points. I hadn't a clue what he was rasping on about, so I just fell back on instinct: smile, and nod.

It was the wrong instinct to fall back on.

His hand soon graduated to my knee…

And then it was resting in my lap.

And then I felt it working its way in deeper…

I couldn't believe this was happening. Was I really sitting in the passenger seat of a Lada, next to a French pensioner who was trying to put his hand down my pants? At least he kept his eyes on the road while he fumbled with my jeans.

At least I was wearing jeans.

If I'd left my package more accessible, this could have been over in a flash – and not the kind of flash I wanted to be giving whilst doing 80kmph down the *autoroute*.

So my number one tip for hitch-hiking, is this: never wear tracksuit trousers.

They offer very little protection against unwanted fondlage.

Still, with all the effort this guy was putting in, even my buttonfly jeans wouldn't defeat him for long. Not wearing underwear was only one of the mistakes I'd made that day.

"*Non! Non, monsieur,*" I told him. "*Arret !*" I added – it was the closest word to 'stop' I could remember, but now I think about it, I'm fairly sure it means 'bus stop'. It's possible that this didn't help my cause.

Either way, he wasn't taking no for an answer.

He kept repeating "*C'est d'accord, c'est d'accord,*" (it's okay, it's okay!).

I think his opinion of 'okay' differed somewhat from mine.

So I opened my door until he stopped the car. Then I got out, grabbed my rucksack, and walked to the next lay-by.

I wasn't really scared, as he was a scrawny old bloke, but if I'd had to slap him to keep him off me I didn't fancy my chances in front of a French judge.

I'd be up for assault of a senior citizen, and possibly attempted car-theft, and I'd be getting the same treatment in prison from someone who was far less likely to be dissuaded.

So, yeah. Groped by a pensioner. I guess it wasn't me who got lucky after all.

That was my first ever attempt at hitch-hiking.

It wasn't a total success.

But my innocence remained intact, if not my dignity.

My second attempt was more successful. Not only did I get to where I wanted to go, but the driver was a mine of information about the local ski industry. None of it was good.

I was not in the best of moods when I arrived, but I was trying really hard to stay optimistic. This was my dream after all, to learn how to snowboard in the hope that it would lead me to the Holy Grail of my youthful life: finally being cool.

It hadn't happened yet, and was looking less and less likely as time went on.

Being touched up by someone's Granddad was not an auspicious start – very few genuinely cool people find themselves in this kind of situation.

However, there was one thing that no amount of positive thinking could change – and that was the date.

I'd gone there in search of winter, so had naturally arrived in October, hoping I'd be early enough to find a job for the ski season.

But the 'Winter Season' in France doesn't directly correspond to what I considered to be winter. You have to understand, I grew up in Yorkshire; pretty much everything outside of July and August counts as winter.

So it wasn't until I arrived, with images of snow covered cabins and whirling ski-lifts in my head, that I discovered my error.

The ski season didn't start until December.

I was two whole months early.

And Méribel – the entire town on which I had based my snowboarding fantasies – was closed.

"I've never snowboarded before," I confessed to the barman at *La Taverne*.

I'd been sent there by the guy who drove me in. He'd told me it was the only thing open at this time of year, and was the only place I was likely to find a lift back down the mountain. He'd not even mentioned job possibilities, which spoke volumes about my chances. Apparently all the ski season recruiters were currently in England, interviewing and hiring their staff as we spoke.

The barman confirmed it. "And they don't really hire people who can't ski already. Too much chance they'll get injured straight away, and have to go home."

"I see."

But he called the manageress over, to ask about the unlikely possibility that she knew someone who knew someone.

I was starting to get worried now; night had fallen, it was seriously cold outside, and getting even more so by the minute. I had nowhere to go, nowhere to stay, and, by this time, very little chance of getting a lift out of there.

And to compound the problem, I was also flat broke.

Basically I was buggered.

Hazel, the manager of *La Taverne*, was a really nice lady and I could tell she genuinely wanted to help.

"Tell you what," she said, as we sat drinking coffee on one of the tables in the restaurant area. "Maybe this will work. You look like a fairly handy sort of a lad."

"Of course!" I was desperate. "I'll do anything!"

"Like painting?"

"Oh, I've done loads of painting."

"Can you do a bit of concreting?"

"Erm… yes? Yes I can," I lied.

"Great! And can you plaster a wall?"

"Ah, yeah… that too."

"And how are you at woodworking? We've got a load of stools that need fixing up, and shelves and things."

"Not a problem. I'm your man."

"What about electrical? Have you done any electrical work?"

"Well, I wouldn't say I've done *work*, as such… but I can probably manage."

"Well okay then! We've got ourselves a deal. You can stay in one of our staff rooms – it's not brilliant I'm afraid, but it's better than nothing – and I'll write you up a list of jobs. I can get the chef to fix you up with dinner every night, so long as you don't mind eating whatever he makes for the rest of us. And if you get hungry in the day, you can make yourself a sandwich or something."

"Sounds great!"

"And you can put a note up on the board, and if a proper job comes along you can stay in the room and pay rent instead of working for it."

I was ecstatic.

I'd made it!

Some slight liberties had been taken with the truth to secure my employment, but that was a minor detail. The point is, I'd gotten myself as far as Méribel, and now I'd managed to find work and a place to stay in one fell swoop.

I wouldn't get rich, but I wouldn't starve, and there was bound to be a chance for more gainful employment – this bar was not just the hub of town, it was the only thing in town. Anyone looking for a job – and anyone looking for someone looking for a job – would naturally gravitate towards *La Taverne*.

I checked into the room, a tiny loft wedged right into the top of the roof, chucked my rucksack on the narrow pad of mattress that passed for a bed, and went back down to see how this list was coming along.

Quite well, as it turned out.

"Jobs kept coming to me, as fast as I could write them," Hazel confessed.

It was very long, very detailed list, starting with the painting of a few corridors and working all the way up to full-scale construction.

Shelve a cupboard.

Concrete a curb around the patio.

Plaster a bedroom wall.

And those were just the jobs I'd expected to see on there.

Rewiring light fittings, speaker repair and fixing up some old gas heaters were next on the list. They would have to wait… until long after I'd left, ideally.

I got started on the painting immediately. There were enough jobs that I felt I could have a go at – like putting shelves up – to last me for a few days at least.

Then Hazel came back with some more good news.

"I've got to make a trip into Moûtiers tomorrow, to get some food for the bar. If you come with me, we can go to the big hardware shop and choose what you need for the plastering and the concreting!"

"Oh… great."

She was clearly excited about this. These jobs must have been weighing on her mind for some time.

I, on the other hand, was quite scared, and getting another notch closer to terrified with each passing discussion.

Because I didn't have a clue how to do any of those things. I was fresh out of an acting degree, for God's sake! I couldn't have been more out of my depth if she'd thrown me into the Atlantic.

It was time to make the choice; either I level with her, and risk getting kicked out before I'd even unpacked, or… I play my ace.

That night I called my Uncle Paul from a payphone opposite *La Taverne*.

Paul, my Mum's bother, was an electrical engineer at the time, but he was one of those incredibly practical people who could do absolutely anything. He took cars apart for a hobby. He'd taken down and rebuilt half his house in Manchester, adding a giant master bedroom above the garage and plumbing in an extra en-suite.

This was a guy who could get me out of any predicament.

I hadn't been in close touch with him for a while, what with studying in Cardiff and then trying to travel, but I felt sure he would understand my situation. Paul was one of the few genuinely good people left in this world, and a bit of a hero of mine. He'd never let me down.

I pushed my phone card into the slot; I had just over ten minutes of credit remaining.

I called Paul's house in Manchester and was relieved when he answered.

"Hello uncle!"

"Oh! Hi Tony. Haven't heard from you in a while. Are you alright?"

"I am uncle, but I'm in a bit of a pickle. I'm in France, and I've had to get a job as a handyman. I've only got ten minutes left on the phone – can you tell me how to plaster a wall?"

There was a brief pause, as Paul processed the information I'd just blurted at him. I could practically hear his brown furrow in concentration.

Then he was back.

"Okay. So first, you have to make sure the wall is damp. Not too wet mind, but moist. Mop it with a sponge is the best way. The plaster you'll need to buy is…"

And just like that, over the phone from the north of England, Uncle Paul taught me to plaster.

It took him less than five minutes.

I never became any good at it of course, but that's hardly the point.

The next day in town, I impressed my new boss by making statements like: "No, that's finishing plaster. It's too fine for this sort of job. What we need is the heavier stuff. It's probably in a darker grey bag…"

And the day after that, I plastered my first wall.

The evening I placed another call to Manchester.

"Hi uncle!"

"Oh! Hello Tony. How'd the plastering go?"

"It went great! Thank-you so much. Not the smoothest, but my boss was happy."

"That's great news!"

"Yes… so here's the thing. I have to make a curb around the patio tomorrow. What can you tell me about concreting?"

Bless him, he didn't miss a beat.

"Okay, so your standard concrete mix needs to be one part cement to two parts sand and two parts gravel. You can measure them by the shovel full, it doesn't need to be exact. Use a big board to mix it on…"

I've no idea if *La Taverne* still has the curb I created for them. Not to devalue Uncle Paul's advice, but he had a difficult pupil and far from ideal teaching conditions.

My workmanship was dire – but I got the job done, despite

having absolutely zero knowledge of the technique less than twenty-four hours previously.

That phone card was worth every cent.

As for Paul, that uncommonly kind, amazingly practical, and utterly unflappable man, he had a much stronger influence on my young life than I think he knew. One of my few regrets is not spending more time with him when I had the chance.

Just over a year ago I ran the launch campaign for my first book from his home office, while he lay in the next room, fighting for his life with Motor Neurone Disease.

It was the only battle I ever knew him to lose.

We all miss you greatly, Paul, and we love you. Rest easy old man.

The Rest Of The Story About Sanding

Sorry about that!

I was supposed to be telling you about sanding.

I guess I got a little carried away.

Anyway, the longer I strung out the work at *La Taverne*, the more obvious it became that I was seriously out of my depth.

So when a couple of English guys showed up in the pub looking for an able-bodied worker, I jumped at the chance to do anything which better suited my skill set.

Which was crap acting, or nothing.

The job was…

Any guesses?

You at the back?

Yes. Sanding.

The two guys were going to be working with me for the owner of a chalet. The job was a fixed-term contract for two months, and they'd been given the option of hiring a third guy to help out. There was a sizeable bonus for finishing ahead of schedule, which meant that both the owner and the two workmen were eager to get it done as quickly as possible.

I was lucky enough to be the only person in the bar that night, sitting in the corner, writing my journal and sipping a glass of tap water. Booze wasn't covered by my deal with Hazel, and even if I hadn't been broke I wouldn't have paid those prices for it. Upwards of ten euros a pint was outrageous for France – hell, it would be outrageous for a celebrity bar in the West End of London! The staff discount didn't apply to me as I wasn't getting paid, and I hadn't been there long enough to make good friends with the few staff currently in residence.

Sitting in an empty bar, with no friends and no booze, is a pretty miserable activity. Luckily, the journal I was using to document my loneliness was stolen off me a few months later, so you're spared any retrospective whinging.

The two guys were pointed in my direction – I was hard to miss! – and came straight over with their proposition.

"So not only do we get a bonus," one guy explained, "but it don't matter how early we finish, we still get paid for the whole two months!"

"It's at least a couple o' weeks of free money," his mate chipped in.

I accepted their offer without hesitation.

Things were finally looking up.

And speaking of looking up… well, it was the only way to take in the enormity of the task ahead of us.

It was four stories high, perched on the edge of a cliff that plunged a good thousand feet straight down the mountain.

Together, the three of us had to sand an entire ski chalet.

Yes I know! Bear with me – you know those enormous log cabin structures you see on postcards? Well they do exist, and they are every bit as impressive as they look. Some of the nicest ones cost several thousand pounds a week to stay at – and even for that you don't get the whole thing. (You do get your own live-in chef and cleaners though.) Being made mostly of wood, these behemoths need regular treatment to keep them looking like they're worth the money. Oh yes – each and every one of the buggers needs sanding down and re-varnishing every four or five years.

It's an even bigger job than you can imagine – mind bogglingly so.

This chalet was a shade of deep brown which the owner had endearingly labelled 'chocolate box'. Unsurprisingly it reminded me more of a certain bodily function – one that, without access to the inside of the chalet, I would have to forego during working hours.

Although it was four stories high, thankfully only the top three were made of wood. But on those levels, *everything* was made of wood. The walls. The window frames. The shutters. The balcony floors. The balcony railings. The underside of the substantial roof overhangs, the eaves, the roof trim, the doors…

Everything.

And most of it had some form of decorative carving, which meant that instead of sanding large flat surfaces – well okay, as well as sanding large, flat surfaces – we had to do the detail work. All by hand.

Imagine you have a small piece of wood in front of you, with three decorative wooden squares fastened to it. On top of those are smaller squares – and on top of those, something festive – like a fleur-de-lis, for instance.

Now you want to remove the overly indulgent poo coloured paint job from it.

How many surfaces and edges do you have to sand?

Don't worry, it's not a trick question.

The answer is simple – too bloody many!

Originally I was told we had to sand off every trace of the current paintwork, leaving the whole place naked so that the owner could have a much lighter shade of varnish applied. It seems there is becoming less and less of a market these days for holiday accommodation the colour of a three-day-old turd.

It took me a week to sand a dinner-table sized hole through all the layers of varnish and wood-stain, right back to the bare wood. The others appraised my efforts, decided it was an impossible task, and told the owner he'd have to repaint it the same colour after all.

Of course, they blamed me for the new bald patch.

The pair of them worked together, with a radio to entertain them. They sent me off to do the harder-to-reach areas, as I was young and skinny, and they were neither. Hence, while they stood on the balcony and rapped along badly to Snoop Dogg and Eminem, I gripped the edge of the roof with white knuckles and fought panic as the icy wind blasting up the mountainside buffeted my ladder.

In order to sand the decorative moulding on the eaves, at the very apex of the overhanging roof, I'd had to brace the longest ladder we had against the railing of the third floor balcony. It was a tiny balcony, private to the top-most master suite, a room which also boasted incredibly high ceilings due to the steep pitch of the roof. The ladder, extended three times, was close to vertical, and I was right at the top of it – leaning backwards to reach the carved fascia boards. I was supposed to be sanding them vigorously, but any violent motion risked upsetting my rather tenuous balance; at any rate, they were so high that in places I could only just brush them with my fingertips. This was on the back side of the chalet overlooking the precipice; it must have made for breath-taking views from the bedroom. If I fell backwards I figured I'd get at least half an hour of free fall in before I landed.

I'd have time to come to terms with it, make peace with my maker, and maybe enjoy the scenery for a bit.

It wouldn't be a bad way to go actually.

Although they wouldn't be able to identify my body because I'd sanded off my fingerprints.

I spent my second week on that balcony.

It was around this time that Méribel got its first dump of snow. Not enough to ski on – just enough to make life miserable for those of us working forty feet up the side of a chalet in one of the few outdoor jobs where it's impossible to wear gloves. My hands were so damaged by bashing them against the wood and catching them on corners that they throbbed all night, keeping me awake in my tiny loft above the bar. They were so cold during the day that I hardly noticed each new injury, one of the few fringe benefits of an aching numbness that also affected my feet, making it even harder to climb and descend the ladder whenever I needed fresh sandpaper. By the time I got home each day my hands would be starting to revive, a sensation so peculiar and painful that it stayed with me all through the night, until at work next morning the chilled air would steal the pain of my injuries again and replace it with the familiar ache of freezing bones and joints.

As I worked on, the job became slightly less unpleasant, and a succession of people from the bar lent me an ever increasing number of jumpers and jackets. I started showing up for work looking like the Michelin Man, and had to strip off one layer at a time as the effort of sanding warmed my body.

Lunch times sucked the most, because the guys would drive off to buy food; I still couldn't afford to, so I scrounged sandwiches from the bar staff each night and sat and ate them on the chalet steps – in a patch of sunlight if I was lucky. It didn't make it much warmer, and any sweat I'd produced during the morning's exertions turned icy as my body cooled.

By the time the guys got back, warm and sated and usually a bit stoned, I was stiff and shivering and seriously contemplating that swan-dive from the upper balcony.

But by the end of my fifth week, I was becoming a veteran. My hands were ragged and bleeding, my nails split to pieces, yet I felt a new level of appreciation from my co-workers. I'd done far more work than either of them, and far more than I'd believed possible at the start of the project. I'd sanded trim and balusters, frames and decking, all the tricky work for the top three floors of the chalet – plus a goodly amount of the large flat surfaces that made up the walls in between. It was only happening an inch at a time, but I could see the end approaching. I even had enough wages to pay my bill at *La Taverne*, and buy a few bits of outrageously priced food to make my sandwiches more interesting.

The deal we'd struck was to split the bonus for finishing early three ways – and I'd calculated that my share would be just enough to keep me in smelly cheese and fresh baguettes until the start of the ski-season.

So I was understandably pissed off when, with less than a week to go, the two guys decided they could finish the job by themselves.

The bastards.

How naïve was I? I'd gone from being groped to being fully exploited in little over a month. It didn't make me feel dirty – just really, really stupid.

And mad.

Of course they'd planned it all along – pay an idiot to take the pressure off them, dangle an incentive to get him to work flat out for sod all – then fire him, finish off themselves and claim the bonus. If this was a gangster movie, one of them would then have killed the other to avoid sharing the loot, and the last man standing would have been shot by police in the last five minutes.

Unfortunately, this was real life; I got screwed, they got happy (and substantially richer), and all this time later I still want to punch them in the nuts.

That's life, I guess.

But at least I got a story out of it.

Gone with the bonus money went not only my chance of surviving until the ski season started, but also my desire to stay there that long.

So I said 'fuck you' to France, and went and got heartily drunk instead – but in Spain, where I could afford it.

My lasting impressions of France were formed on that trip – which is wholly unfair, I appreciate – but to me it will always remain a land of gypsy-murderers, aging perverts, fat con-men and thieves.

And it's left me with three specific hatreds:

Being cold.

Climbing unnecessarily long ladders.

And sanding.

I fucking hate sanding.

More Sanding

No, I'm just messing with you! I wouldn't do that to you, would I? Instead, let's call this one:

A Distinct Lack of Support

Yes, that's much better.

Lenny's team knocked out their second wall with even less warning than the first.

I was past caring by that point, although I was a little concerned that he hadn't bothered to wait until the steel lintel arrived to replace the wall.

The lintel, also known as an RSJ or Rolled Steel Joist, is what would be taking the weight of the two floors above now that we'd removed the supporting wall.

According to Lenny, his supplier was having difficulties delivering it, but should manage to get the thing to us in the next couple of days.

In the meantime he was content to leave the hole as it was – unsupported, despite being a load-bearing wall on the bottom floor of a three-storey house.

Even I knew enough about building to think that was a bad idea. I'd seen exactly the type of programme we were making, and there was one thing they always seemed to need in these sorts of circumstances.

"Acros?" Lenny asked, looking vaguely confused.

"Yes! Acros. Adjustable steel props. To support the house? In the gap where the wall used to be."

"Oh aye, acros. Don't believe in them."

I was momentarily thrown by this admission.

"But… they do exist Lenny! They're not like unicorns. Are you sure we don't need any?"

"Don't believe in 'em," he repeated – and that was his final word on the matter.

His team packed up and left, as I placed a concerned call to Mum in Somerset.

"So, no supports, because apparently he doesn't believe in them," I summed up.

"Will it be okay though?" she asked.

"I don't know Mum, honestly, but it's a bit worrying. I mean, the whole back wall of the house rests on this… gap. That's, like, twenty feet of bricks. And the roof. How do we even know if the beam will come tomorrow?"

"Is there anything else you can do?"

"Not really, that I can think of. I'm not standing in the gap all night holding the roof up!"

"No, I mean, is there anyone you can call? Ring Lenny and check it's okay."

"Well I can, but he already told me. He's happy, and he's not going to change his mind about it. Not on my say-so."

"If he's happy… it must be okay then. He wouldn't let the house fall down because he doesn't want to spend money on acros, would he?"

"I don't know Mum. Maybe."

"Do you want to stay in a hotel? You can get a taxi to the Travelodge and I'll book you a room, just until we get the beam in place."

"No, it's okay. Besides, we can't afford it!"

"Yeah…"

Not really sure what else to do, I thought of one long-shot option.

I called Rachel.

She shit a brick.

"WHAT? No support at all?"

"Nope. I'm a bit worried, to be honest."

"No kidding! Your house is about to fall down, with you inside it! Give me a minute."

The phone went quiet. I hung on, wondering what she could possibly do to help. She'd recorded dozens of building projects. Surely she'd been in this situation before? Maybe she had some contacts in the industry…

Then she was back.

"Right! I've sorted it out."

"Great!" Relief flowed over me. It was going to be alright after all. "So what did you do?"

"I've booked a camera man. He's from Cardiff, so he should be there in an hour."

"And he's going to…?"

"He'll film your end. We'll get another crew out to the presenter, and film you on the phone, asking for her advice. It'll look great!"

"Oh. Right. And, um, anything I can do about the house?"

"The house? Oh, well, that's what you can ask the presenter about. I'm sure you'll be fine."

The camera man showed up exactly an hour later. After a flurry of phone calls between him and his opposite number in London, we were ready to go.

I fake-dialled several times before placing the call, so the camera man had a few of those 'options' they love so much.

"Help," I asked the presenter. "Is my house going to fall down?"

"Ultimately, yes it could," she said. I could hear the gravity in her voice. Was she playing it up for the cameras? Or was she genuinely concerned?

"Okay. Is there anything I can do?"

"Have the builders left?"

"Yup."

"Then you'll have to go and get some acros yourself, and put them up – like, yesterday, ideally."

"I can't afford that! And there's nowhere open now."

"Don't worry about the cost! This is too important. Keep ringing around until you find somewhere."

Which is all well and good, if you live in London. You're bound to find a twenty-four hour tool hire place if you look hard enough. Probably right next to the other twenty-four hour tool hire places. In the twenty-four hour tool hire district.

In Treorchy, in the darkest depths of the Welsh valleys, we weren't so blessed.

We had the B&Q twenty miles away in Cardiff, and a few small hardware shops scattered around nearby towns.

None of which were likely to have acros for hire.

None of which would be open this late.

And none of which mattered anyway.

Because we didn't have a car.

I didn't sleep much that night.

The beam arrived two days later. The crew were there to film it going in, though most of Lenny's boys made themselves scarce whenever the camera turned their way.

"Glad you made it," Rachel told me.

Which was nice of her.

Though I'm pretty sure it was the programme she was concerned for.

I was suddenly reminded that the last bloke they'd been filming had literally died on the job; otherwise we'd never have gotten involved with the crew at all.

It didn't seem likely to happen twice.

I hoped.

That was the last time we saw the crew that year – not because they abandoned us, but because we all decided to take a much-needed break. It was December 20th after all, and up and down the country people were getting ready to celebrate the holiday season with vast amounts of food and booze.

I hadn't had much chance to go shopping for presents.

To be honest, there were only two things on my Christmas list: first and foremost was a day that didn't involve ten hours of digging in a frozen back garden or sanding half an acre of crumbling plasterwork; second on my list was a night in a real, warm bed, covered with nothing more noxious than a clean duvet.

Oh, and I planned to spend at least a day on the toilet.

CRISIS

London, England.

I sat alone in a deserted KFC, munching on a lukewarm chicken burger, and felt like I was the luckiest man alive.

It was Christmas Day.

I'd been lucky to find anywhere open for breakfast; better still, this place was only a stone's throw away from the derelict office building where I was staying. I couldn't wait to get back there. I was exhausted, body and soul, after one of the most difficult nights of my life – after several of them, in fact. I'd lost count how many. All that really mattered now was that I'd found food against the odds, and that somewhere in the middle of that building down the road was a piece of floor with a mattress on it, waiting for me.

The daily grind of the Treorchy project had been getting me down. With two weeks off over the holiday season, I'd hit the internet looking for something exciting to do.

Ever since getting back from Ecuador I'd been trying to recreate the sense of adventure I'd experienced over there. Nothing had come close. There was plenty of drama in my day-to-day existence – a little too much in fact, and none of it good – but there was definitely something missing. Something deeper and more meaningful than the adrenaline rush of constant danger.

It was...

Freedom? Hm. Maybe.

Responsibility? Ha! Not likely. I had more responsibility now than I'd ever had in my life, and it was eating me alive. I'd rather be back in the jaguar's cage.

Friendship...

Yeah, friendship for sure. In fact I missed all those things – but most of all I missed happiness.

I don't think I'd been truly happy since I returned.

Well, not until now, anyway.

I'd found out about Crisis Christmas through a volunteering website I'd started visiting. I'd been planning and dreaming of another trip since the plane flight home. I regularly looked up volunteer opportunities all over the world – but I hadn't expected to find one in England. Yes, I know there are countless charity shops lining the high street of every town in the country, and plenty of people stood in between them shaking collection tins, but that wasn't the kind of action I was looking for. Likewise, sitting around reading to old people, whilst a perfectly worthy contribution to society, also didn't appeal to my desire for the extreme.

Being a Crisis volunteer though, asked for a lot.

I was helping to staff a temporary homeless shelter over Christmas. Every year they were set up with donated funds, giving somewhere to go to the people with nowhere else. It had sounded like a decent thing to do, so I gave them a call.

"Where do you need me?" I asked.

"What do you feel comfortable doing?" they countered.

""I'll do anything!" I said grandly. "What do you need the most?"

"Well, it's always hardest to get people for the night shifts. Especially in the Drinkers' Shelter."

"Sweet. Sign me up."

"That's great! I don't want to discourage you or anything, but it can be tough. And upsetting. It's twelve-hour shifts. There's not supposed to be any drinking inside the shelter, but most of the guests are addicted to drink and/or drugs, so they're often quite… ah, intoxicated. That's why we have to keep them separate from the other shelters. What do you think? Is that okay?"

"That's fine."

It sounded extreme all right.

And so here I was.

Learning the ropes had been simple: Go to shelter. Talk to guests. Help guests with what they want. Pitch in wherever else I was needed.

I doled out sandwiches from bulging black bin-bags, that were delivered each evening by the local branch of Marks & Spencer. They were all the ones about to go out of date, which would normally just be thrown away. This kind of waste is one of the things I'd become a lot more aware of since my time in Ecuador, and it disgusted me. Now though, offering smoked salmon and herbed cream cheese on seeded rye bread to people dressed in rags made me feel rather triumphant. The selection on offer was always eclectic, but gratefully received, and most of my job was to unite the right person with their dream sandwiches whilst avoiding a punch-up. That was part one of the job.

Part two was a bit harder. This was where the 'talking to the guests' came in; I was there to be a friendly face to them, to chat and listen, and to advise them of anything else the shelter could offer them. Clothes, for example, were doled out in a small room on the ground floor; there was always a long queue of people whenever the door to that room was unlocked. Over at the main shelter in the Millennium Dome, there was access to medical care, dentists, computers – all kinds of opportunities which I could inform our visitors about. But most of all they liked to be listened to – to tell the story of their woes, or sometimes just what they had for breakfast, to another human being who was willing to hear it.

This involved hearing some pretty terrible things from people who considered their lives all but over. I doubt I'll ever forget the evening I spent talking with Christian, an eighteen-year-old rough sleeper whose life had been completely taken over by drink.

We chatted a bit about his last year on the streets, but mostly about what it meant to him to be here at the shelter at Christmas – he'd been at every one since he'd been kicked out of home at fifteen.

Close to midnight, I made my excuses and got up to go; most people that weren't already in bed were going at that point, and it was my job to oversee them. But Chris grabbed my arm and looked at me with such desperation that I sat straight back down again.

"Will you stay and talk to me, and keep me awake?" he asked. "Please?"

"Sure," I told him, "Why not? You're not tired then?"

"No, I'm knackered. It's been such a great day, I can't believe how many people I've met up with. So many old mates… But I've been having so much fun talking to everyone, I didn't go out hardly at all. I only begged up enough change to buy these."

He waved at two empty cans of *Carlsberg* in a plastic bag on the floor next to him.

"I'm really, really alcoholic, yeah, and if I don't drink enough I get really bad withdrawal. It could kill me. I haven't drunk nearly enough today. I'm scared that if I pass out now, I'll die in my sleep."

He was in earnest – not in the least bit exaggerating his fear. This was a young man who was genuinely afraid that if he went to sleep he might never wake up. Three years on the streets had put him so far into the clutches of alcohol that at this point it was all that he was living for – and all that kept him living.

He was six years younger than me.

They'd told us at the first briefing about the evils of alcoholism and that some of the guests would be quite far along this path. I'd never known this before, but alcohol is the only drug for which withdrawal, cold-turkey style, can be fatal.

Sitting there in that KFC, all I could think of was how grateful I was for my life being so good. It wasn't right to be lusting after adventure when there were people I'd seen last night that might not make it to tonight. I'd heard rumours of homeless people using the Crisis Christmas to say good-bye, of waiting until this time of year, this gathering of old friends and acquaintances, to see everyone for one last time before they went off to commit suicide. Some people take to a life on the streets better than others; some take to it very badly indeed. And of those, the ones that were suffering the worst, came to the drinkers' shelter.

In comparison, my life was a dream come true.

I was lucky enough to be sitting here, on this rigid plastic bench. Sipping cold coffee from a polystyrene cup I was engraving with my thumbnail.

I was lucky enough to have a family who loved me, and I would be going home to see them after the shelters closed next week.

I even had a mattress on the floor, waiting in an abandoned corner office for my exhausted body to fall into it.

Yes, my life, by comparison, was bliss.

I kind of felt like I didn't deserve it.

And of course, there were other things to be grateful for too.

There was a slight chance that my mattress wasn't the only thing that was waiting for me.

There was a slight chance it was occupied.

Taking Stock

I'd met Maria on my first day with Crisis – she had been the one responsible for finding me a mattress, and deciding which bit of floor I could put it on (this is how I ended up with a corner office).

Maria was responsible for the organisation and supply of the entire volunteers' accommodation – a soon-to-be-demolished office block which had been loaned to Crisis over Christmas, on the proviso that there would be no-one still inside when they knocked it down in January.

She'd been multi-tasking at a breath-taking level, guiding new volunteers to their beds, answering questions from everyone she walked past, still on her way to fetch something vital from the storage area whilst fielding calls on a walkie-talkie. She was bus-y.

"I'll take that, if you want," I said, referring to a huge bale of toilet paper she was on the verge of dropping. "Where's it got to go?"

"Really? Would you? Oh thanks, that'd be great! It's for the loos on the ground floor, near the way in. Thanks so much for that!"

"Hey, anything for you baby!"

This earned me a peculiar look. I cursed myself. Actually I cursed my mouth. Yet again it had tried to make a funny without running it by the relevant part of my brain. I strode away down the corridor before I could be forced to defend myself, as the only explanation I could give was, "I'm sorry. I say stupid things sometimes, because I'm an idiot."

This defence rarely endeared me to women.

Maria was curvy and cute, with straight black hair and a tan so good I was already wondering what it was like all over. I added her to my mental list of 'people to avoid in case I said anything even more stupid to.'

I'd dropped off the bog-roll and retraced my steps through the warren of offices to a huge open room that was being used as a kind of lounge. There was no furniture apart from one table, and that was covered in old kettles. There were stacks of those instant coffee-in-a-cup things leaning precariously against the table; one of the perks of the job, it seemed, was an unlimited supply of out-of-date vending machine coffee. I would later figure out that this was a critical resource.

Until January the building still had power, so there were lights here and there. I didn't need them much because I caught a lift to the Drinker's Shelter at 7pm each evening and didn't get back 'till 9am. But the hot caffeine injection was the only thing to tempt me from the super-warm technical sleeping bag I'd spent all day in. I'd bought it for Ecuador and never used it there, but I was grateful of it now as heating was something the building didn't have. It made it all the more poignant, knowing that with each shift I worked, our overnight guests were one day closer to being back on the streets. It cost Crisis half a million pounds to keep these shelters open for ten days; there was no way they could keep it up for the other three-hundred and fifty-five.

Sleeping during the day meant the building was marginally warmer – out on the streets, at night, at this time of year – I couldn't imagine how anyone could survive.

But the broad daylight made sleeping difficult, so I got up for a wander around the building. I thought it'd be fun to explore a little – and that was how, in a random corridor three floors above where I was supposed to be, I ran into Maria again.

"Hiya!" I said, and made to carry on past her.

"Hi," she replied, sounding startled, and for a second I thought she was going to leave it at that.

And then she asked the question I'd been dreading.

"What did you mean by that, what you said before?"

Oh-oh. Deny everything.

"Ah, nothing…"

She was giving me that peculiar look again. It was unsettling.

"So why did you say, *"Quiero ella!"* when you first arrived?"

Ohhhh… shit.

Now this was awkward.

Because *'Quiero ella'* means 'I want her.'

I'd taken to voicing my inner monologue thoughts in Spanish, so that when they had to slip out, at least no-one would understand them. This one had slipped out shortly after walking in the front door.

Maria, it turns out, spoke Spanish (with a name like that, I shouldn't have been so surprised) – and, like most of the world, she spoke it considerably better than me.

I'd been caught out – twice in one day. There really was nothing else for it.

"I said it because I thought you were hot. And because I didn't know you spoke Spanish."

"You *thought* I was hot?"

"Well, you are hot, I mean."

"Oh. Really."

Then she leaned in and kissed me.

"You're not so bad yourself," she said when she'd finished.

Then a squawk from her radio interrupted us, and the moment was lost. *"That second bus hasn't arrived yet, can you call the driver and find out where he is? We need him here right now."*

Maria squeezed my hand, grabbed the radio from her belt and scurried off, replying to the message amidst bursts of static.

I thought about that kiss quite a lot that night, in between chats with the guests. Whenever I found myself standing around, waiting for another job to do, I replayed it in my head. It was definitely the most pleasant part of my evening.

Things kind of went downhill from there.

I'd been asked to watch over the food, which arrived at fairly random intervals throughout the night. This time soup had been prepared in a vast vat, and set up for self-service by the guests. I was just there to keep the peace, to chat to people in the queue and try to make sure they didn't start arguing.

I failed.

I had no idea what one old bloke was saying to me – quite a few of the guests were falling-down drunk by the time they rocked up to the shelter, but that was why we were here. No drinking (or drunks) were allowed in the other shelters for fear it would cause exactly the kind of problems we dealt with each night. This way most of the trouble was confined to us, and any that wasn't was quickly sent our way.

Drunk people can be hard to talk to. People who have been consistently drunk for years even more so – and this guy was making no sense at all, muttering away in gibberish, but directing it at me as though it was a conversation.

I fell back on my old tactic of nodding, smiling, and dropping in the occasional "Mmm," or "Mm-hm.

It wasn't the first time this trick backfired.

But it was the first time I got scalded as a consequence.

"Gnmnmn mnghuffnr gumnnemmr?" he'd asked.

Faced with no obvious options, I'd nodded, and replied, "Mm."

This was not what he wanted to hear.

Maybe he'd just asked if I thought he was a drunken moron, in which case I'd at least been honest. He took offence at my lukewarm agreement and asked me the same unintelligible question, shouting at me now, trembling with the effort.

I held my hands out to the sides and shrugged, trying to put an apology into my eyes. It didn't work. He got more and more worked up, demanding *something* of me over and over again, and just as another couple of volunteers headed over to see what was wrong, he grabbed a cup of boiling soup from the serving table and emptied it all over me.

He was a damn good shot for a drunken moron.

The stuff was red hot, but my clothes caught most of it. I got a little burn on my wrist, and the guest – who I now felt quite sorry for – was evicted.

Not attacking the staff was one of the main rules here.

Of course, no-one loves to break the rules like a drunk, and we had nothing but drunks and druggies. Mostly though, they kept the peace. Not many of them were naturally violent, and those that were, were quickly identified and removed (the more experienced volunteers from last year inherited this shitty task). It was amazing really, that so many wasted people all herded together didn't cause more problems. Maybe it was because they now had something to lose – perhaps for the first time in a long time – they had a place to hang out, friends to hang out with, full bellies and a bed for the night. It was humbling to see how grateful most of them were for so little.

For my part I was grateful for the chance to meet them, and for the perspective talking to them gave me on my own life.

And I was grateful to Maria, when I got back to the volunteer accommodation. Because she arranged to meet me outside one of the store rooms to which only she had the keys, and in there, on a pile of donated blankets, I got to know her a little more intimately.

Well, quite a lot more intimately, if you catch my drift.

Crisis Averted

After missing my family all Christmas (it was the first time I'd not been at home with them for the holiday), I was over the moon when Gill arranged to meet me in London for a coffee.

She was en-route to Sweden, to meet Roo and some of her other Camp America friends for an epic New Year's Party.

We sat in a disgustingly upmarket café, where she treated me to a real coffee and explained what she was up to.

"You should come to the party," she told me, "there'll be people from loads of different countries there! We're going to make plans to travel all around Europe."

By this point I was knackered. I'd had another tough shift, during which I had accidentally caused a punch-up amongst the guests over how the shelter's beds were arranged. Sweden seemed impossibly far away, as unobtainable from where I was now as international fame and fortune. And requiring about as much effort.

"Nah, thanks, but I'm needed here. And when I'm done here, I want to sleep for at least a week. In a bed, ideally."

"So what's it like?"

"Well, it's… kind of like…"

And then I cried.

I cried and cried for what seemed like hours, spluttering out a few details in between sobs. Every so often the sharing of a particular memory would set me off again, and it would be minutes before I could say something intelligible. I told her how low some of these people had sunk, about the harsh contrast it put my life into. I told her how I'd looked for familiar faces amongst the guests each night, and found one or two missing for reasons unknown. I told her about the bitter cold in the streets of the pre-dawn city, and how many of the homeless believed urban myths that alcohol was all that kept them from freezing to death. Death had always seemed so far away for me, a possibility so random and unlikely it was the bad luck equivalent of winning the lottery. But these people lived so very close to death, always in its shadow. To know that, and then to see how *normal* they were, how real their lives were – how *like me* they were – was every bit as upsetting as it was terrifying.

I laughed too, occasionally. I explained how I walked a knife-edge between gaining and losing these people's trust every time I opened my mouth. Drunks are nothing if not volatile, and it was all too easy to offend our guests with some casual assumption about their lives. It was a mistake I made a dozen times a night, with consequences varying from a terse verbal correction to GBH with a cup-a-soup.

I've never been able to decide if it's my mouth that's at fault, for opening in all the wrong shapes at all the wrong times, or if it's my brain, which waits until it hears something come out before deciding whether or not it was a suitable thing to say.

Gill, for her part, sat there quietly, listening rather than talking (a rare feat for her), hopefully not judging me too harshly, hopefully trying to understand. She frequently passed me napkins, which pretty soon covered the top of our table like giant snotty snowflakes.

She must have been embarrassed as hell.

Sitting there in a trendy London coffee shop with a grown man bawling his eyes out uncontrollably.

She told me afterwards she'd received a few stern looks from other patrons; it must have looked like she was the love of my life, and she'd just finished telling me she'd shagged the band at our wedding.

Poor Gill. She came for a coffee and got a river of salt water. She left for Sweden quite bemused; I can't remember another time in my life where I've cried in front of her. Well apart from a certain climbing frame accident when I was ten, and that was entirely justified – one foot slipped to either side of the bar I'd been standing on, and I landed on my testicles. I dare you not to cry just in sympathy.

But for me, this chance to share had been quite cathartic.

I returned in high spirits to the volunteer accommodation, to my private mattress, and wondered which of my two regular visitors I would see first.

Maria would be along if she got the chance; running errands kept her so busy she struggled to find time for a cup of coffee, let along for conducting an illicit relationship, but she gave it an admirable amount of effort. We frequently had to break off mid-coitus so she could answer her walkie-talkie, but that just made it more exciting. No-one could know; if she was caught in bed with a volunteer, there was a pretty good chance she'd lose her job, and she was hoping to make a career with Crisis.

If she was caught straddling me in the store rooms, which were strictly off-limits even to most of the paid staff… well. Obviously that would be worse, which is why she usually locked us in.

I hope she doesn't still work there. If she does… um… sorry! If you're Maria's boss, and you're reading this, please ignore the content of the last few lines.

My other frequent visitor was a middle-aged woman who had dragged a mattress from one of the larger rooms into the office next-door to me.

"Because all the other people in that room snored," she said.

She was a long-term volunteer and had some vague supervisory powers, which she felt entitled her to a room on her own. But what perplexed me was why she was so often in my room – she popped in and out like we were gossipy neighbours, reminding me when shifts were due to start or telling me how to operate the light switches. I had an odd theory, that she was nipping in and out on any flimsy pretext she could think of, hoping to catch me naked. Maybe hoping I'd invite her to stay.

Maria, when I described this odd behaviour, immediately worried that the woman was trying to catch us together, perhaps after overhearing us doing something we shouldn't. From then on we only met in Maria's private room, several floors above the rest of the accommodation, where she had the ultimate of luxuries: a real bed.

"You can use it if you want," she offered. "I hardly get the chance."

I'd thought I had it tough, working the twelve-hour night shift and then struggling to sleep through the day in spite of half a dozen mini-visits from my nosey neighbour. (Saying things like, "I just thought I'd let you know, it's only three 'o' clock. You've still got a few hours left to sleep." Yeah, thanks for that…)

But Maria was doing the day shift *and* the night shift. She had bus loads of tired volunteers showing up and departing all morning and all evening, and spent most of the time in between solving supply problems for all six shelters. She tried to get a couple of hours sleep two or three times a day, but rarely managed it – the radio allowed her no peace, constantly demanding she rush downstairs in search of spare toilet roll, or a missing volunteer, or to arrange a shift-change.

She was lucky to spend four hours in bed out of every twenty-four that passed; and usually one of those was spent on top of me.

I never told Gill about this aspect of my experience.

There are some things you shouldn't share in the middle of a busy coffee shop, and I'd hate to embarrass the poor girl.

That night's shift was one of the craziest. I'd refined my strategy of 'hot-bedding' – allocating guests to their beds on a rolling basis, so that when one got up to start drinking again the bed could be offered to someone who had just finished. I was encouraging the guests to keep all their belongings with them rather than leaving them stuffed under the beds, which had been the major cause of problems the previous night.

All this was going swimmingly. I had the rare feeling that I could do this, that I was being successful in my attempts to make the shelter run smoothly.

Then Caroline showed up.

She'd been a guest here almost every night, but was usually kicked out by midnight for threatening someone or for stripping off to her bra and panties and stomping around the shelter for no reason anyone could fathom.

I'd managed to steer well clear of her all week, because her hair-trigger temper was well known to the more experienced volunteers. Some of the bigger blokes took it in turns to keep a weather eye on her, so that there was usually someone in range when she decided to kick off.

This caused problems by itself; Caroline was constantly paranoid, and spent half the average night telling her minders (amongst other people) to 'fuck off and stop looking at her'. The situation would generally degenerate until she ripped off her t-shirt and threw it at them, followed quickly by her shoes and her track-suit trousers, and then she would roam around the shelter growling at people until a manager gave the nod to chuck her (and her clothes) out.

Sometimes, though, she gave her minders the slip.

That's when things really got out of hand.

And tonight, I had become one of those minders.

I was a victim of my own success; with the bed system running so smoothly, the bosses had looked for another job for me, and thought to reward me with a little more responsibility. Or maybe I'd impressed them and they thought I was capable of handling it.

Or maybe they suspected I was shagging their Accommodations Officer and they wanted to see me get slapped.

Caroline was built like a heavyweight boxer – only where a boxer would have had taut, toned muscles she had vast, filthy folds of flab.

She had short brown hair, skin ravaged by years of hard drink and drugs, a bucket jaw and a perma-frown. She was constantly inebriated, utterly unintelligible, and had a vicious streak nearly as wide as her ass (which was considerable).

I don't know if I mentioned it, but I'm not a big fan of confrontation.

Caroline was confrontation incarnate.

She scared the shit out of me.

I drifted from room to room, trying to keep as much distance between us as possible. At one point she'd come right up to me, so close I could see the burst blood vessels in her eyes, and mumbled something right in my face. The stench of her breath hit me, overpowering senses already reeling from the smell of her body odour. It was like being tear-gassed; my eyes watered, my stomach clenched and I threw up a little in my mouth.

"Mmm," I nodded at her.

She glared at me and made a sudden move as though to head-butt me – then smirked and shambled off to hurl abuse at a pair of guests playing chess.

I honestly didn't have it in me to intervene, so I just had to hope she would get bored; luckily the other guests also knew Caroline, and none of them seemed eager to rise to the bait.

She moved on.

Around the time she was harassing the tea-and-coffee queue, my opposite number stepped in for a quiet word with her. He was big too, enough to convey a decent amount of intimidation without having to specify it. He had a few words in her ear and seemed to calm her a little, then he gave me a confident nod.

'I've got this,' he seemed to be saying.

I nodded back and even risked cracking a smile – and that was where the trouble began.

Caroline, turning away from the queue, caught my return smile and knew instantly that it was about her.

"YOUFUGGINPISSINABO'MEH?" she bawled.

Oh crap, I thought.

"YOUSE!" She stormed over to me, fists clenched like meaty watermelons. "YOUSESAYN'SOMMERT'A'MEH?"

Ignore, said my brain. *Don't engage.*

"YOUSE!" She jabbed a porky finger into my chest.

"Oh! Caroline! Sorry, I —" I started, as though she'd awoken me from a moment of private contemplation.

"YSEWLLBE!"

It was a mean right hook, a slap rather than a punch, which staggered me sideward. Instinctively my hands came up to protect my head, but she wasn't following up. Not with a physical attack, anyway.

Instead she grabbed the hem of her t-shirt, somehow blackened already despite being fresh from the clothing store that evening – and yanked on it. The t-shirt came apart as though it was designed that way, melting off her body like it really had some better place it wanted to be. With an indecipherable yell she hurled the ruined shirt into my face and stood there, jiggling.

Two other volunteers approached her warily. At times throughout the week various people had had to tackle Caroline, rugby style, but no-one wanted to be the one to initiate such a move. It was one thing to do it while she was clothed, but quite another now she was topless.

Having established her dominance, and shredded her t-shirt Hulk style, Caroline decided to take the show to the troops. She stomped off into the next room, bellowing random insults at everyone she passed. With a shared sigh, the two volunteers followed her.

I breathed again. Somehow disaster had been averted. The only upside to someone that swings from love to hate in the space between belches, is their limited attention span. Caroline was like a three-year-old with ADHD – only trapped in the body of a smelly drunk sumo wrestler. I'd fully expected her to beat the crap out of me, right up until the moment she decided to strip instead. I'd gotten off lightly compared to the pummelling I'd envisaged.

Shouts and shrieks from further down the building suggested that, for the other two volunteers, that pummelling was still a distinct possibility. I felt quite sorry for them – but not enough to get involved. Ferocious wild animals I could handle, often without a thought for my own safety – but this woman was *monstrous*.

Then, without warning, she was back.

Trailing one volunteer, half dragging the other, she surged forward like a freight train made of smelly jelly. She was unstoppable (partly because, as one of the guys told me later, she was so slimy it was impossible to get a grip on her). All that anger, all the power in that gigantic body, was now striving forward towards…

Me.

She shook herself like a dog, dislodging her minders and setting up a rippling effect in every inch of her exposed body. I could only cringe as she lunged forwards, her boobs flopping in and out of her bra like deflated footballs in a sack.

She came straight for me. There was nothing I could do. I flinched, tried to duck away, but she had me. I was afraid she was going to punch me; probably painful, definitely humiliating; but I had no idea how much worse it was about to get. With both sweaty arms wrapped around me, instead of head-butting me, she hugged me, squeezing me lower, thrusting my face deep into her vast cleavage.

Harder she crushed my head into her chest, pressing my face into the dank pit between her breasts as though trying to smother me with them. The two volunteers tried to grab her from behind, and the side-to-side motion as she shouldered them away caused each huge boob to slap me in the side of the face, *left, right, left.*

They were warm.

Tighter she squeezed, her flabby tits clamped around my ears. It was moist in there. Rancid, unwashed flesh assailed my nostrils, a smell so unbearable it was very nearly the worst thing about the situation.

Then, with a sucking sound and a POP! I was free – both Caroline's minders had a hold of her, pulling her back away from me even as she flailed out towards me with both arms.

The two beefy guys hauled her backwards, capturing an arm each and using them like levers to steer her away.

She still fought like a mad thing, shoving and squirming her way out of their grip; neither of them dared risk grabbing her from the front. One of her arms came free, then the other; I think a stray elbow caught one of the minders and he went down.

Now wrestling with only one captor, she gave him a mighty shove, toppling him backwards over a card table. Then she took two quick strides towards me and swung with all her might.

One perfectly timed right hook. With a fist this time. It connected with a boxer's precision and potency, and sent me sprawling, senseless, on the carpet.

It was all over when I came to. Caroline had been bundled off – God knows how, but she had – and most of the staff were clustered around me, reading my name badge at me over and over.

"Tony…? Tony! Tony?"

I sat up, my head still spinning, and tried to figure out what had happened.

"It's okay, she's gone," someone said.

This comforted me enormously.

"You want some water?" someone else offered.

I did.

"D'you want a tissue?"

Tissue? Oh-oh. I could feel the warm wetness of blood on my face. My whole head throbbed, so there was no way of telling what damage had been done. Split cheek? Or just a nose-bleed?

Sitting up, supporting myself with one hand, I gingerly reached up and prodded the side of my forehead. Something was there all right. A viscous, sticky fluid coated me from temple down to jawline.

I braced myself for the worst and looked at my finger. The tip of it was coated with... something *brown*.

It absolutely stank. Reeked. Like... vomit.

It was vomit.

"Ooh, sorry 'bout that mate." It was one of the guys who'd tackled her. A bruise on his forehead proved he'd been in on the action. "She threw up on herself in the other room before she came for you."

So that explained it. The stink from between her breasts. The slick, slippery sensation as she squeezed them around my head. The warm, wet slap of undulating boob-flesh...

Clasped tight in the embrace of those massive mammaries had been more than just my face; there had also been the partially digested contents of her stomach. Her most recent meal in the shelter.

Pie and mushy peas, if I remembered correctly.

The Bombshell

Our first day back in Treorchy was another filming day with the presenter. After a Christmas of luxurious freedom (or in my case, being knocked out by semi-naked homeless chicks), we were reluctant to get back into the house renovation.

There was no choice, of course.

But to celebrate Christmas, and to thank the crew for sticking with us, Mum and Dad bought them each a bottle of wine. Ten bottles of wine, sitting in cardboard boxes in our bedroom – it was almost too much temptation to bear.

With the major building work finished, Lenny and his crew of misfits had stumbled off to pastures new, presumably terrifying other clients with their make-it-up-as-we-go style of construction. I was happy to see the back of them because it made life much simpler. Instead of working as an intermediary between people that wanted to film builders, and builders that didn't want to be filmed, I was now back in my element; regaling the camera with tales of our heroic labours.

The presenter, now heavily pregnant, had only a few days left to spend with us. One would be at the very end of course, when she got to point out all the mistakes we'd made and tell us how it had affected the value of the house – but for now she seemed impressed, touring the rooms with admiration for the amount of work we'd got done.

After filming some of her reactions, the crew set up in the basement to do one of those delightfully awkward whole-family interviews. No matter how many of them we did, we never managed to make it look good; Dad still stared like a rabbit in the headlights, Mum rambled, I quipped and Gill hardly got a word in edgeways. I'm sure it caused no end of amusement for the editors.

The presenter explained our progress to the camera, then moved over to talk to us.

"It's looking very nice down here, I see you've opened up this space nicely."

"Yes, the steel lintel finally went in," Mum said. "Now that it's all finished and plastered we can start to see how nice it'll be in here."

"And presumably you've had all this work inspected by the Building Regulations Officer?"

This threw Mum a little. Her reply was a little defensive; "Oh no. I don't think it needs inspecting, because it's all inside."

"I'm afraid it does," said the presenter. "It's all structural work, so Building Regs will have to see it. They'll want you remove the plaster to expose the steel, to check it's big enough – and you'll have to do the same upstairs."

"WHAT? But it's all done! It's been plastered..."

"That's true, but if they don't inspect the steel then they won't sign your Certificate of Compliance. Without that, you can't sell the house."

"But... no-one said... no-one told us we needed inspections. The builder..."

"The builder should have told you, but it's your responsibility to know these things. You'll have to get the Building Inspector in here straight away, before you do any more work. There might be other things he has to look at too, before he's happy with the build."

"But.... I..."

None of us had any words left. Until the cameras stopped.

"I'm gonna fucking KILL Lenny!" I fumed.

"Oh, fabulous! Can we please get that on camera?" Dave asked.

"Yeah, you're damn right you can!"

"But, ah, without the, ah..."

"Swearing. Yes."

So they filmed a little clip of me saying I'd like to take Lenny, put him in a bag, and beat him with a stick. In truth, I flat out wanted to stab that son-of-a-bitch.

The whole time, Mum and Dad just stared at each other in disbelief.

With the work being all internal, it hadn't occurred to us that anything would need inspecting. We had the letter of consent from the planning department, we had the builders and we had the film crew. None of them had mentioned anything about inspections. Until now.

Dad, putting these facts together in his head, was getting less happy by the minute.

In fact he was furious. I've never seen him as pissed off as he was in that moment. Well, not since the first time I nearly killed my sister (with alcohol poisoning, age 14).

He very graciously allowed the presenter to finish up her piece, gather her things and leave in the car that was waiting for her; then he threw the rest of the crew out of the house and told them never to come back.

"They bloody well knew!" he bellowed. "All over Christmas! They've done this a thousand times, and they knew we were making that mistake, even before we did it. And instead of telling us, they let us do it – and then waited 'til we were on camera to drop the bombshell. Just so they could get their drama. Well that does it. They've blown their chances. They can bugger off and film someone else, and if they don't have a programme ready in time, it sodding well serves them right."

He was right, of course – about everything.

The crew had to have known. We'd discussed every detail of the project with them, even more minutely than we had with the builders. They'd told us all the things they needed to film, and given me no end of grief if I let something important happen without running it by them first. There had been no mention of an inspection – which presumably they'd have been desperate to film – and I could see only one reason for them to withhold this nugget of information from us.

"The magic of TV," I sighed. "I bet Dave was crossing his fingers the whole time, hardly believing his luck that we didn't have any inspections planned and praying to God we wouldn't find out before it was too late. That stuck-up, smarmy, squeaking bastard!"

"Well they've done it now," Dad repeated. "They can bloody well find someone else to film!"

They couldn't, of course.

It took a fortnight of diplomacy; me fielding phone calls from Rachel and passing her messages on to my parents, and them telling me to tell her to "sod off!".

Finally, we reached an agreement.

Dad refused to be filmed any more. Dave apologised to him, and Dad, being the most mild-mannered man who ever walked this earth, meekly accepted. All the while, all he wanted to do was throw them out again and be rid of them for good. Unfortunately it was not that simple.

I'd gotten us into this mess with my desire to be famous; predictably it had back-fired, and now we were struggling to stay civil. My parents didn't blame me (at least, I don't think they did) – but they should have.

I had opened Pandora's Box, and a happy little film crew had danced out.

And shafted us.

One interesting side effect of the bust up was this: with the crew evicted and our parents forced to return home to their day jobs, Gill and I discovered something in a cardboard box in the bedroom. Six bottles of rather nice wine; and another four in another box. It took us exactly two weeks to finish the lot, what with us working so late we often fell asleep on our pizzas. It was a great reward for our efforts, and compensated us mightily for all the stress we'd had from being in the middle of the situation. Part of me wanted to tell the crew that they'd screwed themselves out of their Christmas presents – so I did.

"They didn't need to buy us wine…" Rachel said, sounding a bit embarrassed.

"No, they didn't. But I'm glad they did."

"Oh really? Why's that?"

"Because it was delicious."

I don't think she liked me much anyway.

The Buildings Inspector came the following week. It goes without saying that the crew were there to film it. It was probably already written in to Dave's 'story', just ahead of the bit they were up to.

'Next scene to film: Chapter 27 – The Slaters Realize They've Made A Big Mistake…'

If so, then Dave's story was bang on.

Because he *had* seen this a hundred times before.

Hell, he'd probably *caused* it a hundred times before.

The Buildings Inspector wandered around the house making notes, mostly ignoring the camera which followed him from room to room.

The interview was set up in the garden, where he was to tell me his findings; the crew had acquired a taste for capturing live upset, and wouldn't settle for it any other way.

He started with the good news.

The two lintels were both adequate.

My relief was so strong it was like a drug.

I'd been dreading this moment ever since the inspector had booked his visit, because I knew something that he didn't.

I knew that, rather than going down the conventional route of ordering an appropriately-sized RSJ, Lenny and his crew had gone back to their roots and simply stolen one.

According to one of his workers (who was obviously so impressed with their cleverness that he couldn't resist telling *someone*), they'd waited until the time felt right, and paid a night-time visit to an abandoned factory – quite possibly one on the industrial estate where I'd had breakfast with the drug-dealing plumber.

Lenny had measured up and lopped off a chunk of steel from the end of something – a girder supporting the roof perhaps? And brought it home on the back of his pickup.

Lenny himself had told me he was getting the girder 'from a factory down the road'. He'd just omitted to mention what part of the factory.

Hence, the beam was not really designed for residential use. It was huge, 'I' shaped in cross-section, and its surface was a dull orange from many years of oxidization.

Fortunately, Lenny had gotten something right. When revealed for inspection, the beam proved more than adequate.

Quite a lot more. It was absolutely massive.

The building inspector said it could have supported a train.

As far as I knew, at this time there were no sections of track missing.

But we got the inspection holes covered over as quickly as possible, just in case – because, honestly, I wouldn't have put it past him.

So, the girder was fine.

The footings beneath the kitchen lintel, where the wall met the floor, were not fine, because there weren't any. The bricks of the kitchen wall – on which the lintel, and consequently the weight of top two floors of the house rested – were sitting on bare earth. The lovely concrete floor Lenny had poured went up to the bricks, but not under them. There was no foundation, and apparently it was a miracle that the house was still standing at all.

This was still the good news.

The insanely steep staircase was okay, but only because there was no conceivable way to make it any different.

The bathrooms all needed mechanical ventilation, which meant ducting and new electrical cables would have to be run in the ceilings, leading all the way to the outside.

A 'soil pipe' had to be fitted, which had to rise higher than the highest toilet in the house – or, in our case, about thirty feet up the back wall; and the main drain had to be replaced.

"How... how do we replace the main drain?" I asked the guy. My mind shied away from the enormity of the other problems, so I fixated on the one that made the least sense.

"The waste from the toilets can't be plumbed straight into the existing pipe. It's too old. What you'll have to do is dig down through here…" he stamped on the ground beneath his feet for emphasis, "find the chamber where your drain meets the main drain, and fit a new pipe into that."

"But… where is it?"

"Oh, probably a few feet down. It runs behind all the houses, see, down the back gardens. It'll be under here somewhere."

And it was.

Somewhere.

Dad was appalled. The film crew were delighted. At least, they were until I told Rachel what this could mean.

"There's no way we'll finish now, not in time for the programme," I said.

"But you have to! We've almost got enough footage! I'll see if we can extend the deadline." She was in a panic. I had the guilty satisfaction of knowing that she'd helped shoot herself in the foot, as if we didn't finish it would be her that would be in trouble. Dave would be kicking her ass – if that's even possible with a wooden leg.

If it is, I bet it hurts like hell.

I had another thing to feel guilty about as well.

Because this was a crucial part of the house project, with emotions running high and an already impossible workload about to triple – and I was about to leave for two whole weeks.

I packed a bag and caught a bus to London, leaving Dad knee-deep in a hole in the back garden. Shovel in hand, miserable in the driving rain, the poor man dug forlornly in search of the main drain.

Back when I'd been looking for something to do over Christmas, I'd come across a kind of volunteering I'd never heard of before.

A kind of volunteering that was paid – and paid well.

Naturally I'd applied for a position, and had just been asked to come and take my place.

In hospital.

Because this was medical volunteering; also known as conducting a clinical trial.

Also known as, being a guinea pig.

Oh yes – for the next two weeks, instead of sweating away in the middle of a busy building site, I'd be lounging around on a hospital bed – whilst a team of research scientists pumped me full of experimental medicines.

I have to say, I was a little bit nervous about it.

Hospitalisation

I've always had a phobia about needles.

It's a ridiculous, pointless fear – but then, that's what a phobia is.

Mine was so bad that when it came time to have my travel vaccinations before going to Ecuador, I point blank refused to do it.

My Mum, being a nurse, was disgusted with me, and had decided that extreme measures were called for. So she brought the needles home and hid them in our fridge until the moment was right.

I was minding my own business in the kitchen one evening when I heard her shout: "NOW!"

And Gill and my Dad pounced on me, dragged me to the floor and pinned me in place while Mum stepped in and gave me the jab.

Tricked! In my own house!

Man, was I pissed off about that.

But I'd been through a few things since then, and it had occurred to me that if I wanted to be a professional adventurer (I feel certain such a profession exists *somewhere*) then sooner or later I would have to get over my fear. As the doctor always said, "Why is such a strong young man afraid of such a tiny prick?"

(The answer of course being that it's not the prick I'm scared of, but rather the needle the prick is holding.)

But anyway – it had to end.

So it was that I made the journey to London, and checked myself into hospital. It was to be the ultimate immersion therapy; I planned to emerge richer – hopefully unchanged by the medicines being tested – and cured of my irrational fear.

Because one thing I could be sure of; there would be needles enough to cure a dozen such phobias in the next two weeks.

I was told that at least five times a day – even more in the beginning – nurses would be drawing my blood to see how well the drug they'd given me was metabolizing in my system.

It was for the same reason that they also collected my wee.

There was a huge fridge full of gigantic brown bottles of urine; anytime I needed the toilet I had to find a nurse, get her to unlock the fridge, find the bottle with my unique number on it, then allow her to escort me to the nearest bathroom. She would unlock the door and thankfully remain outside it whilst I rushed in and tried to remember to unscrew the lid of the bottle before widdling into it.

I'd like to say I was successful every time – but I'd be lying.

Afterwards I had to close it up (and/or wipe it off) and hand it back to the nurse, whilst trying not to make any jokes about how she was taking the piss.

It really was quite odd.

The pay, though, was astronomical. Ludicrous. For two weeks in hospital I was getting over two grand! It was a staggering amount of money. The official reason for this was that we were being paid for 'working' around the clock – back to back twenty-four hour shifts in the hospital, of which I spent the most part sleeping. There was absolutely no mention of the pay being related to the amount of danger we were in, which was comforting.

When I say 'we', I am of course referring to my fellow medical volunteers; there were thirty-eight of us on that study. This was the first of the downsides to chasing such a grand prize; I was far from alone in wanting to be paid for doing nothing. There was one long corridor lined with twenty beds on each side – so many that they didn't even have space for curtains around them. Now, I'm not big on demanding privacy, and those flimsy plastic curtains don't afford you much anyway, but with nearly forty blokes in one big room, things were bound to get... fragrant? Sleeping each night, if possible at all, was done to the accompaniment of synchronised farting, snoring in stereo and the ever-present buzz of thirty-plus sets of balls being scratched.

It was like being in a giant college dorm room – except one where nurses came in at 5 o'clock every morning to stab you in the arm.

Dinner times were even less pleasant. Many of the guys moaned about being hungry all day, and fell upon their evening meal like starving tigers. I wasn't too bothered to be honest, having done nothing but fart and scratch my balls all day, but that didn't matter; everyone had to eat *everything*.

I hate vegetables. In fact I try to avoid anything green, just in case it's been anywhere near a vegetable.

Alas, whilst on a medical trial you have to eat a balanced – and carefully prescribed – diet. It goes without saying there are vegetables involved, but this place went completely over the top. Meals would consist of a dry piece of grilled meat – a chicken breast, say, or a pork chop – and half a plate piled high with one kind of vegetable. Presumably this made it easier to calculate the calories and nutrients we were getting, but there are few things more off-putting than a mountain of garden peas – at least a tin's worth – with nothing on them. And the next day, the meal would be the same – only a triple-sized portion of sweet corn had been substituted for the peas.

I hate sweet corn. It's not food. It goes in, rattles around inside you and comes out completely unchanged – which I take to mean, it's indigestible. Like swallowing the toy gun from your Action Man – you could conceivably fish it out, wash it off, and eat the damn stuff again. It can't possibly provide you with any nutrition – hence, not food.

But I couldn't convince the nurses of this. I had to eat every single kernel. Every pea. Every piece of limp broccoli. And on the day they gave us a sachet of tomato ketchup to liven up our meal, I forgot about it and was sent back to eat it after presenting my plate as empty. I literally had to open the sachet, squeeze the contents into my mouth (under close scrutiny to make sure I didn't try and hide it in my pyjamas) and eat it. Ugh!

On the upside we each had our own TV's, hanging from the roof on chunky metal arms; on the downside, only a handful of them worked. The rest of us fought over the single TV on wheels, and the one ageing PC in the rather grandly titled 'Computer Room'.

Or at least, we did for the first few days. Then the drugs started to kick in, and most of us never left our beds. A few people quit the trial straight away, some claiming unfinished business in the outside world that they'd forgotten about, some admitting plainly that they were scared. It didn't bother me, as sleeping eighteen hours a day was something of a luxury after the last few weeks in Treorchy. We'd been working so hard recently, sanding and painting late into the nights, that I felt doubly guilty about leaving Gill to it. But what else could I do? I needed the money if I was ever going to make it to Thailand, and fulfil my dream of blatantly copying Toby's dream (of becoming a professional diver).

So I toughed it out, and allowed myself to relax; I let the drugs take hold, and I dreamed of a better place.

It wasn't hard to imagine – pretty much any place was better than here.

A Change Is As Good As Arrest

A few more downsides emerged as the trial progressed.

Every second morning a bunch of doctors would come around changing all our cannulas. These were tiny plastic tubes inserted into a vein in our forearms – the same things people always rip out of their arms in movies, when they're determined to escape from hospital. Ours weren't linked to anything; they just ended in a little plastic tap that was taped to our wrists. Several times a day the nurses would shake me awake, attach a small phial to the tap in my arm, open the tap, and let a measured amount of blood flow out of me into the bottle.

It was such a regular occurrence I hardly even noticed it happening, and was usually asleep again before they'd closed the tap.

But the tap needed replacing regularly to avoid becoming infected, and this particularly unpleasant experience could only be delivered by a doctor.

My doctor one morning was an old bloke with noticeably shaking hands. I worried when it took him five tries to open the packet with the new tap inside; no matter how he held it, his hands were shaking too much to get a firm grip on the packet. On the forth attempt he accidentally threw the thing halfway across the room; it was then that I started getting really nervous.

Being afraid of needles was already in my past. But being afraid of a needle in those hands? I wasn't so sure...

Let's just say, it hurt. I mean, really hurt! I could feel the guy fishing around inside my arm with the point of the needle, searching in vain for the vein he'd been targeting.

Getting frustrated, he pressed in hard causing me to cry out.

"AAARGH! I don't think that's right!"

At this he gave a muttered curse and withdrew the needle.

It was bent.

Whatever he'd done with it inside my arm, he'd managed to bend the narrow steel shaft so that it stuck out at an angle.

His hands shook uncontrollably as he dropped the broken needle in a sharps bin and reached for a fresh packet.

"Are you okay?" I asked. I wanted to say, "Please don't touch me ever again you fucking nutjob!" – but that didn't seem polite.

The old man had another go.

It hurt like hell, but I tried to ignore it. I'd had this done a dozen times already, and I knew that if I could shut up and let him get on with it, it would be over all the quicker.

It wasn't. It took him an age – and another needle – before he found a vein. I was a bit pale by this point, and on the verge of throwing up, but at last the deed was done.

Then the doctor turned around to reach for a sticking-plaster, caught the tap in my arm on the pocket of his white coat, and ripped it right back out of there.

I shrieked.

Blood spouted from my arm, one short sharp spray which nearly reached the guy in the next bed – then it seemed content to trickle out, running down the back of my hand and dripping off my fingertips.

"Can I help?" A young South African doctor was passing the end of my bed, and looked concerned when he heard me yelling.

"Yes please! Can you look at this? I'm not letting this pillock near me again!"

The old doctor stormed off in a huff as the new one slid in to replace him. At the same time a brace of nurses arrived to see what the commotion was about.

With far less fuss than I'd feared, the young doctor opened a cannula and embedded it painlessly in my arm. It took about three seconds from start to finish. "That better?" he asked.

"Yeah! Whew, thanks man. That guy was scaring the shit out of me! It's never been as painful as that."

"Don't worry," he said, "I'll do your cannulas from now on."

It hadn't occurred to me until then, but I still had an awful lot more of these things to go in and out of me.

"Thanks for that," I told him. I decided not to ask what was wrong with the old doctor – I was half afraid to find he was a patient from the other end of the hospital that had wandered in and made himself at home. Either that, or a smack addict going cold-turkey.

"No problems, my friend," said the doctor. Then he was gone, leaving the nurses to move in clutching wads of blue tissue paper.

"I'll just clean this up," one of them said, as she began dabbing ineffectually at the mess on my arm.

"I think you might want to sort that out first," I said, glancing down at her feet. She followed my gaze.

She was standing with both feet in a puddle of blood the size of a dinner tray.

"Oh! Yes!" she looked a little sick herself. My heart went out to her. She was probably worried about her shoes. "I'll... I'll go get a mop."

It took me quite a while to get back to sleep after that one.

For some reason.

By the time I'd been there a week, there was less than ten of us guinea pigs left. It was the sleeping bit that had scared most of the others off; there was something vaguely disturbing about the drugs having such an obvious effect on our systems. The last few of us were like zombies, hardly moving from our beds except to go to the bathroom.

I was a bit worried myself, mostly about what would happen if the sleepiness didn't wear off as soon as the drugs were withdrawn; I couldn't afford to be kept in longer for observation, and I needed all my energy to put back into Treorchy.

After a week with only one person on site, time was bound to be getting tight. After another week... well, I'd be returning to desperation central, I knew that.

The nurses changed our beds around, wheeling them together to close up the gaps. It made monitoring us easier, and we were past caring. Wires from electrodes on my chest led to a heart-rate monitor next to the bed, which was an absolute nightmare; turning over in my sleep was quite hazardous. I'm a hairy bugger, and nowhere worse than on my chest; the wires would only stretch so far before the machine would yank them back, performing an impromptu waxing on a small circle of my body hair. I had a nice little pattern of bald spots ranging up and down my torso, which would be hard to explain if anyone saw me naked.

Well, other than the nine dudes who saw me naked all day, every day.

It was too damned hot for pyjamas.

And the bloody bed sheets were made of rubber!

But at least they wiped clean easily.

One day there was nine of us. Then eight. People were giving in to fear, which seemed pointless to me as they'd already been taking the drug for a week. What was it going to do, that it hadn't done already? And anyway we were being closely monitored 24/7. Our blood work was being checked every couple of hours. If there was something going wrong, the administrators would know about it – they weren't about to take a risk with the health of a whole roomful of young men.

I hoped.

And then there was a big commotion a few beds down.

An alarm had gone off on one of the monitors – itself not a surprising thing, as mine was going off all the time. I must have been fitter than I thought, as every time I fell asleep my already low heart-rate would dip low enough to blow the alarms. They'd had to recalibrate my machine to stop the bloody thing waking me up every ten minutes.

But this was different. Nurses were rushing back and forth around the bed, stage-whispering commands at each other in tense voices.

That afternoon they stopped our drugs.

We were kept in for another couple of nights, until tests confirmed that the last of the medicine had left our bodies, then we were sent home early with only half our pay.

The buggers!

But I had to admit, I was grateful to be getting out of there. Not because of the food – or not only because of the food – and not because of the needles.

Because while he was asleep, the guy in bed number six had had a bit of a turn.

His heart had stopped.

Thankfully the nurses had been on hand straight away, and had managed to resuscitate him.

But the rest of the trial had been cancelled, because just as I'd thought, the hospital bosses took a dim view of doing long term damage to a whole roomful of young blokes.

To say nothing of killing them.

Homecomings

When I got back to Treorchy, Dad was still digging a hole.

It was the same hole – only bigger.

Much, much bigger!

First Dad had dug a hole – then a wider hole. Still not finding the elusive main drain, he'd dug a little deeper – then a little wider. Then his hole had become a trench. Then it had become a crater. By now Dad's hole extended right the way across the garden from shitty wooden fence to ugly concrete wall. It was four feet wide and four feet deep, except in the middle where he was busy widening and deepening it. It seemed to have gotten a bit out of hand; if Dad stayed there much longer, either he'd drop dead from exhaustion or he'd hit China. Possibly both.

There was nothing else for it; forcibly removing Dad from the hole he'd spent most of the week in, I took a turn on the shovel.

For three days.

When my spade finally struck pipe, I nearly cried in relief.

Every evening, after darkness forced me to stop digging, I'd had the thought; this is all for nothing. The inspector was wrong. There is no drain.

Realistically, it could have been anywhere in the garden – so just how deep do you dig, before you abandon your efforts and try somewhere else? And how many somewhere else's do you try before you give up completely and dedicate the rest of your life to murdering every Building Inspector you can find? I'm telling you, it damn near happened – about once a day, on average.

And yet there it was! An enormous concrete well, covered over with paving slabs – buried nearly six feet below the surface of our back garden. In fairness to the inspector, it was exactly where he'd said it was: 'somewhere under here'. Only about two metric tonnes of soil deeper than we'd thought possible.

I'd dug down through the First World War, the Renaissance, the Roman occupation, at least three iron-age hill-forts and was about to discover a new species of dinosaur.

"My arms are dino-sore enough," I quipped.

Thank God this incredibly poor joke did not make it onto your TV screens; I'd have been lynched.

There was one unexpected benefit though: as a direct result of this part of the programme, I received three requests for a date and one proposal of marriage from the girls who worked in my Dad's office. Whether or not Dad got any proposals, he never said.

There was no two ways about it though – this monumental mission had set us back. We had less time than ever, in spite of a few extra days' leeway being granted by the TV crew. Not only was there a staggering amount of work still to do to the house – not to mention furnishing it and 'dressing' it for the final reveal – but the crew also had things they needed to get done, and it didn't come as a surprise to find out they would be hindering, rather than helping us.

It began with a trip to Holly Cottage, the ancestral home of the Slater Clan for over ten years.

(In other words, we were going home.)

I love my parent's house in Somerset, for all its eccentricities – of which there are many.

But this was exactly the wrong time for a visit. Pretty much the worst possible time. Mum and Dad had both taken another week off work. All four of us were working around the clock, sleeping maybe four hours a night at a push. We worked as we ate. We worked in our dreams, what few of them we had time for. The pace was frantic, and every one of us was close to breaking.

I'd been wanting to go home practically every night since the project began, but I'd only managed it a handful of times in the last three months.

And yet, right now, for the first time in recent memory, I really did *not* want to go home.

None of us did.

There simply wasn't time.

"We need you to come home," Rachel told me on the phone.

"WHAT? No! No, I'm sorry, there's no chance. No way."

"But we have to film you there! We need to show you some 'mood boards'."

"But we'll never make it! We're getting so close… can't you do it here? We can take an hour out, maybe take it in turns to look at your boards…?"

"No, it has to be at your house I'm afraid. And it had to be this week. We're bringing the presenter."

Ohhh… Shit! I'd forgotten. Or rather, I'd stopped counting. And caring. We had not one but *two* presenter days left, which meant there was no way at all we would be getting out of this trip.

I told Rachel if we missed the deadline by a day, it would be all because of this.

She said she'd try and get us an extra day on the schedule.

But she didn't sound hopeful.

So we downed tools one morning and, instead of flicking the kettle on and grabbing more tools to do something while we waited for it to boil, we piled into the car and drove for two hours down the motorway, back to our comfy cottage in the middle of nowhere.

We arrived just before the crew, and set about a lightening-fast clearing up of all the clutter. Housework, when anyone had even been there, had become a very low priority.

One thing we couldn't hide though, were the clocks.

Amongst his many strange hobbies, my Dad also collects clocks; he has well over a hundred, covering every spare scrap of wall-space, cluttering the mantelpiece, lining every cupboard and bookshelf in our quaint little cottage. The effect is overpowering; in moments that would otherwise be dead silent, the minute clacking of dozens of clock movements escalates to machine-gun-like proportions. When Daylight Savings Time begins and the hour goes forwards, it takes him most of the night to change them all – and costs at least £10 in new batteries. First-time visitors to the house display a variety of reactions, from amusement to bafflement to horror; it certainly gives an impression, though perhaps not the one he thinks it does.

To me it says, 'This is the house of an unhinged psychopath who is almost certainly about to kill you and eat you.'

But it doesn't bother me because I live there.

Rachel's reaction was one of the few moments I wish they had been filming, when they weren't. She did about three double-takes back to back; the first presumably to check she wasn't hallucinating, the second to confirm the results of the first, and the third to look for axe-murderers hiding behind the door.

But nothing fazed her for long.

Soon we were presented with two wooden boards, each about a metre square, both covered with an assortment of floor surfaces and lighting fixtures.

Rachel had mentioned that this bit of filming would involve 'mood boards'. No-one had bothered to tell us what mood boards were, because all that had been taken care of by the crew – for which we were more than grateful.

It seems some enterprising researcher had watched the footage so far, decided what style Gill and I were trying to decorate the property in, and knocked up a fairly random assortment of samples. They'd done the same for Mum and Dad – gluing hideous tasselled lamp shades straight out of an old people's home onto the board, above strips of vinyl floor tiling and dark brown carpet.

It was quite over top, and it wasn't hard to see what kind of conflict they were hoping to generate between us as we each defended our apparent styles.

Of course, it also ignored the fact that the lights, the blinds, the décor, had not only been chosen already, but had all been installed; the carpets had been ordered and would be going down as soon as we could make room for them.

None of that mattered.

The crew explained the rules. The presenter would interrogate us about our 'choices', and give us her verdict on what we'd picked.

Except, we hadn't picked them.

"They're awful!" Mum moaned, indicating the lamp shades. "I would never even think about having something like that!"

"Ah, I see," said Dave. "Well we can't worry about that now. Just pretend it's what you've chosen."

"But…"

"Don't worry. Oh, here she comes!"

And the presenter's arrival signalled an abrupt end to the negotiation.

Poor Mum had to go on camera defending the nastiest interior design decisions since the house had last been decorated – and she had to make out they were her own.

The presenter ridiculed her choices, obviously, and rebuked me for choosing lighting options that were way out of our budget. I had no idea what they cost, as I'd never seen them before in my life. The glass-and-chrome spotlight on my mood board could have been bought from a swanky London lighting designer for a thousand pounds for all I knew – it may well have been out of our budget, but I didn't really care.

The gorgeous recessed lights I had chosen had been fitted weeks ago.

The laminate floor on Gills-and-my board was actually quite

similar to the stuff Mum had picked out for the basement – which had been fitted shortly after the lights.

Bless her, Mum defended the lino, although it had never been on the cards, but I could tell she was getting ready to pop by the time filming finished.

"Just one more thing, *dahling*," Dave asked her. "We need a shot of you flicking through the Yellow Pages. Remember at the start, when you were looking for a builder?"

"I remember at the start, when you lost us our builder and I had to find another one."

"Yes, of course! We'd like to film you looking through the phone book. Can you remember how you felt back then?"

Mum took a deep breath. "Pretty much," she said.

Dave didn't even spot the irony. "That's marvellous! Okay *dahling*, let's move this into the kitchen. Remember how difficult it was, that's what I want you to talk about…"

I left them to it. Gill and I had a race to the shower; the experience of being clean was something we dimly remembered from the last time the crew had dragged us home. Then we got to experience a rare moment of serene calm.

Dave asked us (Gill and I) to sit on the sofa – and do nothing.

Absolutely nothing!

We flicked through a couple of magazines, gazed idly around the room, and tried not to think of the million and one other jobs we could have been doing at that moment.

"I don't understand," I said to Dave, afterwards. "What do you need that for?"

He waved away my curiosity and muttered something like 'general background footage'.

How odd! But I thought nothing more of it. Relaxing, however temporarily, was one of the few perks – along with a night in a real bed – before the morning's inevitable charge back down the motorway to Wales.

To be honest, we were getting quite sick of the place.

Waterworks

Having a working, flushing toilet fitted in the Treorchy house was possibly the most exciting point of the entire project. A day later we also had a shower, although none of us dared use it – with the final – and now extended – deadline only a couple of weeks away, it seemed like it was tempting fate too much. I mean, everyone deserves a toilet. But a shower? Were we worthy of such a luxury? Would we be punished for our vanity by having it explode in our faces the first time we turned it on?

If our previous luck with plumbing was anything to go by, the answer was a definite yes. That shower was almost certainly a time-bomb, and none of us dared test the theory. There simply wasn't time to repair flood damage and install another one – not while there were skirting boards still going in, doors to be oiled, ceilings needing painting, carpets to get laid... it was a measure of how insanely busy we were that I hadn't even thought about getting laid myself.

Which is probably for the best, as I spent most of the week looking (and smelling) like a long-dead member of the Addams Family.

We needed only two things to make the plumbing complete; first, there were myriad holes chopped out of the floor in the most unlikely of locations, each one lying in wait to catch an unsuspecting ankle. They needed repairing, although so much damage had been done already that we'd had to abandon the idea of polishing up the floorboards. Dad was thrilled that he could have the entire house carpeted, and by this stage Gill and I were just glad we didn't have to hire a floor sander. Carpeting was a job we would contract out, and it would take less than a day – but it still couldn't be done until the missing chunks of floor had been replaced.

The second thing we needed our plumber for was a Gas Certificate. You can't get the final okay from the building inspector without this, making it one of the most valuable pieces of paper in our universe at the moment – except that, there wasn't one in our universe at the moment.

And we couldn't sell the house without it.

Unfortunately, James had stopped coming to work. The longer he stayed away, the more we worried. He'd also stopped answering my calls for no discernable reason; yes, I might have been a bit more forceful than usual when complaining about the hatchet job he'd done to the floor, but we were holding on to the last of his cash until after he'd finished. Surely it was worth it to him, a couple more days with a hammer and nails, to get his final payment in full?

Except that, at the back of my mind was always the worry that our plumbing might be less important to him than his 'real' job; as time went on, it had become increasingly obvious that James' main source of income was selling drugs.

Now, I always knew that James was selling drugs – mostly because every half-hour or so throughout his rather short working day, he would stop, roll a spliff, smoke it, and then ask me if I wanted to buy any.

But the final confirmation came when Dad and I went around to his house to confront him about the work he still had to do, and demand that he return to finish it.

But we could only find his girlfriend.

Because James was in prison for selling drugs.

It didn't look good.

The first time we'd lost a plumber, we'd had an almost impossible task finding someone else to take over. Or rather, Mum had. Now it was back to her again – and the Yellow Pages – to find our saviour. Ideally one who would work all weekend. And all night. For free.

As I may have mentioned, it didn't look good.

And unsurprisingly, it never happened.

Our new plumber was shockingly expensive and we were beyond broke, but we had absolutely no choice.

He was efficient though; he wasted no time in ripping up all the floorboards we'd been carefully nailing back down, starting with one by the lounge door that was making a squeaking noise. He muttered to himself, as most tradesmen do, but we tried not to read anything into it. He seemed to know what he was doing.

He delivered his report to the whole family – we took a break from group-sanding our new skirting boards, and stood in a defensive semi-circle to protect ourselves from the news we felt was coming.

"It's the wrong size," he said.

"What is?" Mum asked.

"The pipe."

"Oh! Which bit?"

"All of it."

It turned out that James had run some quite tidy lines, amongst his other less-tidy lines. His approach to carpentry was about as poor as could be expected, as he'd sawed almost clear through a couple of the joists supporting the first floor. But the real killer, the bit that was going to sting us the most was this; he'd used the wrong gauge of copper pipe, presumably because it was cheaper, on the whole house. Everything was at least one size too small, including the pipes carrying the gas – and these had dimensions that were regulated by law.

Every bit of James' pipework was going to have to be redone – it would be as though he was never here. Which was pretty much how it had felt most of the time he had been here.

That was pretty much the worst thing he did to us.

Oh, except he never could have given us that gas certificate, because he wasn't qualified.

When he'd joked with me about how simplistic and pointless the CORGI gas fitter's exam was, I never once thought that might be because he hadn't taken it.

The bastard.

Dad swore that evening, as he hammered the floorboards back into place for the second, and in some cases third, time. He swore and hammered, swore and hammered, cursing James, Lenny, the Welsh, our luck – then there came a time when his swearing grew louder, and more frantic.

By now we were so well-drilled in the face of an emergency, we were all there before he'd thought to call us by name.

Frustration, tiredness and a desire to outright murder some bastard Welsh plumber, had combined in my Dad to give him tunnel-vision. He'd pounded nails hard into the floor, and not always with 100% accuracy.

Result; he'd driven a nail clear through one of the under-sized copper pipes that fed cold water into the house.

When we arrived he was on his knees in a puddle, both hands under the floorboards with his fists clenched around the leak. Panic was in his eyes as he tried – and failed – to stem the flow. He knew –

we all knew – this was the mains water, coming in from under the doorstep. It was supplied at enough pressure to rise up three storeys to the new toilet on the top floor – only now it was being supplied at a similar pressure to the kitchen ceiling below.

"Tape!" Mum called.

"It's too strong!" Dad said. "My hands can't hold it."

I took over from him, gripping the punctured pipe with all my strength. There was a spray as we swapped over, soaking all the others who were bending over to get a closer look. Then my fist was around the problem and the water was dripping slowly from between my knuckles. Dad sat back, rubbing his hands. Already I could feel the pressure building, a spot of pain burning into my palm, my grip weakening.

"Call the plumber! I'm not gonna be able to hold this for long."

Then Gill came to the rescue.

"Here – try this!" She thrust something at me on the end of her finger and I looked up, confused.

"Gill, what the fuck is that?"

"It's chewing gum. I was chewing it."

"What the… are you fuckin'…" words failed me for a few seconds.

Then I tried it. That is how desperate we were in that moment.

And it worked.

Kind of.

The gum stuck into the hole and adhered to the pipe, slowing the flow immediately. It had the makings of a solution – but one piece would never be enough. Gill ran for the packet, then doled it out to Mum and Dad.

Four pieces left.

"I'll run to the shop," I said. "Gill, can you…?"

Gill took over, wrapping her hands around the gum-covered pipe, and I took off for the corner shop like the hounds of hell were after me.

I bought all the gum on offer – twenty-six packets, each with ten tabs in them – and raced back to the house.

And so we sat there in a circle on the floor, chewing gum as though our lives depended on it.

We crammed in as many pieces as we could fit, chewed until the consistency was right, then spat it out, moulded it onto the growing lump around the pipe, and stuffed in another mouthful.

It was a little awkward, as I don't normally masticate in front of my parents.

Finally the leak was sealed. A wet, sticky ball encased the pipe, glistening with saliva. Occasionally a bead of water squeezed out of the mass and dripped kitchenwards. It was a solution as crazy as it was ideal – and as precarious.

The plumber was called and would be here in the morning – with the water under control, we hadn't dared ask him what the emergency call-out fee was.

"No running water at all," Dad said.

I agreed. Any changes or surges in water pressure could blow the lid right off our solution.

"Just like before, if you need the loo use the one in the café."

"Café's shut by now."

"Okay, so wee in the back garden. I'll go and buy some bottled water from ASDA and we can have a cup of tea and go to bed."

And that was that. Gill was clearing away the chewing gum wrappers when she discovered our next problem.

"Oh bloody hell! Look what it says on the packet!"

We all crowded round to see it, written on the back under the ingredients.

In tiny letters:

'WARNING – EXCESSIVE CONSUMPTION CAN CAUSE A LAXATIVE EFFECT'".

If we weren't in the shit already, we soon would be.

The End

The presenter's last visit was the most fraught of all.

From the very start, she'd taken issue with our bathroom arrangements. I always felt this was more because she had to find fault with something to create some conflict, and she'd seized upon the bathroom issue because she knew there was no way we could change it.

Her on-camera suggestions had been to chop off the end of a bedroom on the top floor to add a shower to the upstairs toilet we were building. The local estate agent told us this was madness because it would turn one of the two double-sized bedrooms into a single, effectively downgrading the size and value of the property by one band. Since people from outside the valleys never bought houses there, and all the terraces were identical, it was unlikely anyone would be horrified by the lack of a shower on the top floor – he doubted there was a house in ten miles that had one.

The presenter also believed we should squeeze all the rest of our bathroom facilities into the old coal hole, where we'd put the bath. She was adamant that it would have fitted, and solved the problem of having the bath and toilet in two separate rooms.

Unfortunately in order to do this, we'd have had to run a large-bore toilet waste pipe through the floor from the front of the house, all the way out the back to that drain under the garden. Almost the only part of the whole house that hadn't needed replacing was the huge concrete slab which formed the basement floor. Like the rest of the basement (before Lenny's crew started attacking it), it had been renovated recently and was in good condition. Digging it up to run a pipe down the middle – with enough of a downwards slope to ensure your business didn't sit in the pipe making its presence known – and then re-pouring a new floor over the top – would have cost us about three grand.

So instead we stuck to our original plan, and put the new toilet where the existing toilet had been.

Some people like having the loo separate, we figured, so they could still use it while someone else was taking their time in the bath.

The presenter thought otherwise. Standing in the middle of the open-plan basement, she pantomimed the problem. I was half expecting the crew to play Benny Hill music as she scurried around clutching an imaginary towel.

"So you're in the bath, with no clothes on. But you want to use the loo, so you've got to run through here, past all your guests sitting at the dining table, use the loo, then run back, in your towel, into the bathroom. And when you want to go to bed you've got to run upstairs, with no clothes on, waving to all your guests again. How bizarre is that?"

To which I replied:

"But surely, if they were having a party, most people would have a bath before dinner? Or after it? Or both? And:

a) who has a bath while they have dinner guests sitting at the table?

b) who goes to bed – naked – while their guests are still eating? And

c) maybe it's a bloke thing, but – wouldn't you just pee in the shower?"

Apparently, this rebuttal was not considered appropriate, as it was cunningly left out of the programme. Maybe viewers took the same issue with her scenario as I did. Or maybe, like everyone who believes what they see on television, they exchanged shocked glances and comments like "She's right! You'd never want to run from the bath to the toilet past all your guests! What were they thinking?"

Remind me to invite all these people for a dinner party in a three-bedroom terraced house in South Wales. And then to go and have a bath while they're waiting to be served. Oh, and then run past them, naked and dripping, to use the toilet in the middle of it.

It'd give them something to talk about, over coffee and mints.

But at least the house was finished. I had some good news to tell Rachel.

"We've had it valued! It's worth £87,000!"

She wasn't as excited as I'd hoped.

"Oh! You can't do that! We arrange the valuing, and film it as part of the programme. You'll have to pretend you don't know about it, and try to look surprised when you get told about it."

"Ah… okay then. I guess we can do that."

"Great. So, can I have the number for your estate agent? We'll get him round to give his valuation on tape."

They also brought two other agents to see the house. Being in a desperate bind for time, they plucked the first two agents they could find from the Cardiff phone book – neither of whom had ever set foot in a valleys house for reasons of valuation – and brought them along to give their professional opinion.

We'd been asked to find people to pose as potential buyers, to view the house and give their opinions on our handiwork.

Our estate agent brought one – a young lady who had already been in touch with him about buying the house. We supplied the others. Our next-door neighbour was one; he was eager to see what we'd done with the place, as he was a few months out from finishing the same job on the identical property to our left. Without artificially imposed deadlines, his schedule was more relaxed, allowing him to work mostly on weekends. He asked us if we thought it had helped, having the TV crew round to film us.

We thought about that for a moment.

"No, not really," I said.

Oh yeah, we found one other person to pose as a potential buyer. He was also really keen to see the final product, because he'd been getting a blow-by-blow account of our progress every other night for the last four months.

Usually whilst waiting for our pizza to cook.

He was the owner of the takeaway down the road.

In a caricature of the rest of the project, the deadline had reduced us to this: while the crew filmed their 'after' shots and followed the buyers around the top floor, Gill and I squatted in the alleyway assembling the last pieces of flat-packed furniture.

"It's done," she'd hiss, passing me a low bookcase with both hands to keep its feet out of the mud. I'd peer around the back wall to make sure there wasn't a camera pointing out of one of the upper windows, then I'd scurry down the garden path, slip my shoes off at the back door, and tip-toe inside to place the thing beside the dining table. No sound could be made in the house while these vital interviews were recorded, as members of the public tend to get annoyed when their fourteenth take is spoiled by some idiot dropping a bookcase.

One by one we put the dining chairs together in that alley, working on a filthy sheet of cardboard placed over the mud. We sniggered – very quietly – at the ridiculousness of the situation. Taking it in turns, we silently snuck them in, then wiped them down and arranged them for shot just as the crew brought the camera downstairs to film them.

We'd finished in time by the skin of a gnat's nether regions.

Maybe even less.

It's a long time since I looked at a gnat that closely.

According to the format of the show, the presenter sat us all down at the shiny new kitchen table to let us in on the final figures.

First Dad had to reveal how much we'd spent, and explain why we'd gone over budget. He was not allowed to say "It's because you didn't tell us about the building inspections until it was too bloody late! You lost us our builder and consequently our plumber, which resulted in us hiring a bunch of maniacs and paying to have the same pipes done three times!"

I also couldn't mention that 10% of the total overspend was my phone bill from calling them every day.

Instead, the presenter laid out the rules. Three valuations; then take an average of the three. This final score was the price she recommended we place the house on the market for.

Of course, the two Cardiff estate agents hadn't got a clue how to value the property. More used to looking at rather grander properties in the suburbs of the capital, their rough estimates were quite a lot lower than our current asking price. Mum had no choice but to tell the presenter that we'd be holding out for the top figure.

"That is *quite* high," she replied, putting just enough stress on the words to imply that she knew something about the local property market. Which of course she didn't. "You'll be putting off potential buyers by trying to get that price."

We had to sit on our hands and bite our tongues.

How badly did I want to blurt out "But that 'higher' price is the only real valuation! Given by our agent! And not only is the house already on the market with him at that price, but we've already received an offer on it!"

Oh, no. We'd been cautioned not to say anything that would upset the presenter's logic, as we'd only have to start again, and keep filming until we got it right. And re-takes took time; time that, for them, was rapidly running out.

So we nodded, and tried to look thoughtful, and racked our brains for a way to defend our position.

There wasn't one.

The presenter wrapped up by concluding that we'd done an amazing job, but that our overspend had proved her point; if Gill and I hadn't worked for free for all those months, we'd never have made a profit. She explained that the peculiar arrangement of bathrooms would make it a tricky sale, and that by holding out for the higher price, we might struggle to find a buyer.

The show aired three days later.

The whole family sat down to watch it, with glasses of wine all round and a tape in the VCR ready to record. We even wheeled Granddad over to see us on the telly.

And then the programme started, and a few minutes into it I finally realised the full implications of Dave talking about 'the story'.

We were horrified.

What was unfolding on the TV in front of us bore so little resemblance to the job we'd just completed, that it was a surprise to see ourselves on the screen.

It had obviously been scripted well in advance.

Then they'd cut out bits of footage from all over the project, and put them back together in a completely different order – so that instead of showing what actually happened, it told precisely the story they wanted to tell.

This was the real magic of television.

The arguments they'd asked us to stage had been kept in, some run together into a montage to suggest we'd spent most of our time doing this.

And then, to add insult to… well, to other insults – they showed the footage of us at home.

I may have mentioned how much we protested at the time, on the grounds that we were working flat out, eighty hours a week, living on site with barely enough spare time to visit the café for a crap. And all of this was because their schedule was so tight, and they'd made us promise to be finished by their deadline. But they'd insisted, so my family had driven all the way home to let them film us sitting on the sofa, leafing through magazines.

The presenter's voice over, presumably recorded in the studio to fit the footage, went something like this:

"With Carmel still unable to find a builder, work at the site has ground to a halt. With nothing else to do, Tony and Gillian have come home, and are sitting around, twiddling their thumbs."

Our mouths fell open in perfect unison.

"But…"

"*Twiddling?*"

"Those *miserable* bastards!"

"We came home *for them!*"

The same smug voice-over gave Mum a harsh critique on her search for a builder. She was accused of having failed to arrange one before we started work – even though the crew had directly forbidden us from doing this. In fact we'd had a builder – who Mum had found – and who had quit due to the new time constraints imposed on us by the crew when they decided to film us.

Mum was most upset about that.

But perhaps the single biggest blow came at the end.

The house looked gorgeous, belying all the crises that had occurred and our ridiculous last-minute decoration effort. Then came the scene where first the estate agents, and then the 'potential buyers' were shown around.

Somehow every one of them mentioned the strange bathroom layout; the presenter had had her way after all, and was proved to be almost omniscient in predicting our mistakes.

Reading between the lines a bit, it was easy to see how the same rather creative interview technique that had worried us, had been used on the unsuspecting buyers.

"Are you happy with this bathroom layout?"

"Well, yes."

"But don't you think it's a bit strange?"

"Why?"

"There are so many bathrooms with different things in each."

"Oh. Dunno. Maybe."

"Well, don't you think that's weird?"

"Um… yeah, I guess so."

"Great! ROLL CAMERA! Now can you say that in a full sentence please. Start with the phrase 'I think the bathroom layout is weird because…'"

And thus, the presenter's predictions were borne out.

Her legend grew a little further.

SEE! We should have followed her advice.

We probably would have done, had it been possible. And not wrong.

Every single man, woman, child and dog who lived in the valleys was watching that show. It was the most exciting thing to happen in Treorchy since… well, ever. Daily throughout the project people had been asking us about the rumours; were we really being filmed for the telly? We'd been more than happy to spread the word. A few local papers had even run stories about us, showing photos of the house and announcing the upcoming programme. Every potential buyer for miles around tuned it to watch us develop that house, to see if they fancied buying a slice of TV history.

What they saw was the goddess-like presenter chastising us for trying to sell the house at nearly ten thousand pounds more than it was worth. Backed up by the false valuations, with her apparent gift for prophecy displayed at every turn, who could deny that what she said was the truth?

Before the end credits rolled, a familiar voice-over chimed in; "Two weeks later, the Slaters' house is still on the market."

Which was not entirely true, because
a) we'd been on the market for less than a week, and
b) we'd sold it.

Unfortunately, two months later that sale fell through because the couple who wanted to buy it hadn't managed to sell their own house, and then the poor bloke lost his job in the recession.

Shortly after that, the sub-prime mortgage incident happened and threw the economy of the world into disarray. Partially because of that, and partially because the programme made us look like argumentative, incompetent, money-grabbing idiots, we never managed to sell it again.

My parents still own that house.

"People would never believe what's happened here," Dad said afterwards. "With the crew trying to screw us over to add drama, half the builders turning out to be criminals, beams stolen from a factory and a plumber in prison for dealing drugs! One day I'll write a book about this. I swear, it'll be a bestseller. We'd probably make more money from the book than we ever will from that bloody house!"

Ah, Dad, about that…

Sorry! I'm afraid I've beaten you to it.

But you know what?

You were right.

Booze Cruise

So once again, I was in a bit of a bind.

I imagine it's a situation familiar to most people; I desperately wanted to disappear on a crazy adventure to the other side of the world – but I couldn't, because I had no money.

Being broke sucks.

Being young, not particularly gifted, and broke, sucks even more.

I needed a plan.

I was already scouring the internet for volunteering opportunities, but even the ones that didn't charge much would cost a fortune to get to. Flying to Costa Rica or Bolivia simply wasn't on the cards for now, no matter how reasonably priced the project. Being penniless in a foreign country was one of the least pleasant experiences I'd had to date (friggin' France!), and I wasn't anxious to repeat it. Yes, it was boring at home, but it was also safe.

I knew that when we sold the house, I'd get a cut. That would help. Until then… well, I could get a job? Ha! The very idea was ridiculous. What was I good for? Other than being a chew-toy for big cats and small crocodiles? I couldn't face the thought of a nine-to-five existence – escaping that sort of life had been what prompted me to flee to Ecuador in the first place. No, there had to be something else…

Some kind of adventure that wouldn't cost me anything.

Something to keep me occupied until I could get on to another medical trial – preferably one where they didn't try to kill me.

In the few hours I'd been awake during the aborted trial, I'd taken full advantage of the laptop I'd borrowed from Gill. I'd persuaded her to give it up by pointing out how important it was that I work on writing my first book, 'That Bear Ate My Pants!'. Grudgingly she'd agreed that my writing was a more productive use of the technology than her using it to watch movies, so I'd left her alone in Treorchy with a crappy wind-up radio as her only source of entertainment. If she'd known the only radio stations we could get in the valley were in Welsh, she'd probably have put up more of a fight. Then I'd spent a week as a victim of drug-induced zombification, and hadn't written a single word.

I'd like to think we suffered equally – even though most of my suffering had been done horizontally.

But what I had done, when I'd felt able to do anything, was scour the internet for the kind of adventure I was craving.

Organised expeditions, rail trips, round the world flights – they'd all been dashed by the premature end of the trial. But there was one avenue which still looked promising…

Sailing.

I'd taken a sailing course shortly after I finished university. I'd been trying to add strings to my acting cv, in the hope (no, don't laugh) – of becoming a stunt man.

Yes, okay, you might as well laugh.

Suffice to say, as one of the clumsiest individuals alive – and one of the few people who can be convincingly mauled by a domestic cat – I soon discovered I wasn't stunt man material. But along with studying kung-fu, archery, snorkelling, trampolining and gymnastics, I'd also had a go at getting my Competent Yacht Crew qualification.

I was crap at it, of course.

But I'd rather enjoyed sailing.

So I created a profile on a website called 'Crewfinder', and placed an advert that said 'Position wanted as crew member on a boat. No real experience. Will go anywhere.'

It wasn't long before I got a reply:

'Hello Tony, my name is Paul. I'd like you to consider accompanying me on my powerboat. I can pay for you to fly here to America. I'm male, forty-five. I'm planning the trip now, a few weeks to a few months, with no real destination in mind, just sailing around and enjoying ourselves. Eventually I hope to sail all the way to Australia, which will take a minimum of one year, but depending on how much fun we have, could be as long as 3-5 years. I hope you're interested! Please let me know as soon as possible.

And I'm gay, but don't worry, that won't be a problem.'

Quite why this wouldn't be a problem, he didn't say.

Maybe he was in a relationship? Although he never said so.

Maybe I wasn't his type? Yeah… it wasn't likely he preferred them old and fat.

Maybe he felt he could control his urges? I know I struggle in this regard – I think most men do. But maybe he was a stronger man?

Maybe he really could avoid hitting on me?

For upwards of a year. Alone on a boat together…

Or maybe he was just saying that because he planned on drugging me.

Yeah. I had a feeling this wasn't going to work.

Especially when I noticed that his email address was 'Paul@whoopee.com'.

I confess, I checked 'whoopee.com' out of idle curiosity. It was a man-on-man porn site, presumably owned by Paul.

So I politely declined his kind offer.

I'll admit though, I was quite flattered – it was the first time I was *literally* invited on a gay cruise.

So, with my own advert pulling in entirely the wrong kind of fish, I started browsing other people's, and came across a few possibilities. The year-long journey from the US to Australia was a popular one, and I exchanged a few emails with a middle-aged couple who were planning on making the same trip. Still, a year seemed like a long time to commit to. I'd had a ball in Ecuador, but after three months at least part of me had been ready to come home. The part of me that was left, anyway.

A full year, with just one couple for company, trapped aboard a tiny boat… No. I am a child of the twenty-first century. I wanted an amazing experience, but I didn't want to have to *commit* to it!

And then I found an advert for a yacht delivery company. They always needed crew because they had a business to run, and they were perfectly happy to find me a place on one of their runs.

Of course, they were paid to move X amount of yachts from A to B. If they could find people to do it for free – even people with no clue how to do it – they would increase their profit margin dramatically. At least until some idiot crashed one of them.

And who could crash a boat in the middle of an empty ocean?

That sort of thing almost never happens.

So I told them I'd like to volunteer in exchange for some sailing experience, and they agreed to give me a job.

Just one. As a test.

What could possibly go wrong?

I packed a bag, took a train bound for the south coast of England, then another train and a bus, and finally strolled into Port Solent harbour. There I was to meet the crew who would be sailing with me over 2,000 nautical miles, to Lanzarote on the west coast of Africa.

Tony Bevan, a small, mischievous looking fellow, was to be the skipper of our little expedition. He was an old-school sailor, the kind who'd being messing around on boats since you had to build them yourself with nails and a plank of wood. I admitted to my complete lack of experience straight away, in the hope he'd find me something easy to do on the voyage – like watch.

"Not a problem at all," he said, in a way which convinced me he was sincere. "Geoff and I–" he waved a hand at his substantially taller first mate, "have got enough experience for all of us. We'll show you the ropes!"

He then proceeded to show me the ropes.

There were many. Clusters of them ran from every point in the boat, gathered together at the mast and then ran back individually to a series of locking levers on either side of the great steel steering wheel.

"That is a lot of ropes," I told him.

"Nope! No ropes! Not a single one. Not on-board a yacht. These are sheets, lines and warps." He indicated various collections of ropes as he said this, which stirred my memory a bit.

"Of course! Sheets are the ones attached to the sails…"

Tony was impressed, and told me so. "You see! We'll make a sailor of you in no time. You'll be sailing this thing by yourself before long!"

"Really? How long?"

"Well hopefully by tonight, because Geoff and I will be downstairs getting drunk."

"Oh? Um…"

"No, I'm only joking lad! We'll be doing the cooking."

"Oh! Oh. Ah."

"Unless you can cook?"

"Um, no. Not at all."

"Oh well. We'd best work on your sailing skills then."

"Yeah…"

He gave me a tour of the boat, starting in the cockpit. This was at the back of the boat, and was all one piece with the moulded plastic of the hull.

"It's a thirty-seven foot *Jeanneau Sun Odyssey*," he said of the yacht, "which is so flat it probably handles like a surf board."

I didn't know if this was a good thing or a bad thing, so I just nodded.

"She'll be fast though, under sail. We should make Lanzarote in less than three weeks – two even, with the right winds. There's a whole load of us going – ten boats in all, all owned by a charter company called *Sunsail*. We're relocating them for the summer season. Most of the others left this morning, but there's no rush; we'll be sailing straight there with no stopping, so it shouldn't take us long to get there."

Downstairs there were three cabins – one oddly triangular one nestled into the very front of the boat, and two at the rear, while in between them were sofas, a table, the bathroom and the kitchen. It was compact yet perfectly formed, with gleaming wood everywhere and ample space for the three of us.

"Fridge and freezer," Tony noted, opening hatches in the galley, "and this great big one is where we'll store the booze!"

"I see," I said. Tony was clearly the kind of person I would get on well with.

"Technically, this company operates a 'dry boat' policy," he explained. "No alcohol to be brought aboard at all, much less consumed whilst in command of the vessel."

I nodded soberly. I wasn't about to argue with my first skipper.

"I'm old fashioned though," he added. "I think a man should be able to have a beer after a long day of sailing. Otherwise, what's the point of being in the middle of nowhere? So I had Geoff get us a few supplies…"

I swear his eyes twinkled, like those of a cartoon bad guy.

He led me back up the ladder, out of the hatch to the cockpit.

Geoff was on the dock, struggling to unload a series of cardboard boxes from the boot of his ancient blue Volvo.

"Geoff lives in Gibraltar," Tony explained. "They don't have the same tax on alcohol as we do. Isn't that right, Geoff?"

Geoff balanced a box on the lip of the boot and slid a litre bottle of gin out of it.

"Three pounds, this cost," he said.

"That's the other reason I asked Geoff to come along," said Tony, that twinkle making another appearance. "We'll get the rest when we go shopping."

Tony wasn't lying. That afternoon, after a good look around the boat, he took us into town to the biggest supermarket he could find.

We spent two hours in there.

Well over three-hundred pounds later we emerged with a shopping trolley each, all piled high with every conceivable kind of pasta, kilos of rice, tins of meat, long-life milk by the gallon… we had enough food to feed us for a month. Which was long enough to make the trip twice over, depending on the weather, but Tony had plenty of his budget left over, so why not? A giant bag of mini Twix's also found its way into the trolley, which was fortunate as I ended up living almost exclusively on them.

Then we hit the booze aisle.

"Just a beer per man, per day," said Tony, "to give us something to look forward too. And I think we should get a bottle of wine for each way-point, to celebrate our progress."

We did this, though with rounding up to the nearest week, plus a few extras on top, some spare beers just in case and a few odds and ends for the road, we managed to fill another entire trolley with alcohol.

They didn't need to buy cigarettes though, as Geoff had brought a thousand with him from Gibraltar. Again, 'just in case'.

It wouldn't do to be caught out miles from land, without the essentials.

It was comforting to know they were well prepared.

That Sinking Feeling

We were all loaded up and inspected by late afternoon, so we motored out of the harbour and set sail for Lanzarote. The weather forecast had been for blustery conditions (which, let's face it, could mean anything), and our trusty skipper thought this would be ideal for my first proper sail.

Trusting the forecast, as you must at sea, we hoisted the sails, keeping them small and under plenty of tension to help me keep control.

Tony watched me at the wheel, imparting tips on how to read the sails, how to correct course when they started to flap or to ease off our heading if the boat leaned too far over.

It was an exhilarating experience, though not always a pleasant one. Bumbling around the Caribbean with the sun high overhead, chicks in bikinis sun bathing on the deck and chilled cocktails in a pitcher of ice – this is what I normally think of when someone mentions sailing.

Or I did until that moment. Now I know it for what it really is; freezing spray coating your face, chill wind whipping at it; three layers of clothes, thermals and waterproofs struggling against the odds to keep your body warm and dry, and, most of the time, failing miserably. The boat heeled (leaning) well over so that standing upright is impossible; one bent leg takes your weight and soon starts to burn with the effort, but there can be no relief for it while your turn at steering lasts. We were flying along. The sails would snap taut and the boat would lean deeper, leaping forward like the Hand of God had grabbed a-hold and was yanking us towards him.

Then Tony would grunt and nudge my arm, I'd ease the wheel a smidgen and the boat would slow and sit upright again, responding instantly to the slightest touch.

It was magic.

As darkness fell and my confidence grew, we sailed out of the protective shadow of the Isle of Wight, into the middle of the English

Channel.

Right into the teeth of a Force Nine Gale.

There's a scale for measuring the destructive power of wind, called the Beaufort Scale. It starts at one, with something akin to a silent fart, and builds up potency as the numbers get higher. It only goes as high as twelve – which I'm pretty sure represents the extinction of all life on this planet.

So our Force Nine, or 'Strong Gale' as they call it, was quite something. On land it would be uprooting small trees and breaking branches off bigger ones; at sea, with nothing in the way to slow it down, it was insane.

Massive waves crashed over the boat, drenching us as we crouched in the cockpit. Tony recognised the danger and called out to Geoff.

"We've got to get the main sail down!"

I could hardly believe he was serious.

Lowering the sail meant climbing forward along the roof of the boat, right up to the mast, then wrestling with ropes and levers in some form of co-ordinated effort with someone in the cockpit. It was dark; the sky was pitch black, the only illumination coming from the glow of our compass and a tiny signal light atop the mast. The boat was plunging into waves now, rising and falling like the chest of someone having a seizure. We were all fastened to it by straps and harnesses and chunky metal clips; going outside of the cockpit had to be suicide.

But that's exactly what Tony was proposing. Geoff moved around and started doing things with ropes and levers. Suddenly it occurred to me that whist this blatantly impossible task was being attempted, I would be left on my own to steer the boat. A wave slammed into us from the side, ripping the wheel out of my hands and slewing the boat around in its wake.

"NO!" Tony called. "Keep her steady!"

I gritted my teeth and clung to the wheel, hauling it around against the pressure of the water. The boat leaned over again, as more waves crashed over the bow. I was soaked to the skin already, and shivering with the cold, but neither Geoff or Tony seemed the least bit fazed by it.

"What do I do?" I called out.

"Just keep her steady!"

"But how? The waves are–" I was cut off by another pounding, and threw all my force onto the wheel to keep the boat from spinning away again.

"Every wave pushes us round sideways!"

"Yes, so just keep her steady!"

"Keep her… keep her steady? For how long?" I had the wheel in a death-grip by this point, straining against the wave action with all the tension my body could muster.

"Yes, just like that, you're doing great," said Tony.

He must have been talking to someone else, because I was not doing great.

Waves smashed into us, flooding the cockpit as it heaved to and fro.

The gigantic mainsail flogged and flapped, then caught the wind again and snapped straight against its ropes. The boat lurched forward, ploughing nose deep into another wave before leaning back as we sailed up the face of it. I could see sky, almost as black as the water, then we levelled out and teetered on the top of the wave, before crashing back down into the trough behind it.

Clunks and crashes came from below – I could imagine lockers shaking open and spilling pots and pans everywhere, like an earthquake in a kitchen.

"SORRY!" I screamed, and considered adding 'HELP!'.

The wheel went loose in my grip, losing all tension as the boat came upright – then in a spilt-second it span, nearly breaking the fingers I'd curled around its spokes for extra leverage. As the wheel span so too did the boat, bringing the beam holding the bottom of the sail slamming across from right to left with unprecedented violence. The sail gave two great flaps, then filled again and we lurched forwards – or was it backwards now? The next wave in sequence lifted us, soaking me as it broke across our bow, and the wheel strained against my grip as I hauled on it with all my strength.

My arms were about to come out of their sockets, my legs were struggling to keep me upright and every time I dared open my eyes the sea filled them with salt water. The sail flapped and flogged again, and Tony yelled at me to "point up!".

I didn't have a bloody clue what he meant, so I steered back into the waves and fought the wheel to keep us there.

Geoff was hauling himself around the cockpit, releasing some ropes and tightening others. Tony had long since left the safety of the cockpit, fastening his harness to a rail and climbing hand over hand along it towards the mast. Then the main sail started to come down, and the effect was instant. The wheel slackened off, the flapping noise returned with a vengeance, and Tony grabbed the loosened sail and pulled it down, folding it back and forth across the horizontal boom to which it was still attached.

He made it seem entirely normal that he was out there, folding a massive sheet of canvas in the middle of a hurricane like my mum folds shirts in our front room. Geoff paid out the rope, I manned the helm, and Tony tied the sail down with a load of long coloured streamers.

Then he was back to take over on the wheel, and I was more than happy to relinquish it.

Except my hands wouldn't let go. Between the cold, the tension and the stress, they'd seized up on the wheel and needed prying loose.

"You did great!" he told me, as I wrapped my uncooperative mitts around the nearest fixed object.

"Shit man, that was crazy! I thought I was going to kill us all!"

"Course not! That went perfectly. Bit windy though."

"A bit? I thought I was going to be blown overboard! I nearly wet myself." I shook my head, showering water around the cockpit. "Not that you'd be able to tell! Thank God I was fastened to the boat!"

"Oh yeah…" Tony took the loose end of his harness strap and clipped it around a ring built into the deck. "We call them 'Murder Lines'," he shouted.

"What?"

The wind was stealing our words, so I strained closer to hear what he was telling me.

He tugged on his strap, checking it was secure. "They've got to be long enough to let you move around the boat, right?"

"Yeah!"

"So, they're just long enough to let you fall in the water! You get pulled along behind the boat at whatever speed it's doing." He pointed at the electronic speedometer mounted beside the hatch that led downstairs. It glowed '12' in the darkness.

"They reckon no man can pull himself out of the water speed if you're doing more than five knots. You just get dragged along upside-down until someone thinks to stop the boat and come and get you. So if you're on your own…"

"What?"

"You drown."

"Oh."

"So when we start doing solo watches at night – don't fall in."

For once, he didn't look like he was joking.

Not even a little bit.

The storm got worse.

Both Tony and Geoff took turns battling the elements, but all of us were struggling. The two men had tried to reduce the size of our one remaining sail, which was designed to roll up like a window blind; unfortunately it had jammed, and I had to agree with Tony when he said, "This isn't the best weather for going out there and fiddling with it."

No shit!

I was dreading my next turn at the wheel.

"Jesus Geoff, I don't think I can do this. What if I sink us?"

"Ha!" Geoff's laugh was like a bark. "Boats don't sink!"

You've never been on a boat with me then, I wanted to tell him. But a mouthful of sea-spray made me choke instead.

"Here, take over," he said. "I've got to see how Tony's doing with our position."

Tony had been downstairs for a while, trying to get a fix on our location and plot the rest of the night's sail. It was probably taking so long because he was being thrown around the cabin like a rag-doll.

"I don't know about this Geoff! If you hear me scream, it's because we're sinking!"

"Hah!" Geoff was more amused than ever at the panic in my voice. "We won't be sinking!"

There was a shout from below. "GEOFF!"

"Oh-oh! Looks like the Skipper needs me," Geoff said. He winked at me. "You'll be fine, right?"

And he ducked down into the boat.

This was not going well at all.

I wrapped my hands around the icy steel spokes of the wheel and peered through the rain at the horizon.

"Oh FUCK!" I could just make out the shape of the wave ahead, a blacker edge against the dark grey, and either we were pointing down into it or else it was towering above us. Whichever way, it wasn't likely to be good news.

"Hold on," I shouted, though there was zero chance of anyone hearing. Up we rose, the nose pointing skyward, the deck shaking beneath my feet. I clung to the wheel like a lifeline, white-knuckled in the deluge of rain and spray as the boat climbed like a rocket after take-off. Again we righted atop the wave, the wheel loosened and I had the terrible thought that we would swing sideways, rolling down the back of the wave like a barrel and ending up upside-down at the bottom of it.

I wrenched the wheel, swinging the nose back to make a right angle with the wave, but it was only an instant before we crashed down its backside, slicing an angle across it rather than shooting straight down vertically. My heart, which had stopped at the top, beat about a thousand times before we came to the bottom. Our angle by then had slipped back; I was losing my struggle for supremacy with the wheel and it was pulling us parallel with the edge of the waves.

"HELP!" I shrieked. "Geoff, HELP ME!"

There were clunks and clangs from below and the hatch cracked open. "you okay?" Geoff called.

"NO! Shit Geoff, I'm gonna kill us! I can't do it, it's going everywhere!"

"Just keep her steady," he boomed, shouting over the deafening crash of waves and slap of the sail.

"But – "

And Geoff was gone, vanishing back inside, sealing the glimmer of light within.

The wheel tore at my grip again as the boat heeled over and started to rise.

As the next wave lifted us we were completely broadside to it and there was nothing I could do.

It picked us up, span us completely, and flung us down in less time than it takes to tell. The sail slapped, ropes sang under tension and I half-drowned as water filled the cockpit to knee height.

Amazingly I had the presence of mind to feel bad about the ride I was giving to the guys down below – it must have been like a plane crash, with all the lockers spilling baggage and people falling all over the place.

The hatch cracked open and Geoff's head reappeared. "You still okay?"

"NO! Geoff help me, please help! I'm gonna die, I know I am. I'll kill us all Geoff, please just help me!" I was on the verge of hysterics. No, scratch that – I *was* hysterical. Tears flowed down my cheeks, unnoticed because I was soaked to the skin and ankle deep in water that was re-filling as fast as it was draining.

"SHIT Geoff, we're going again!" I braced myself against the cockpit seats and dragged on the wheel, fighting to bring our nose around as we rode up the next wave.

Geoff scrambled out of the hatch and grabbed the wheel just as we crested the wave, and between us we guided the boat safely down the other side.

"I'll take it," he said, his huge hands latching on to the wheel either side of mine. They looked strong enough to bend the steel in half, let alone steer it – and now I knew why. "It's bad this," he added, nodding into the weather. "Bad…"

"Geoff I'm fucking scared, man," I told him. "This is really fucked up! I can't do this."

"It's not normally this bad. You're doing good, lad, very good. You've kept us afloat!"

I was gripping handholds now, concentrating on keeping myself in the boat as Geoff swung us into the next wave. Until then no one had confirmed it as a possibility; the fury of the sea had terrified me, but the gravity in Geoff's voice brought it home. I had kept us afloat – but barely. Meaning, there had been a chance that I wouldn't have.

"Geoff, what the hell is going on?" I shouted over the wind and the rain.

"Oh, it's nothing to worry about, really…" But there was a strain in his voice that I could hear in spite of the sheeting rain.

"Geoff?"

"Yes?"

"What's up?"

Geoff thought about it as he skilfully slid us down the back of another wave.

"We're sinking," he said eventually.

Right then there was another crash and a string of swear-words from below. The light seeping from the hatch went out. And again, the call came from below.

"GEOFF!"

"Grab the wheel lad," he told me, and waited while I took a reluctant grip. "You're doing fine! Just point us into the waves."

And then he was gone. Again.

R&R (Relocate and Repair)

Looking back on that night, I have no idea how I survived.

I guess, boats are designed to float, and sail, and they are generally pretty good at it.

And I had two excellent crew members to help me and guide me.

Neither of them did, though.

Because downstairs our situation had worsened.

Tony had gone below to study the navigation charts, and figure out where we were.

He'd not been down there long when he'd discovered that the floor was floating.

Now, in a boat this is not exactly unheard of. Water gets in there all the time, though not normally enough to fill the bottom right up to the level of the floor. But it can happen, and doesn't exactly spell disaster; Tony just turned on the electric pump and went back to his charts.

The pump didn't work.

That was the first major problem.

With Geoff down there helping him, and me at the wheel turning the boat into a roller-coaster ride, he had quickly established that the pump was knackered. This was more of a problem.

But there was a back-up, a manual pump operated from the cockpit by a long metal lever. Geoff had scurried up to start that process when I'd had my first meltdown, and he'd taken the wheel to give me chance to calm down.

Then the lights went out, and suddenly we had a real problem, because all the rest of the electrics had failed with them.

That was when Geoff had vanished for the second time.

Now, I was about ready to call it a night. I think the only reason I hadn't already shit myself was that I was in shock. The horror of the task I was trying to achieve, to keep us afloat and alive when our whole environment wanted the opposite, was driving me to desperation.

I clung to the wheel and fought, and yelled and swore, and slid around the cockpit like it was lined with grease. The rain beat down, or occasionally up depending on how far into the sky our nose was pointing, and waves crashed over the deck with such ferocity that all I could do was put my head down, hang on and let the water pummel me.

In fairness, it can't have been much fun downstairs, in the pitch black, ankle-deep in sea water, fiddling with electrical connections whilst falling all over the place.

When the skipper and the first mate emerged, they were wearing most of our pasta.

The electrics were shot. Geoff manned the pump while Tony took over the wheel, still praising my efforts but with a terse, subdued voice.

He altered course, guiding us out of the worst of the storm and into calmer waters.

"We're turning back," he told me.

"Are we going home?" I couldn't disguise the hope in my voice. "To Portsmouth, I mean?"

Tony's reply was somewhat grimmer than I'd hoped.

"No. We won't make it."

"Oh…?"

"We're heading into Poole Harbour. It's a lot closer. We should be able to manage that."

Which was reassuring.

"What went wrong? Is the storm too bad?"

"No, we can sail in that. It gets a lot worse at sea."

This wasn't something I wanted to hear.

"But the real problem is, I think we have a split in our skin fittings."

"A what? In the what? Tony, are you telling me there's a hole in this boat?"

"No, I mean there's… it's like a…" he sighed. "Yes. There's a hole in the boat."

Geoff was perched on the back of the cockpit, working the lever back and forth with all his might. "And we've lost our main pump," he added.

"Oh. That IS bad, right?"

"It's not great, lad. And what's worse, is this one just stopped working as well!"

Tony looked back at him. There was no humour in that stare.

Geoff wiggled the lever up and down to demonstrate; there was no resistance to it, as though it was connected to nothing.

"It was working, but now… it must have got blocked."

I was a pace behind their thoughts, as all this was still new to me.

"Will we still make Poole?" I asked.

"Yes, we'll make it. We have to." There was steel in Tony's eyes, and in his voice.

Which was good, as I was shaking like a jelly.

We limped into Poole, our engine shuddering, our one sail pulled defiantly taut, and navigated between a series of red and green beacons all the way into the harbour. I was sailing again by this point, although I'd spent most of the last two hours in my cabin, feeling like I wanted to die. Once the shock of sailing alone into the storm had worn off, my stomach had realised it didn't know which way was up anymore, and I'd lost everything I'd eaten since breakfast down the marine toilet (which for some reason is known as 'the heads'). I'd had to make room to be sick; the toilet bowl was already full of spaghetti, which had originated in the kitchen cupboard opposite.

A couple of hours had been enough to get my guts under control though, and I was so eager to see land again that even the biting cold couldn't keep me from being up on deck.

The red and green guidance lights were a mystery to me; being colour-blind was proving to be more of a handicap than I'd expected.

But for now I didn't care. I wanted light, I wanted warmth – oh, man I wanted warmth – I wanted food, and I wanted sleep.

And I wanted never, ever, to set foot on a boat again as long as I lived.

We motored in past ranks of gleaming white yachts, all packed tightly together as though they were stopping each other from falling over. Navigating the narrow lanes of clear water between the other boats was not made any easier by having a sail still up and flapping around, but my expert crewmates were up to the challenge.

We moored up – itself a tricky procedure in such a crowded harbour – jumped off the boat and made straight for the pub.

I needed the Dutch courage of a stiff drink or two inside me, while I figured out how to tell the guys that I was leaving.

Because my regular courage was all used up.

My confidence was gone.

I was dreading telling Tony and Geoff, as they'd impressed me so much in such a short time that I already considered them more than friends. They were mentors and guardians; they had saved my life. They were heroes.

And I was going to thank them, and apologise, and run screaming for the hills.

But how to do it?

I was twenty-five now, and had been judged a man by the toughest standards I cared to experience. I had been to Ecuador and wrestled wild animals; I'd been deemed praise-worthy by the world's toughest midget. I was supposed to be strong and confident, the master of my own destiny.

Yup, the way I saw it, there was only one thing I could do:

Call my Mum.

She'd know what to say, how to handle the guys and how to let them down lightly.

Because no matter what happened, I was not getting back on that boat.

Later, back on the boat, I reflected on one of my deeper character flaws.

I'm bloody useless when it comes to getting my own way.

I could face down all kinds of scary creatures and had an almost unhealthy desire to do things which were bound to cause me injury sooner or later; but I was a complete coward when it came to confronting people. I still felt the need for their approval, hungered for it even; I couldn't face the thought of anyone being disappointed with me.

And I couldn't, for the life of me, say 'No.'

A few drinks is all it had taken. In front of the guys I laid my fears bare – whilst cunningly pretending they were my mother's fears, to avoid looking as weak and pathetic as I felt. I painted a picture of a terrified parent who was convinced her only son was bound for a watery grave. The tactic had seemed perfect when I conceived it on the phone, with one ear listening to my dear old Mum express exactly that concern.

But when I presented this argument to my salty sea-dog companions it didn't take them long to find the crack in my dam of logic.

"You're what, twenty-five?" asked the skipper. "Man up. Tell her to get over it. You're a sailor now."

And that was that.

Bollocks.

By midday the next day, an emergency team from Sunsail had arrived to restore our yacht to sea-worthiness. I bloody well hoped they would do it right. If I came any closer to death this time out… well, I'd be dead. And that would *really* piss my Mum off.

I had imagined a titanic hole in the side of the boat; the kind of damage Jaws might have done for shits and giggles. Alas, I was to be disappointed. There was no need to bring in some epic crane, to haul the boat out of the water and reveal shattered planking and tooth-marks that would have Steven Spielberg reaching for his typewriter. Although to my delight, one of the engineers did utter the phrase "You were lucky!"

You have to appreciate the glass-is-half-full-iness of a statement like this. Ten boats set sail for Lanzarote that morning, and we got the only one that sank. This didn't make me feel particularly lucky. We'd survived because two of our three crew knew what the hell they were doing – and the third one was stupid enough to do it anyway.

The team wasted no time in identifying our problem. ('What's the problem?" the lead engineer had asked. "The boat's full of water," Tony had replied. "Oh. Shit." said the engineer.)

They'd discovered that the water was getting in somewhere above the front cabin, by the simple tactic of opening the door to the front cabin and causing a miniature tsunami. Everything in there was soaked through, which made me glad we'd only stored our 'spare' stuff in there; things like books and magazines that we had no room for in our own berths. All were ruined. Tony was even less impressed, as he'd planned on sleeping in there. Now it was looking like he and Geoff would be getting closer than ever.

"Well, this water must be coming in somewhere," said the engineer. Helpfully.

It still sounded to me like there was a bloody big hole in the boat.

But this wasn't true.

According to this crack team of experts, our problem (when they found it) was merely 'an unsealed portal in the hull'. Portals apparently differ from holes in that they are designed to both open and close. Although this particular portal was achieving one of these states considerably better than the other, this was easily remedied with a huge tube of glue.

Now I know what you're thinking – but don't worry. This was not just any glue – it was special Boat Glue.

It was around this point that I started getting nervous again.

Because there was a very real possibility that we would be sailing again soon; only now the hole in our boat had been glued shut.

I wasn't completely convinced. I was less than thrilled at the prospect of taking any boat out of sight of land again – especially not one with uncooperative portals.

I've seen those adverts where they dangle a man over a shark tank by his jacket, which is stuck with super-fast drying *Lock-tite* to a plank. You CAN entrust your life to glue, seems to be the message. But then I've also seen an advert where a fifty-foot tall squirrel crushes a row of cars, and frankly I place about the same amount of faith in both of them.

So, the vast amount of water, which had taken us most of the morning to bail out of the boat, had (in layman's terms) gotten in through an unsealed hatch – the irony being that it was an inspection hatch that had not been sufficiently inspected. Inside the nose of the boat (hereafter called the bow, for fear any sailing types reading this will burst a blood vessel at my disregard for nautical terminology), there was a locker. In this locker was our anchor. It may sound medieval, but this big lump of spikey-assed metal is still the way you get your boat to stay where you put it. It's heavy and slimy and needs to be kept on its own for fear of getting tangled with anything else. Naturally, lockers have lids; unfortunately, this one had a lid which was about as good at its job as I was. Hence, water had been flooding into this locker every time the bow of the boat dipped underwater – basically every time we'd plunged into another gargantuan wave – which was about every thirty seconds.

It wasn't my fault, I was reassured to hear.

There was no point at all trying to place the blame in a situation like this, the Sunsail engineers explained – conveniently ignoring the fact that it was their fault.

Their report concluded that 'our primary problem was excessive ingress of water', which for anyone not familiar with the jargon means 'these poor bastards nearly drowned because some idiot forgot to shut this locker.'

The vast amounts of water sloshing around inside had shorted the electrics, including lights, navigation systems and the all-important pump, which is why they weren't working, and when we'd turned to the manual pump to replace the electrical one, a bit of floating rubbish had blocked it – a situation that was impossible to remedy in a force nine gale, under the floor of the boat in total darkness.

All that remained was to feel grateful that this particular set of circumstances had arisen and combined to screw with us less than a day out of the docks; if it had happened a little later in our trip, like say, fifty miles off the coast of Africa, I might well have been dictating this book via a medium.

'Cheer up lad,' Geoff had said as we'd motored in to Poole Harbour last night. 'Worse things happen at sea!'

Into The Blue

We set sail that afternoon. Leaving dry land again was one of the hardest things I've had to do in my life. Luckily, I had no choice. It was a bright sunny day and I was trying not to think about what it would be like once darkness fell. In truth, it was easy to get enthusiastic again, when the sails billowed and the boat began to heel over. This was my chance to gain valuable experience in controlling her – experience that might just keep me from killing the lot of us come nightfall.

I steered at an angle to the light breeze and felt the joy of the rudder in my hands. There's an almost imperceptible feeling on the wheel, a tension between the hull of the boat and the water, both of which left to their own devices would be going in very different directions. Feeling that slight vibration, feedback from the helm that the rudder and sails are perfectly balanced and acting together and against each other at the same time – I have to admit, it's magic.

The wind dragged us along, and out, and once more we were surrounded by deep ocean waters, well out of sight of land. The waves were rough and gave us a battering, but with a little instruction I was handling it. The boat rose and fell in tune with the waves, slicing through them instead of fighting them; but then, they were only small. They wouldn't have put up much of a fight anyway.

If we could just keep these conditions all the way to Lanzarote, I might actually have a chance of surviving the trip…

The sun on my face helped. We all took turns in steering, three hours on then six off, though we weren't as strict about it as we'd have to be after dark. The guys promised to stay with me for the first night, more for moral support than anything else. I was managing to sail her quite well by this point, and as far as the others were concerned there was no difference between the day and the night. But there was for me. The day was a relaxed and enjoyable drift, with the promise of a beer around five-ish and dinner soon after. The sun warmed my face, Tony and Geoff bumbled around, imparting snippets of advice in no particular order; in short, it was fun.

But the night brought with it a nauseating fear.

Controlling the boat was achieved either by feel or by eye. After decades afloat, my fellow crew members could sail in their sleep. Not so me; I felt the pull in my guts that told me how well the boat was sailing, but I didn't trust it yet. I still relied on looking at the horizon, then the compass, then the shape of the sails, then back to the horizon, in a never-ending cycle of nervous anticipation. I was waiting for the moment when it all went wrong – when a freak wave would jolt me, the boat would spin and I'd have sails slamming across the cockpit at head-height…

It happened often enough, on that first night.

Because boats don't have headlights.

So I could see absolutely nothing, even when my eyes adjusted – because there was absolutely nothing to see.

Unless we were about to be run over by a super-tanker, in which case I got a few minutes' notice from the warning lights bearing down on us. It was a singularly nerve-wracking experience, never being sure if a tiny correction on the wheel would lead to a better angle for the sails – or a sudden and dramatic about-turn! Both Tony and Geoff told me that I'd pick it up eventually, but I started to worry – and worried that they had started to worry – that I wasn't cut out for this sailing lark.

At dusk on the second day, the sea got choppy. It always does at dusk, and again at dawn, due to winds caused by the rapid temperature change between day and night. This scared me, because this was to be my first solo night shift. Three hours, during which time the others would be fast asleep down below – assuming they trusted me enough to be able to sleep. I wouldn't have.

The wind seemed light, but the sea, the Atlantic now, threw deep, rolling waves my way. The boat's movement was so dramatic, riding up the front and sliding down the back of each wave like a roller-coaster car on a track. Except, the only thing keeping us on track were my hands on the wheel. The merest twitch in the wrong direction led to an instant response – too far one way and we'd stall, sitting dead in the water with loose sails, at the mercy of the waves who would push us around to whatever direction they saw fit; too far the other way and the sail would suddenly reverse with a deafening 'SNAP!', sending the boom crashing across the boat and spinning us off in another direction entirely. To stay on course, and on the wind, was a difficult and intensive task, relying on minute adjustments, total concentration and the kind of sensitivity I'm always being told I don't have.

The size of the waves turned the deck of the boat into a steep slope up, then down again, each time with the threat that it would topple over completely if I moved my hands just a fraction in the wrong way. I crouched behind the wheel as we dove, and hung off it as we climbed, each time marvelling that we were still upright, afloat and in one piece. With the others there to guide and advise, it would have been exhilarating. With them fast asleep in the cabin beneath my feet, and no other living human within fifty miles, with the bottomless ocean beneath me and all around me, all shrouded by the inky darkness and chilled to the temperature of a meat-locker – it was bloody terrifying!

I survived though.

Perhaps because I spent most of my three-hour shift praying.

The next morning I awoke not only to fried eggs being made for breakfast, but also to praise from the crew.

"I slept like a log," said Tony, which actually worried me more than if he hadn't. He meant I'd given him a smooth ride, and he was happy with that; all I could think was that if I had had an emergency, I wouldn't have been able to wake him by stomping on the deck.

I was glad I hadn't known that when I started my shift.

"I kept us going, but only just," I told him, and then in a moment of honesty, I confessed my fears about being the worst sailor a man could be.

"You'll get it," said Tony, not seeming the least bit bothered.

"But when?"

"Tonight will be easier. Because you've done it once already, and you didn't die. That'll give you some confidence."

And he was right.

The second set of night watches passed without incident. I was calmer, more resolved to getting through the three hours without scaring myself shitless. I started to rationalise my thoughts, to temper fears that I could capsize the boat at any moment with the logic that people all over the world had mastered this skill, and that boat sinkings were fairly rare; and anyway, we'd already had one. By the law of averages alone, we should manage the next few weeks without going under.

And so I came through the shifts, one at dusk and the next at dawn, and got my first proper sleep as the guys took their coffee on deck to share the morning sail. I slept like the dead, in spite of the boat's motion; I woke up to find myself bruised all over from rolling backwards and forwards along my bed, bouncing off the cabin walls with knees and elbows at every turn.

"You learn to sleep like a starfish," Tony told me later. "That way you slide a bit, but don't roll. Otherwise, sooner or later you're bound to end up on your head on the floor, and that's a shitty way to wake up."

"Especially if you've been sick," Geoff chipped in.

And especially without a working shower aboard…

I could well imagine the horror.

I made myself useful bringing coffee and sandwiches, and taking my turn at the wheel. It seemed crazy to think that although we weren't moving much faster than a slow jog, we'd make the Canary Islands in a couple of weeks. It's the twenty-four hour nature of sailing, where you take turns to keep the boat on course and moving ceaselessly, day and night.

It struck me as a wonderfully efficient way to travel, except for the fact that you had to spend up to nine hours a day standing stock-still at the wheel, regardless of the weather.

I was saying this to Geoff, when he came back with a corker:

"It's a pity we don't have autopilot."

"Ha-ha!" I joined in the joke. "Yeah, that would be totally sci-fi."

"I mean, you can't just leave it," Geoff continued, "you still have to keep watch – especially at night – or you might run into something, like an oil tanker. But it means you don't have to stand there steering the whole time."

I blinked at him. I still couldn't decide if he was pulling my leg or not.

"Honestly? This thing is real?"

"Of course, yes."

"There's an autopilot? That works?"

"Yes, it's like a motorized box that turns the wheel. It just keeps you going in the same direction, like."

"And… boats have these things?"

"Yes, most of them I'd say. Apart from this one."

"But… what..? Why? Isn't..?"

"Don't worry about it! Think of it as a bonus. Without autopilot this sail will be much more *real*." His eyes shone with enthusiasm as he said that.

Real. A dangerous word in my experience. Sailors, I've discovered, tend to be the worst kind of sadists. They scoff at an easy life, drifting lazily around palm-fringed islands or sun-bathing on deck in perfectly calm waters. No, they are a peculiar breed, whose enjoyment seems directly proportional to the pain and suffering their hobby inflicts on them.

Rather like cyclists. I've seen cyclists force their way up a 1 in 3 incline by sheer willpower alone, going so slowly a hedgehog could outpace them. But when asked about such an experience they usually reply, "That last hill nearly killed me! It was AWESOME!"

Oh yes, sailors are famed for this delight in adversity. With their boat leant over at some ridiculous angle, feet trailing in the water, waves crashing over them, gales blasting stinging salt water into their faces and rain pummelling them from above, they're always grinning madly, calling back to their sodden mates "This is what sailing's *really* about!"

It seemed I was stuck on this voyage with just such a pair of deviants. A pair of… *enthusiasts.*

Unfortunately, the revelation came a bit too late.

Dry land had long since receded and there was nowhere to get off; we were bound for Lanzarote, come what may. Hell and high water, I imagined, though probably not in that order.

To Be, or Knot To Be…

Sitting in the sun, passing chilled beers around the cockpit, was far more to my liking. This is when I felt like a proper sailor. I could handle almost anything the boat threw at me during daylight hours, scurrying around to trim the sails, working the vast array of winches and pulleys, tidying up the loose ropes by coiling them, and taking my bearings from both compass and weathervane. I could steer with a beer, and chat to the guys, dividing my attention between them and the ocean like a seasoned pro.

Geoff, especially, was a mine of stories about his days at sea – starting with his very first trip, an almost unheard-of solo crossing of the Atlantic in a boat he'd built himself. If ever there was a man to rely on when it came to sailing problems, it was Geoff.

"I had no idea you could just make your own boat," I said.

"Yup, if it floats, you can register it. Not like having an MOT on your car."

"That's incredible."

"Yeah? I knew this guy who made his own boat out of concrete."

"You're shitting me! Concrete can't float!"

"It does if it encloses enough air. He made a mould, see, and cast it all up himself. Waterproof concrete of course. It had to be big because it was so heavy, so he cast it up in sections and took it down to the dock to put it all together."

"No way!"

"It was an awful boat though. Didn't steer very well, and ugly as hell. But eventually he got crashed into by a tug boat in Brighton harbour."

"Did it wreck the boat?"

"Oh, yes. Didn't sink it, but smashed it up pretty good. The tug's insurance people couldn't figure out how to value my mate's boat, 'cause they'd never seen one like it! In the end they gave it a rough guess, based on a normal boat of about the same size, and coughed up nearly fifteen grand. My mate couldn't believe his luck. He put the cheque in the bank, nipped down to B&Q for a few bags of ready-mix, and a week later he was back on the water. It cost him less than £200!"

Stories helped pass the time, as did our copious supply of alcohol. We never allowed ourselves to be drunk in charge of the boat, because that was unprofessional, and these guys took their work seriously. But once a shift was done we would typically have six hours before the next one, so a swift gin-and-lemonade never hurt.

One afternoon we were sitting in the cockpit, Tony steering lazily with one hand and leg, when he decided we should have our beers early. It was such a nice day; the sun was blazing overhead, not a cloud in the sky, and we'd all been inspired to break out our shorts and t-shirts. From here on, it should be plain sailing, or so our skipper thought.

Geoff brought the beers and an opener, popped off his bottle cap and flung it over the side.

I did a little involuntary gasp, as I'd been carefully collecting all my rubbish in separate bags for recycling in Lanzarote.

Geoff noticed my squeamishness, and gave me a shrug.

"It doesn't matter. We're over very, very deep water here."

And I guess a couple of bottle caps was small fry compared to the wreckage of hundreds of sunken ships in the area.

I chucked my beer cap overboard and felt immediately guilty about it.

If I'd been on a boat coming up behind ours, I'd probably have shouted at me and given myself some shit for being a litterbug.

But there was no-one in sight. We were alone from horizon to horizon. It was very liberating – the Captain makes the rules on board ship, and his word is law whilst out of sight of land. Luckily, we had a very laid back captain – I couldn't imagine what it would take to get on the wrong side of him.

We lounged on the cockpit benches with our beers, feeling the elements play all around us. It was at times like this, I could see why these guys loved to sail.

The sea was flat, but not too flat. The motion of dipping and then rising between the waves was so ingrained I hardly noticed it.

The boat was heeled over, but not so far as to be uncomfortable.

The sails thrummed, the wind caught the small clouds of spray we threw up and fanned them out away from the back of the boat.

And we sat sipping our beers, Geoff taking his turn at steering with one hand resting on the wheel. It looked casual, but I could feel the warring forces through the hull and knew Geoff's hand, steady as a rock, was applying quite a bit of pressure to keep the boat in line.

It was as close to paradise as we'd been so far.

A second beer followed the first.

"It's a beautiful day," said Tony, "might as well take advantage of it. At this rate we'll still have half the beer left when we get there."

This didn't seem like an insurmountable problem, but it did represent the fact that this trip had been more difficult than anyone expected.

I fetched three ice-cold beers from the fridge, replacing them with warm ones from a locker. It was a system that worked well so long as everyone remembered it and did their part each time – much like everything else on the boat, from steering the thing to cleaning the sink after use. Every part of life on board was carefully thought out and planned for, which is why it ran so smoothly – providing everyone cooperated.

I handed out the beers to contented sighs all round.

Tony opened a beer for Geoff and one for himself, then handed the opener to me.

It was a shackle key, a basic steel sailing tool not dissimilar to a bike spanner, with a bottle opener cleverly incorporated. What caught my eye, though, was attached to one end of it; a gigantic white knot, a round ball the size of my clenched fist, which seemed more incredibly intricate the longer I studied it.

"You can't keep this in your jeans' front pocket," I pointed out.

Tony laughed. "No, and anyway it's too precious to get dirty."

"What do you call it?"

"It's a kind of Star Knot," he said, "or it started out as one. It used to be a hobby of mine, fancy knot-work. I built it up in layers, just figuring it out as I went. It's basically a really big Star Knot made out of lots of little ones, but I think there's about thirty different types of knot in there in total."

Tony's face became more animated as he explained, the flash of enthusiasm giving me another insight into the soul beneath that calm exterior.

"It's incredible," I told him, and I meant it.

It was string – quality stuff mind, but not rope – miles of string, tied and built up, knots over knots over hundreds of lesser knots, every one placed with such precise regularity that it created the overall symmetry of the piece. It was a mind-boggling effort, almost worthy of a documentary; like someone who's collected enough beer cans to fill their house or built the world's biggest elastic band ball – only this was a thing of beauty.

"It must have taken you forever to make this thing!"

"Oh, I just worked on it whenever I had spare time. Evenings mostly, during long crossings… I reckon it took about three months, on and off."

"Wow…" I marvelled again at the combination of massive effort and perfect form.

Carefully, I used the shackle key to prize the top off my beer bottle.

Then I turned and casually threw it into the ocean.

There was almost a whole second of calm before my brain computed what I had just done. Then it went very still. Everyone in the back of the boat was still too. All eyes were fixed on the point where the key had disappeared into the water. I was frozen, arm still half outstretched, as the full horror of my action flooded into my brain.

The key and the bottle top had been in the same hand. I'd let go of both at the same time. I'd just… my mind shied away from the enormity of my cock-up.

Eyes were now on me. There was a half grin on Tony's face, as though he thought I'd pulled some sleight-of-hand trick and was about to dazzle him with my cleverness.

But no. I had in fact just chucked his favourite possession into the ocean.

"I don't suppose it floats, does it…?"

The smallness of my voice and the panic in my eyes alerted them to the truth. This was not a joke.

"I'll jump in and dive for it," I offered.

Geoff waved a calloused hand at the instruments. The water beneath us was over two miles deep – and we'd already put several dozen meters between ourselves and the unnamed, unmarked location.

There was a bit more silence then, during which Tony placed his open beer in a holder and lowered his head into his hands.

I didn't dare utter 'I'm sorry' – somehow it just didn't fit with the magnitude of the mistake.

"I'm a good swimmer," I pleaded instead.

"No. It's gone," said Tony.

He was rather quiet that evening.

The Long Way Home

Amazingly, our last week of sailing passed almost without incident.

We were followed by a pilot whale for a day, which was exciting for the first few hours, then kind of mundane afterwards. He was eating the plankton churned up by our passage, so he stayed behind us most of the time and came to the surface regularly to blow a plume of water from the top of his head.

Then there was a night of giant ocean rollers, where the boat sailed almost vertically up the front of each wave, hung suspended over nothing for several seconds at the top, then dived back down the far side with reckless abandon, clocking up speeds we hadn't seen all journey. At one point, angling slightly too far into a wave, the boat had shot up so steeply that my feet had left the floor, leaving me hanging, just for a moment, by both hands from the wheel as my legs flailed above the stern.

Had to change my underwear after that one.

I named the freak wave that caused this 'Eric', and I talked to him like Ahab did to Moby Dick, chanting my defiance afterwards, as though surviving Eric had proved my mastery over all his kind.

Then, a few nights later, Eric had had his revenge; coming out of nowhere, completely at right angles to the rest of the waves, a massive wall of water crashed over the boat, flooding the cockpit completely and forcing it's way down the hatch into the boat. They call it being 'pooped', apparently, when this happens; you go completely underwater for a short time as the wave engulfs you.

I emerged triumphant and grinning like a maniac, as I'd felt in control the whole time. The rest of the crew were less sure, and soon emerged on deck to see what had happened.

"Rouge wave," Tony nodded, "it can happen. You okay?"

"Fine, yeah! I enjoyed it. Sorry to wake you though!"

"Yes well, sleeping like a starfish can only do so much. That wave threw me out of bed, through the door, past the kitchen and into the saloon!"

"It wasn't all bad news though," said Geoff. "look – you've caught a squid!"

And there it was, draped across the floor behind me; carried into the cockpit by the surge of water and unable to escape when it drained, a two-foot long, gelatinous squid. Geoff threw it overboard when I confirmed that I wasn't interested in calamari for breakfast.

And then, almost before we knew it, we'd arrived.

Actually it was long after we'd known it; I'd been keeping a detailed log in my journal of number of days remaining, number of nights, number of watches, then the whole thing divided up by an estimate of hours and minutes.

Sailing was fun, but I was really, really looking forward to getting off that boat.

The crew, in spite of my errors, had embraced me fully. I felt like I'd become one of them, although I had no desire to continue with them. They would be off on another trip almost as soon as we'd finished this one, and that sort of total dedication to sailing was not something I could imagine having.

Sailing for fun would be just that; but sailing for a living sucked ass.

Getting off the boat and onto the jetty gave me my first taste of 'land sickness'. After almost a month afloat, my internal balance had been re-calibrated to take account of the boat's constant movement. For the first couple of weeks I'd fallen everywhere, always expecting the deck to be somewhere it wasn't – beneath my feet, for example. Now those same feet had supposedly gotten used to the deck rising to meet them, or falling sharply away at an angle, and they'd developed an unconscious appreciation of the boat's rhythm. Suddenly on land, bereft of that rhythm, they couldn't adjust straight away. As far as they were concerned, the ground must be moving – my eyes were obviously malfunctioning – so they stuck to the rhythm they were used to.

It's a surreal experience when your brain and your body don't trust each other – like if you've ever been sitting on a train when the one next to yours pulls out, and you're convinced that you're moving backwards.

I've never been the most elegant creature on land anyway, so the result was to make me even less co-ordinated than normal.

I'd hoped I would be proudly identified as a sailor by my rolling gait; instead I fell on my face roughly every three steps, all the way from the jetty to the bar, where they refused to serve me on the grounds that I was already a danger to myself and others.

And yet I'd suffered the same lack of agility on the boat, damn it! I'd never even developed sea legs.

So the most noticeable effect of my great ocean voyage was to make me stagger around like a drunk who's been hit by a car, no matter where I was.

I could handle both land and sea with equal ineptitude.

Now, I'm ashamed to say I had a typical Englishman's view of Lanzarote. Yet another hedonistic party island, I'd lumped it in with Majorca and Ibiza, the sort of Blackpool of the beach world; crammed with wasted blokes on stag do's and hordes of women wearing police uniforms and 'L' plates. I'd assumed it would be much like any Mediterranean sun-trap – blue ocean full of jet skis, white beaches barely visible under the sea of lobster-red flesh, the occasional strategically-positioned palm tree.

But Lanzarote, happily was not like this at all. It's not even in the Mediterranean, something I had only realised when we sailed right past that seductive stretch of water with a week still left to go.

Lanzarote was off a much more volatile coast, both politically and geographically. It wore its volcanic sleeve on its heart, with bizarre black-sand beaches and cinder-block rocks which looked for all the world like stone sponges. Most of the marina was built out of this rough honeycomb-like stone, chopped into blocks and stacked up to make walls, buildings and sea defences.

Yes, Lanzarote was shaping up to be a unique and fascinating place.

There is part of me that loves to seek out the new and the exotic, that craves the experience of different cultures and is keen to explore them.

But there are other parts of me. One of them saw an Irish bar, thought 'bollocks to the rest of it,' and dragged me in there to get drunk.

And that was my experience of Lanzarote.

The following day, Tony called the yacht delivery company to give them his report.

He told them I was very useful (a lie) and that I was very likely to do another job for them in the future (also a lie). This must have been what they wanted to hear, as they agreed to pay for my flight back home to England. Score! They even booked it for me, leaving me with two days to help clean the boat before it was time to leave.

Most of the other boats that had set off from Port Solent on the same day had arrived already and their crews had fled, but there was one other boat still in dock being cleaned.

It was in a sorry state. The crew had been cursed with a foul-tempered captain, a whole bunch of equipment malfunctions, much like us – but the real biggie was that their boom – the beam that holds the bottom of the main sail out straight – had snapped in half! This is the sort of catastrophic damage that can really spoil your day, and the crew had spent the rest of the trip motoring, with none of the delicacy and decadence of sailing – just a pounding, churning, vibrating engine chugging away 24/7, right between their cabins. They said it had been the journey from hell, and even I was tempted to agree with them.

They'd arrived in port desperate to get as far away from the boat as humanly possible. So they'd hired a car – being soundly ripped off in the process – and then missed their flight home when they crashed it on the way to the airport.

All in all, it made me feel a lot better about my experience.

This sorry little group agreed to give me a lift to the airport, as their new flight left just after mine. They picked me up late, burst a tyre on the fifteen minute drive, and were amazed that we arrived just before the check-in desk closed. My natural good luck had evened out their terrible streak, but I worried about them once they were alone again. I didn't hear about any planes crashing in that area though, so maybe they survived.

For me the good luck continued, as I was seated next to a cute blonde chick called Lisa, who was returning home to England after spending a year working at a tourist bar in Lanzarote. She was sick of the life, and sick of the boyfriend she'd left behind. She wanted to cut loose, and if there's one thing I can't resist, it's a loose woman.

We got chatting straight away, comparing the mistakes we'd made whilst attempting to express ourselves in Spanish.

One of the stewardesses passed by and mentioned to me that we both looked (and sounded) very happy.

"Couldn't be happier," I said. "We've got our whole lives ahead of us and we both love adventure! I think we'll travel forever."

"Ooh, that sounds worth drinking to! Hang on a tick."

She nipped off towards the back of the plane and returned a few minutes later with two glasses of champagne.

"Here, compliments of the crew!" And she handed us each a glass.

"Wow, thank-you so much!"

"Just call me when you need a refill."

"Thanks, I will!"

And I did.

During the four-hour flight we chuckled and chortled our way through at least a bottle of champers apiece.

At one point I staggered back to the prep area and gushed with thanks at the stewardess there.

"That's nice," she said, "so, how long have you two been together?"

"Oh, we're not together. We just met right here, on the plane."

"Oh! Oh? Oh… we all thought you were newly-weds! On the way back from your honeymoon."

Of course, it all made sense now! That's why they were plying us with copious amounts of free champagne.

"Ah. Well, um, we're not, but thanks anyway!"

"Alright. Just, shhh! Don't tell anyone else, okay?"

And she handed me the refilled glasses.

I was so drunk I followed Lisa right out through airport security, through the baggage reclaim and out to the taxi rank, where she was expecting to get picked up by a friend at any minute.

It wasn't long before she spotted her friend's car, stuck behind a fleet of taxis that were queuing past the front of the terminal. She was moving towards us very slowly.

"Let's dance for her!" I said.

So I strutted my funky stuff while Lisa shook her booty, then we slow-danced together as the line of cars inched past, honking their appreciation.

When Lisa's friend pulled up, we gave her our best grand finale, spirit fingers and all, to thunderous (imaginary) applause.

The friend got out, took one look at me, bundled Lisa and her luggage into the car, and drove off without a word.

I had that horrible feeling that my balls were hanging out of a hole in my trousers again – but for once, they weren't.

It must have been something else I did.

All of a sudden I didn't know what to do. I had booked a seat on the coach home, but I didn't feel like taking it. I wandered over to the airport information desk. "How do I get out of here," I asked the lady.

"On the train?"

"Yeah, that'll do."

"Into the city?"

"Yeah, wherever."

"The shuttle train to Paddington Station leaves in five minutes – you might just make it."

"Thanks!"

I followed her directions up to the shuttle platform and made it inside before the doors closed. It entered my head that I didn't have to go home at all – from the centre of London I could go literally anywhere in the country. Anywhere in the world, even! I had my bag with the basic travel essentials, even some clean clothes, as I'd only bothered getting changed twice in nearly three weeks afloat.

The downside of this was that I had a bag of exceptionally smelly clothes tucked away amongst all my clean ones. It was well wrapped in about a dozen plastic carrier bags, for fear it should melt through a less formidable defence and contaminate the contents of my rucksack.

The journey to Paddington Station was over in minutes. I jumped out and wandered through the concourse, looking for the board with the train destinations on. If there was one leaving soon…

Maybe I'd just go with the flow. Take it to wherever it was going, then figure out how to get back afterwards. Have a mini adventure. It was nearly midnight; the witching hour! Anything was possible.

"Excuse me, what train are you waiting for?"

It was a station official, suited and booted, and wearing his official hat. I tried not to sound too drunk, or too weird, when I told him, "I haven't decided yet, I'm just looking to see what's available."

"There are no more trains until five-thirty," the man informed me. "And the station is closing. I'm afraid you'll have to leave."

What? I glanced back at the board, trying to make sense of the glowing names and numbers. No trains…?

"But, what am I supposed to do until then?"

"You'll have to wait outside I'm afraid sir."

And that was that. Brooking no argument, he herded me and about fifteen other unfortunates out of a side entrance, drawing the folding steel barriers closed behind us and locking them.

I'd hardly figured out where I was, and now I was outside, in the frigid night air, in one of the least savoury places in all of London. The crowd of loiterers dispersed. I must have been the only one who genuinely didn't know where he was going. There were still people hanging around here and there, but none of them looked like they wanted to be approached. There was a kebab shop opposite, running a brisk trade to a queue of people waiting at a bus stop, and that was about it; the bleak backside of the station, and all else surrounding it, was closed and dark.

The next coach, which left from an entirely different part of London, wasn't until 6:15am.

That was a long time away…

I was shivering, still wearing the t-shirt I'd left Lanzarote in.

A young bloke in dishevelled going-out clothes sauntered up to me and asked where I was headed. It struck me as odd, until I remembered I had an enormous rucksack on my back. It made me an even bigger target for nutters – as well as making it much harder to run away.

"I'm going nowhere until the station reopens," I told him. "I'm bloody freezing cold though, and I'm busting for a wee!"

"Yeah, me too. You can pee behind those bins up there," he waved at a recess in the wall of the station. "Everyone does."

"Okay, thanks. I might have to."

"I'll watch you, you watch me," he slurred.

I thought about correcting the expression to 'you watch out for me', but it seemed like too complicated an issue to explain.

I just stood in the corner behind the bins and peed, looking back over my shoulder defensively to find that my new friend was as good as his word.

He was stood there, watching me wee.

Then we went for kebabs. There didn't seem like much choice.

My new friend insisted on paying for my food, which was a surprise. Maybe traveling drunk was the way forward? I surely wouldn't have ended up in this situation if I'd been sober. We stood outside the kebab shop scoffing our food in the wash of fluorescent light – but it was too cold to stand still, even whilst eating.

"So, what next?" I asked.

"To the bus stop!"

He set off, weaving horribly as he walked, threatening to veer out into the road. Even at this time there were enough cars zipping around to make this dangerous. I put a hand out to steady him, not stopping to wonder if this was a good idea. The hand did not have the effect I envisaged; he looked at me and smiled, laid his free hand over mine, and squeezed it tightly.

Then he lost control of his legs and fell face-first onto the pavement.

He hit the ground with a slap which echoed above the sound of the traffic. All eyes turned to him as he lay there, dazed, one arm stretched out in front of him, the hand still clutching his kebab.

Taking his time, he pushed himself up using his other hand, then carefully dusted off the kebab. "It's okay!" he said, offering it up for inspection.

I thought this was a bad time to mention that he was bleeding from his nose and a cut on his cheek.

"Are you going home now?" I asked instead. "Because you probably should…"

"Yearrr mate! I'm off on the bus. You should come with me!"

"Err, yeah, I think I'll go and wait for my coach. I don't want to miss it."

"No, you should come back to my place. We can get hammered."

"What, more hammered than this?"

"Yeah! I got whisky."

I weighed up my options. On the one hand, this was a pretty dubious proposition, from a complete stranger who was already so drunk he could barely walk. But then, he might need my help if he was going to make it home. And it was so bitterly cold outside the station that I was starting to sober up. A few shots of whisky could fortify me against the wait for the coach… and wasn't I supposed to be all about embracing life's unexpected adventures? Who knew where it could lead?"

"And we don't even *have* to have sex," he concluded.

Ah.

So that would be a no, then.

He chose this point to fall flat on his face again, with no warning – like a tree felled in a forest, he made no attempt to save himself. This time it was too much for the kebab, which threw itself halfway across the road in an attempt to escape.

I had a similar urge myself. So I helped him up, guided him towards the line of people waiting for the bus, and walked briskly in the opposite direction.

The coach station couldn't be *that* far away.

And suddenly, I did feel like going home.

To where it was safe, and warm, and where my family, though utterly taken for granted, still loved me unreservedly.

And they almost never asked me for sex.

The Lesser Evil

And once again I was at a loose end.

I didn't have any travel plans.

I couldn't afford to make any travel plans.

I didn't have a job.

I didn't really want a job.

But somehow this stalemate had to give. Although I'd studiously avoided the nine-to-five lifestyle expected of a recovering student, I was by no means work-shy. I knew I had to put myself out there if I was ever to afford to travel the world again, and although I was writing a book about my adventures in Ecuador, it was proving to be a long, slow process.

Because, truth be told, I guess I am a little work-shy after all.

What I was waiting for was some kind of sign; a coincidence or moment of serendipity that would spirit me away into the middle of some new excitement. No matter which way I looked at it, I couldn't believe that getting a real job was what Fate had in store for me. After everything that had happened to me recently, I felt like there had to be more. Something else… something different.

But there wasn't.

So instead I toyed with the idea of applying for another medical trial (without mentioning to my family exactly what had caused the last one to be cancelled, of course).

After the loneliness I'd experienced on the boat in spite of close friendships with Tony and Geoff, I'd decided to be more appreciative of my family. I couldn't be away having adventures all the time, much as I'd like to, and my sailing odyssey had reminded me that every time I was away, I missed my family intensely. Very few people, on their death-beds, regret the lack of adventure in their lives. The vast majority have only one belated wish: that they had spent more time with their loved ones. I resolved not to be amongst them; I would spend as much time with my family as I could, and be sure to tell them all how much I loved them and how grateful I was to them for being a part of my life.

Because if my attempt at sailing was anything to go by, there was a fair chance that next time I wouldn't be coming back.

Appropriately enough, it was around this time that someone from my local bank made an appointment for me to come and have a chat. He was a Personal Financial Advisor, which presumably meant he drove an Audi and bought his clothes in entirely different shops from me. He'd been calling regularly while I'd been away at sea and had left messages requesting a meeting, which unnerved me as I know nothing about money. I used it whenever I got hold of it, but not usually in the wisest of ways. I had a nasty feeling he had some bad news to tell me.

I showed up, nervously, in plenty of time. I even put my least-ripped pair of jeans on. The man who'd been calling me shook my hand, and led me into his office. I took the chair opposite his desk and tried to relax.

"Right, Mr Slater," he opened. "I'd like to talk about your future."

"Oh? Well, to be honest, at the moment all I'm thinking about is getting out of England as fast as possible!"

He furrowed his brow at that.

"I mean, not that there's anything wrong with England."

"Okay. So, what are you doing at the moment?"

"Doing? Well, I was sailing, but I'm not very good at it. The boat started sinking less than a day into the trip! So I don't think I'll do any more of that. I'll probably have to go back to selling my body to medical science."

"Excuse me?"

"Oh, sorry! I mean, I do medical trials. You, know, let them test experimental drugs on me."

"Ah? And, is that... stable employment?"

"Hell no! But it pays in big chunks of cash, which means I can bugger off at a moment's notice, and I don't have to worry about taxes and things like that."

Then I remembered where I was, and decided to shut up.

"Right. So it's not regular work?"

"No, I'm trying to avoid getting a real job for as long as possible."

"Avoid?" He seemed quite surprised by this.

"Yeah, I just can't imagine what it'd be like to spend every day in an office, or..." I trailed off as I looked around me. Enemy territory.

The man leaned back in his chair. "I see. And have you made any plans for your future?"

"Well, I'd like to get back to volunteering with animals. I worked with big cats in Ecuador – ideally I'd love to work with lions and tigers – you know, the really dangerous ones! But I've no training in it, of course."

Now he was looking at me like I had three heads. "I mean in the longer term," he said.

"I guess I just want to travel until I fall over, really. Or until I get eaten. Which is probably more likely."

He sighed. "What I'm getting at, Mr Slater, is have you made any provision for your pension?"

This was too much for me. Suddenly I understood the man, and his questions, and it all seemed utterly ridiculous. I cracked up right there on his desk, which was probably not the politest thing I could have done.

"Oh man," I said when I could, "I'm sorry about all that! I didn't know what you meant. Pensions eh? It all makes sense now!"

He cleared his throat. "So, have you considered your pension?"

"Nah man, not really. You can't even use them until you're sixty-five, can you?"

"Yes that's correct, your pension is about providing for your retirement."

"Well, thanks and all that, but I don't need a pension. There's no way I'll live past forty."

He seemed a bit taken aback by this.

"Don't worry about it though," I told him.

"Ah, no…"

But he still seemed a bit nonplussed. So I thanked him, stood up, shook the hand he offered, and left his office.

He didn't call again.

And still, I needed cash.

There was only one obvious way that was going to happen: prostitution.

To the medical fraternity, of course.

Though it amounts to the same: I would be letting them put things inside me for money.

It would be awkward, and uncomfortable, and a bit degrading.

Only with death in place of STI's.

No, I'm only kidding! Medical trials are as safe as houses. But I decided not to go with the same company as last time – just in case.

Unfortunately, they turned out to be the only ones who had anything decent on offer.

I only had one shot at this, otherwise I'd have to wait another three or four months before I could try again – so I could only afford to take a big trial, with plenty of time in hospital and an equivalently large pay-out.

So it was that I ended up back in that long straight ward, plastic curtains the only barrier between me and over twenty other lads my age, as we prepared ourselves for the unpleasantness ahead.

There were two strange things about this study, and it was a toss-up as to which was the more off-putting. On the one hand, we didn't have to collect our urine; this meant that the toilets would be unlocked, so an urgent bladder release in the middle of the night wouldn't have to be preceded by finding a nurse, checking my bottle out from the fridge, getting the door unlocked and fumbling with the bottle's screw-top.

No, this time they weren't taking the piss.

Instead they were collecting our poo.

Which meant that, while we could skip to the loo as frequently as we saw fit, whenever we wanted to go number two there were procedures to follow.

We had to request a clear plastic bag from one of the nurses. There was much discussion amongst the volunteers as to whether it was entirely necessary that the bag be clear.

We then had to use one particular bathroom, which had a special chair in it. This chair had a toilet seat on top and a bowl underneath, and we had to lift the one and place the plastic bag into the other. I won't draw you a diagram – I think the picture is already, like the plastic bags, perhaps *too* clear.

We would then present one bag of freshly steaming turd to the nurse, who would whisk it away to the lab and return to her packed lunch as though she hadn't just been handling a sandwich bag full of someone else's shit.

I admire nurses. I've never wanted to be one, and I was starting to think I'd never want to date one either, but it has to be said: they can put up with a lot of shit.

The other issue with this trial was The Tube; known to the professionals present as a 'naso-gastric tube'; and to everyone else as, "Fuck off, you'll never get that thing inside me!"

They were wrong.

The tube was inserted up my left nostril – itself an incredibly distasteful process, a feeling of something scratching *inside*, where I couldn't reach to smooth out the abused tissues – and then inched its way down my gullet, which required it to be continually swallowed for about ten minutes.

It could have been achieved more quickly, except that every time I gagged on the thing it came back up a little, forcing me to swallow a length that had already gone down once. With a handful of people clustered around the bed watching, a stern-faced doctor pushing the tube in faster than it really wanted to go and the sound of the guy in the last bed trying to cough his tube back up again, it was a bit of a 'two steps forward, one step back' process.

Eventually it was in; a narrow plastic pipe that coiled in my stomach, ran up my oesophagus, right over that sensitive part of the back of your throat that activates your up-chuck reflex, on up into my sinus cavity and back down out of my nose.

It's hard to describe in words just how violated this made me feel.

The more I thought about it, the more parallels I noticed between medical trials and a life of prostitution. On top of developing a complete disregard for my own privacy and an immunity to my fear of needles, I was now learning that if paid well enough, I could swallow absolutely *anything*.

I lasted two days on that trial. I'd just been given the good news – that I wouldn't be dosed with the study drug, and so would require considerably less blood tests than most others in the group – when the trial was withdrawn, citing some unforeseen complication with a member of a previous test group. I was so close – but yet again, no banana. And so it was time to find a new trial, and a new activity to keep me occupied while I waited for the money to come through.

It was all getting a bit repetitive.

I'd been back in England for nearly a year at this point.

I'd rebuilt a house, sank a boat, corrupted the youth of several different countries and got to see what my poo looks like in a little plastic bag – but I still wasn't any closer to getting away again. My search for adventure – which I was starting to realise was really a search for friendship, acceptance and love – was still only a glimmer of an idea in the distance.

This pissed me off a bit.

So I went ahead and booked some flights.

Three months in Thailand, with a spot of volunteering and a dash of diving thrown in for good measure, all centred on the notorious party island of Koh Pha Ngan. That ought to do the trick.

I figured that having the tickets would keep me sane, would give me something to work towards, and would convince me to do whatever I had to do to make it happen.

God bless credit cards, eh? Where would we be without them.

Not in Thailand, that's for sure.

Richer, but not in Thailand.

I could have gone straight away if my bank had approved me for a loan, but after our last meeting they didn't consider me a strong candidate for repaying it.

I can't imagine why.

Doing What I'm Told

Now, it's worth mentioning at this point that I am an extremely suggestible person.

Perhaps it's part of my need for acceptance, developed when I was young and insecure, and never fully shaken; this insatiable desire I have to become popular by amusing people?

I was legendary for it as a student. Once, after a particularly hard drinking session in the Union, I came home to the house I shared with nine other students. They were having a party of their own, daring each other to do increasingly stupid things, and had just hit the ceiling in terms of challenges that no-one would attempt even whilst blind drunk.

Enter; me.

One of the housemates had been cultivating a small, spiny cactus, and he reliably informed everyone present that even to stroke it was to be tortured for a week, as the microscopically-fine hairs covering its surface worked their way in and out of the pores on your fingers. He'd done it once, and vowed never to make that mistake again.

Would anyone present be fool enough to repeat this act of lunacy?

Then they noticed me – probably because I slammed my way in through the living room door, fell down the single step that always surprised me with its existence inside the living room, and announced in a loud voice, "I'm wearing TWO belts!"

My arrival was exactly what was required to take this party to the next level – because I was obviously stupider than anyone else present, even when I wasn't drunk.

And I was raging drunk.

So they dared me to lick the cactus, and I proved my amazing awesomeness by not only licking it, but having a damn good go at deep-throating it like an actress in a porn film.

My housemate was right on both counts; it was a mistake, and it was torture for about a week. Though I don't think he predicted that I'd lose the ability to speak and would only be able to eat liquids during that time.

The following week they dared me to pour over-proof vodka into my eye. That also turned out to be a mistake.

I'm telling you all this to paint a picture of how dangerous this media-filled world is for me.

Infomercials are particularly bad territory – all night the airwaves are groaning with gadgets of such awesomeness it constantly amazes me. Sure, some of them have fairly limited usage for a penniless, homeless backpacker such as myself; incredible new power tools in particular, unless they can be used to fix a tent.

But that doesn't stop me wanting them. On occasion it doesn't stop me buying them. In my weaker moments – which is pretty much anytime there isn't someone sitting next to me ready to place a restraining hand on my phone-arm – I have been known to make some less-than-wise investments.

The Multi-Cutter was one such item; incredibly versatile to the point of deviousness, the presenters assured me it could cut through PLATE STEEL – in pretty patterns, no less! The potential was unlimited. I could unleash my inner creative spirit through the medium of metal, creating and selling unique sculptures to fund my future travels – is there anyone, anywhere who wouldn't want a Tony Slater Original on their mantlepiece?

Sold, in a heartbeat.

My family know about this trait; they know that there are times, when watching TV, that are particularly dangerous. They've been well trained in the art of sitting on me while I make frantic grabs for the phone, desperate to acquire some miraculous kitchen utensil before the limited-time-only offer expires.

They'd been doing so well at it too.

Months had passed since the last debacle with the 'Ab-Force Training Program', and I hadn't done anything even marginally stupid. Well okay, I hadn't *bought* anything even marginally stupid. Mostly because I hadn't had access to a TV for much of that time.

But neither Gill, nor my parents, could possibly be ready for a new round of TV ads that launched in the summer of 2005. In fairness, it was a bit of a departure from my usual trend. How were they to know?

'Be The Best,' said the ads, appealing straight to my deep-seated desire to be the best. Which blatantly wasn't fair. Surely, everyone wants to be the best?

It was almost like they knew me.

None of my family even thought to grab the remote, much less the phone.

So it surprised the hell out of them when I joined the army.

Okay, so I didn't actually join the Army. I joined the TA – the Territorial Army. Also known as the 'weekend warriors', the TA are the volunteer forces, the reserves that get to do all the same training as the regular army, but in a kind of piecemeal fashion, spread out over many weekends. Once the training is complete there's every chance of being deployed in the field – so long as the boss at your day-job allows it, of course.

I had no day-job.

I really *did* want to be the best, but I figured the regular Army would chew me up and spit me out in minutes. I may dream of being Indiana Jones, but I have less courage than his make-up artist. The TA would be a way for me to test the water without getting in too deep (and ending up drowning).

And also, their advert came on first.

So it was that I found myself in a tiny office somewhere in Taunton, being inducted into the ranks of the Somerset Light Infantry (weekend division), or as it was shortly to become known, The Rifles.

I was excited, because Richard Sharpe had been in The Rifles. He was a fictitious character of course, but then according to the 'proper' army, so was my entire battalion. They don't much like the volunteers, on account of us doing the same job as them but getting paid less. And rumour has it that we can't drink as much either.

Back to the office. In a chair in front of me sat my new Commanding Officer, or 'CO'. In my hand was a card with the Pledge of Allegiance on it, which I had to read out loud in order to confirm my willingness to die for my country (as long as it didn't happen on a Monday-Friday).

It was such a cheesy statement, dripping with patriotic sentimentality – my head filled with images of men in white dress suits saluting the Stars and Stripes. I had to fight to keep the fake American accent from creeping into my voice. Instead I focussed on reading it *with feeling*. I took my time and made eye contact with the Captain in the pause between sentences. I poured my pent-up emotions – and my love of the movie 'Independence Day' – into the speech. If space aliens attacked us tomorrow, I thought, I would fly a plane right into their mother-ship. As long as we had CGI on our side, we couldn't lose.

So I went for the Oscar.

As I finished speaking, the Captain stood up and I swear I saw a glistening in the corner of one eye. He thrust his hand forward and gripped mine tightly enough to count the bones in it.

"Slater eh? I've had recruits read that thing out in this office a hundred times – but that was the best I've ever heard it said."

In a rare moment of thinking before I opened my mouth, I managed to stop myself from replying, "Why thank-you, I'm an actor!"

Somehow I don't think that would have enhanced his opinion of me.

Instead, I applied my Most Serious Acting Face (one of three I'd learned to pull off, thereby proving I didn't waste the thousands of pounds it cost my parents to put me through acting school) – and said, "I meant it, *sir.*"

I honestly thought he was going to cry at that point.

The big girls blouse.

So I was a soldier! Or trying to be. I had the much-feared Basic Personal Fitness Assessment to take, and I much-fearfully passed it; working hard in Treorchy had helped me get back into the kind of shape I hadn't been in since Ecuador. In case you're wondering, that shape (post-fitness test), was sprawled out like a starfish, flat on the floor, with snot coming out of every orifice.

I ran 2.4km (chosen instead of 2.5km by the army for reasons no-one could understand) in nine minutes and nine seconds, and managed to do more than sixty press-ups in two minutes. Hardly Iron Man, but it was a good start.

I had a long way to go to prove myself to these people, but I'd been in that situation before. Hell, I'd been trying to impress people for most of my life. Maybe it was time I got a dog instead?

I think Mum would have preferred a dog, given the choice.

She was most displeased when I told her I'd joined the army.

"But... but you only went out to buy socks?"

"*Army* socks, Mum," I told her. "And the recruitment office is right there on the street. It's impossible to miss!"

She was furious. "You'll be the one that's impossible to miss! What will I do if you get shot?"

"I won't get shot! I'm way too lucky. I almost never get hurt."

At this, she just looked at me.

"Okay, I *sometimes* get hurt. But I won't get *shot.* I promise."

"And what if you have to shoot someone else? Have you thought of that?"

"I could shoot a bad guy."

"Tony, you can't even kill a spider. You made me buy those humane mouse-traps, remember? The ones that never work? The mice just use them as temporary accommodation. I don't think you could kill anything, not if your life depended on it."

"Well I won't have to kill anything! There's loads of jobs in the army. They even have cooks…"

"You can't cook."

"Well, they have drivers."

"You can't drive."

"Well, there's engineers and things like that too."

I received another look. Presumably she didn't think it necessary to point out that I wasn't an engineer. Or that the army's 'Acting Division' is notoriously non-existent.

"I know, but honestly, it's safe Mum. Almost no-one actually fights anymore. There's tanks and things for that."

"Really." She wasn't convinced. "So what are you… in? You know, what type?"

"Type of regiment?"

"Yes."

"Oh. Right. I'm in the Infantry."

I won't write what she said next, because it was very un-motherly.

Nocturnal Manoeuvres

I loved being in the army.

I was terrible at it, of course.

There are some qualities that are highly desirable in people that make up a country's elite fighting forces; hand-eye coordination is particularly useful, as is a basic degree of common sense.

I know! You can already see where this is heading…

Because I have neither.

Walking and breathing at the same time is a skill I've only recently mastered. My grip on it is still tenuous; if I try to talk whilst walking, I sacrifice any attempt at observation, and end up hopelessly lost; if I try to eat whilst walking, it's only a matter of time before I choke on something. If I try to walk, talk *and* eat – well, there's a strong possibility I'll end up in hospital.

I was once told by a close friend that I was the 'least ninja' of any person they had ever met. They were right.

And nothing about this has changed.

The sergeant responsible for our little batch of recruits was quick to spot my inadequacies.

He was every inch a soldier – which was important, because at five-foot-four, if he'd had any inches that weren't a soldier he'd have struggled to fill the uniform.

He was as fit as it's possible for a man to be though, a block of sculpted muscle like a scale-model bodybuilder. Because he was the shape of a child in a man's world, he'd taken it upon himself to become the toughest mo-fo in the whole army. Like so many small men, what he lacked in stature he had learned to make up for in attitude. I knew he was a nice bloke really. I could tell he was a nice bloke. But he had to put on the persona of a hard-ass drill instructor because that was his job – and I'm sure he enjoyed every minute of it.

A large part of this job was finding out which recruits were the least capable at any given task, and kicking their arses until they got better at it. It's a tactic which works quite well with me, because of how much I hate to disappoint people. Unfortunately, there are some things which I am just plain bad at, and not likely to improve no matter how far up my arse the teacher plants their boot.

Shooting is one of these things.

We studied the principles of marksmanship. I learned how to lay supported on my elbows, perfectly still, and how to breathe out as I gently squeezed the trigger.

It didn't help.

I still couldn't hit shit.

"SLAT-uh! You're the worst damn shot I've ever seen! If you get sent for deployment, I'm going to recommend they don't issue you with a rifle. You're more dangerous to yourself than you are to the enemy!"

"That's okay sir. I don't like guns anyway."

"Call me SERGEANT!"

"Yes sir!"

"SEREANT!"

"Yes sir! Oh, I mean sergeant."

"Don't like guns, Slat-uh?"

"No si… sergeant."

"Why the hell not?"

"They, ah, scare me."

"Then why the bloody hell did you join the army?"

"I just wanted to be the best."

"Well you've got a bloody long way to go!"

"Yes sergeant."

"In future, if anyone wants to know where the safest place on the battlefield is, it's directly in front of Slater's rifle!"

There were sniggers from the rest of the group.

"Now, who's put in for the sniper course?"

Four people raised their hands. I was one of them.

The sergeant looked at me long and hard, then shook his head.

"God help anyone who's in front of you."

I wasn't a whole lot better at marching, though it took another weekend to find this out.

I could keep the rhythm in my head well enough, and I appreciated the logic behind taking shorter steps at one end of a line and longer steps at the other end, so that the whole rank seemed to wheel almost on the spot.

What I couldn't figure out, for the life of me, was how to turn.

Or more specifically, which way to turn.

"ARRRRright, TURN!" bawled the sergeant.

In perfect synchronisation, seventeen recruits made a perfect quarter-turn to the right, stamping their left feet in unison to punctuate the movement.

And right in the middle, standing eyeball to eyeball with his neighbour, was the one soldier that had turned the wrong way.

Again.

Yes, that was me.

"SLATER!" The sergeant's yell was now familiar. "Come here! Are you trying to wind me up, Slater? On purpose?"

"No si... sergeant. I just keep forgetting!"

"Bullshit! You're a clever lad, I know that. You've got a degree, haven't you Slater?"

"Yes sir. Sorry! Sergeant."

"Then why haven't you applied for Officer Training?"

"Because my degree is in Acting."

"Oh. Right."

He thought about this for a while.

"So what's your problem with marching? Are you bored of listening to me?"

"No sir! I just... sergeant, sorry! I just... I don't know my left from my right."

"WHAT? That's bullshit for sure!"

"No, SER-geant. I can't tell sir, without looking at my hands and deciding which one I write with."

"Bloody hell! I can see why you went into acting. You're either the world's greatest liar, or the world's biggest idiot."

I wisely chose not to respond to this.

"Look, put an 'L' on your hand or something. You know we always go off the right foot first, so focus on that. And sneak a look at your hand before turning, or you'll always be the only bugger facing left when everyone else turns right."

"Yes sergeant."

"That's better." He stared at me again, which was quite unsettling. "You could still be an officer, you know. If you wanted. They're all bloody idiots."

And with that, he turned to direct his attention at the only other person who'd screwed up the turn.

Because there were two recruits that regularly failed to achieve this manoeuver. The other one, a chubby moron who we'll call... um... The Chubby Moron, was one of those guys that can't get anything right. I'm talking tying his shoe laces. Dressing himself. Uttering words that didn't start and end with him drooling down his shirt. Every time he made a mistake, the whole lot of us got punished for it, in theory to try and spur him on to get better. It never worked; the simple truth was, he was already operating at maximum capacity. I haven't named him here because to be honest I felt sorry for the guy – it wasn't his fault he had the intellectual capacity, body density and personal fortitude of a homemade pancake. I usually change the names of people when I write negative things about them, but in this case I can't see it being necessary. I know for a fact that The Chubby Moron can't read.

Anyway, the point is, this guy was causing trouble for everyone. Lesson after lesson we watched him get it wrong, waited for the inevitable lecture and the resulting press-ups or extra guard duties (known as being 'on stag'). I wished he would just quit; it was blatantly obvious he had zero chance of passing the course, so why did he continue to put himself through it all?

We did a route march with full rucksacks, and he didn't finish it.

He failed every part of his fitness test, every single weekend.

I wasn't surprised when he couldn't memorize the Phonetic Alphabet – you know, 'Alpha, Bravo, Charlie, Delta' and so on. I honestly don't think he could spell his own name in ordinary letters.

He was still a better shot than me though.

Eventually, a decision was taken by the lads to punish him for getting us all in trouble. I'd like to say I played no part in making such a decision, but I wasn't blind to it occurring – it was my turn on stag duty, so I chose to ignore the small group of lads conspiring in the corridor when they should have been sleeping – which I guess makes me an enabler.

Their plan was taken straight from *Full Metal Jacket*, with encouragement by one of the guys whose brother was in the regular army, and had ensured him it happened all the time in basic training.

They would wait until everyone was asleep, slip out of their beds and gather around Chubby's. On a signal they would each grab an edge of his mattress and flip it over, dumping him out of bed in the process. Since Chub was in a top bunk this would be a particularly unpleasant experience – to go from a deep sleep, through five feet of fresh air to the cold, hard tiles. By the time he knew what had hit him – or what he'd hit – the perpetrators would be back in bed, faking sleep in case the disturbance brought trouble from a patrolling guardsman.

To anyone investigating, the bed would appear unmolested; it would look like Chubby had fallen out of bed on his own. It was the perfect crime; calculated, vicious and untraceable – because no-one would dare spill the beans and invite a similar fate the following night.

My turn on watch had long since ended, and I was tucked up in bed, my uniform neatly folded in my locker, when I heard the first stirrings. I knew what was about to happen, even though I wanted no part in it, so I lay there – sleep eluding me – listening to the guys climb down from their bunks and make their way across the dorm.

All in place at last, the countdown was given in a hoarse whisper. "Three, two, one, PULL!"

All of them grabbed an edge of the mattress and hauled with all their might. But this being the top bunk, they couldn't get the best of grips. It was dark; at least half of them were pulling the wrong way anyway, and there was a great big fat bastard lying on top of the thing they were trying to move.

The result; they tugged hard on the mattress from all four directions, and succeeding in shaking it up and down quite a bit, but nothing more. It was just enough to wake Chubby.

"Uuuhh? Whass goinon?" He mumbled.

"Shhhh!" hissed one of the gang, as though expecting him to conspire in his own torture.

"Now!" someone stage whispered, and the guys gave the mattress another heroic yank. It was about as effective as the first had been, only this time Chubby, struggling to sit up, wobbled too; one flailing arm connected with his chief tormentor, an accidental blow that sent the lad ploughing backwards onto the bottom bunk behind him.

Complaints erupted – all delivered in as-close-to-silence as anger allowed – and the ringleader jumped back up, determined to wreak his vengeance.

I was trying not to laugh, both for myself and for the room. If we got inspected now we'd all be in as much trouble as the idiots who were out of bed. The guy whose turn it was on stag was hovering nervously outside the door, obviously concerned with the sudden increase in noise level.

"Fuck off will you, I'm trying to sleep," moaned Chubby.

So the lads resorted to Plan B. Mustering their finest English fighting spirit, they gave one last ineffectual tug on the mattress – and fucked off.

They scurried over to the furthest corner of the room, chuckling and congratulating each other on their achievement. The whole room was awake at this point, and a few annoyed "SHHH!"s were tossed in their general direction.

They weren't to be beaten so easily though. I listened as they hatched a plan, as cruel as could be imagined, to wake up in shifts, go over to Chubby's bunk, and try the same trick every hour throughout the night. Sooner or later, they reasoned, it was bound to work, spilling him out of his bed like a half-baked pudding – and if nothing else, they'd keep him from getting any sleep. With an arduous day ahead of us tomorrow, that would be punishment enough.

Evil geniuses one and all, they dispersed to their own beds, sniggering at their combined cleverness, and fell asleep.

It was an infallible strategy.

Except that none of them woke up again.

In Confidence

It was quite surreal, to spend one day sitting in my parent's front room, typing away on what would eventually become 'That Bear Ate My Pants!', and the next day find myself in the middle of Salisbury Plain, fitting bullets into two spare magazines before a 'live-fire' exercise.

The army has a whole town up there, made of houses that look normal from the outside, but are just bare concrete shells once you get indoors. That was where we were sleeping – seventeen men to a floor and a separate room for the one woman in our little group.

She was popular, I can tell you that.

But she held her own and gave as good as she got insult-wise, and it made us seem more like one big family.

Well, we squabbled enough.

The instructors encouraged our rivalries, most notably between me and one other bright spark, a South African bloke called Butler. Both of us had migrated into leadership roles within the group, him by intent and me (as always) by accident. There's only so long you can watch a bunch of guys struggle with some team-building task (like making a raft from string and oil drums, or getting from A to B on a series of planks without touching the floor), before you have to step in and tell them how it's done.

The post-Ecuador me had a fairly eclectic skill-set, including the ability to make just about anything out of a few scrappy planks and a load of old rope. Chuck in a couple of battered oil drums and I could do a convincing job of world domination. Honestly! I'm like a one man A-Team.

And it might be hard to believe, but I am also quite a logical thinker. Although it doesn't translate itself into anything as useful as common sense, there was always going to be a time for this aspect of my nature to shine.

This was it.

No-one could solve those human-sized puzzles like I could, something that did not go unnoticed by the sergeant.

He liked to make a game of it – challenging Butler and me to out-perform each other at every turn. Bullet-stuffing was today's little exercise.

Everyone had to fill their magazines personally before doing any shooting – that way, if a bullet didn't go off, or got jammed due to being badly positioned in the magazine, it was no-one else's fault but yours. This wasn't likely to be comforting when under heavy fire from the enemy, so we practised this one skill regularly. I'd developed a technique using both hands, grabbing for the bullets and jamming them in left, right, left, with the magazine gripped upright between my knees. Butler did it all with one hand, and this was one challenge he won – by milliseconds – when the sergeant decreed that we both had to use one hand to make it fairer.

Ah well.

I got my own back when the live-fire exercise was cancelled the following day. The shooting range was over-booked, and some real soldiers needed to practice, so we got elbowed out into whatever space wasn't being shot at.

It was one of the best things that could have happened to us.

With no plans for what to do, the sergeant had to improvise – and improvise he did, coming up with an inspired lesson on 'improvised weaponry'.

What this translated as is, he taught us how to make and throw Molotov Cocktails.

How cool is that?!

Downstairs in one of the empty houses, we filled milk bottles with flammable liquids, stuffed a rag in the top and left them to soak. It was every fourteen-year-old's dream; the ultimate chemistry lesson! And as we may have covered, fourteen is about where I stopped developing – at least as far as my sense of humour goes.

So all chuckling maniacally, we gathered upstairs, to look out of a glassless window at the mock street below. Parked right in the middle was a battle-scarred tank, a gigantic steel beast almost as big as the floor plan of the house.

The army have rules for everything. Rules, and instructions. In one of the most unlikely situations I've ever encountered, our pint-sized sergeant imparted the Official Technique for Discharge of an Improvised Weapon. Seriously – there were hand-outs and everything.

What it boiled down to was:

1) crouch down while you light the thing,
2) lob it at the tank, and
3) run like fuck!

Hardly surprising – but there were other bits of knowledge to appreciate, like the benefits of throwing our firebombs at a vehicle after it has passed, so that its occupants are less likely to spot where the missile came from.

And not holding onto one for too long, causing you to burn your hand on it, drop it at your feet, and immolate your entire squad.

Oh, and yelling, "Eat THIS mutherfuckaaa!" while you throw it is also (apparently) frowned upon, for some reason.

Impossible to resist of course, but there you go.

I scored a direct hit, putting my shoulder into the throw and being rewarded when the fireball blossomed right over a hatch open to the tank's interior.

Woohoo! Enemy solders, frying tonight.

Butler missed completely, his bomb proving more dangerous to anyone cowering on the pavement than to the massive war machine, but I was magnanimous enough not to point it out.

I didn't have to – the whole group was giving him grief for it!

"Jesus Butler, is that not a big enough target for you?"

"We'll have to bring yo' moma's ass in here and see if you can hit that!"

Even the sergeant chipped in: "Bit limp-wristed are we, But-lah? I'd cover your arses when you sleep tonight lads, in case Butler comes looking for a bit of action."

Politically correct he wasn't.

But it was bloody funny – especially seeing as it wasn't aimed at me for a change.

And now, when the revolution comes, I'll know exactly what to do! Or I would do, except I haven't seen a glass milk bottle in close to a decade.

I don't think it works nearly as well with a plastic carton from Tesco's…

Next on the improvised agenda was a trip around the army's Confidence Course. The sergeant's introductory spiel caught my interest immediately.

"This course will test your confidence – and your fears. It's designed to show you the kind of things you might have to do in a battle, the things that might stop you because you're scared of them – like heights, tunnels and drops. In a battle situation you have to keep going because your whole section is depending on you. If you fall behind, they might have to rescue you – and that puts everyone in danger."

"The point of this course is that you WILL get scared. It WILL test you to your limits. When you get scared, you have to go on and do it anyway. That's what this course is about – don't think, just do it. Nothing here will kill you – but the enemy will, if they catch you. So don't stop to think. Don't let the fear take control of you. Don't give it time. If you get stuck on any obstacle, help each other to overcome it – that's what you'd have to do in a real situation."

It was possibly the most exciting briefing I'd ever heard.

Pushed to the limits?

Pah! If I could capture an (admittedly very small) crocodile bare-handed, then there was nothing they could throw at me here that would bother me in the least.

I waited until half the recruits had started the course, because I didn't want to look like a show-off.

Even though I fully intended to be a show-off.

Then it was game on.

Most of the course was about sprinting between buildings. Inside the buildings were ladders up to bare-beam second floors, planks to cross from one house to the next, roofs to scale and ropes to slide down. It was like an adult version of a kids adventure playground, and I was loving every minute.

At one point there was an oil drum protruding from the ground, which we had to climb into. It led to a maze of underground tunnels, all just big enough to squeeze through on my knees and elbows – and all in the pitch black. I could see how anyone the least bit claustrophobic would have issues with this part of the course. I couldn't see my hand in front of my face, so when I ran into a dead end I did it literally – usually with my nose. Turning around was impossible; even backing up was tough, especially if the next person down the tunnel had followed too closely, and was still pushing forward as I tried to reverse through them. In the end it was as much about cooperation as anything else, and I led the guys behind me through by calling out "Left!" or "Right!" or "Ow my fucking nose!"

Emerging into the daylight was blinding – the more so because there were fireworks rigged to go off – and the next stretch was a crawl through mud, under a net, with little bangers exploding all around us. It was like being in the middle of *Call of Duty*.

Finally there was a rope climb, followed by a further climb up a scaffolding tower, ending up in a leap of faith off the highest obstacle of the course so far. It was about three stories high. There were mats of course, to cushion our landing. By this point I was so enthused I was running on pure adrenaline. It was all I could do to keep from trying a somersault off the rickety wooden platform.

The sergeant was waiting for me with his stop-watch as soon as I hit the mat.

"Well done Slater," he growled. He was always cautious with his praise – especially around me. "You've got the fastest time so far. What did you think of our confidence course, eh?"

"It was easy!"

"SERGEANT!"

"Sorry! It was easy, sergeant."

"Easy? EASY? You're too good for our course, Slater, is that it?"

"No sergeant."

"Then obviously, you want to do it all again?"

"Yes sir! Sergeant, I mean."

He eyed me, weighing his options. Did my enthusiasm warrant punishment? Or was I taking the piss? I could tell he wasn't sure. To be on the safe side he poured extra menace into his next threat.

"You're too cocky for your own good, Slater. I can do it you know – I'll send you right back to the start, and you'll have to go through the whole course again."

"Yes sir, I'd love to, sir!"

He looked hard at me, then back at the course behind him. And then at his watch.

And said, "Well you can't 'cause it's nearly dinner time."

Vital Instructions

With every weekend that passed, I learned more awesome things.

For example, I learned how to strip, clean and reassemble my SA80 rifle. We cleaned the things far more often than we got to fire them, which to be honest was probably for the best.

I learned how to hold it when I was on guard duty. I learned never to leave it lying around on the table in the mess hall (a mistake you only make once – the second time you get kicked out on the spot).

I also learned how to hide effectively, which is something I haven't tried to do since I was about eight. It constantly amused me, the kind of things the army had an instruction manual for. They can dress it up with fancy words all they like, but Concealment and Camouflage is still a lesson in Hide and Seek.

It began with identifying all the things that make a person stand out from their surroundings. Shape was the most obvious – we're all hard-wired to recognise another human shape, so that's the first thing to disguise – in this case by ramming armloads of foliage down our trousers and into the elastic webbing on our helmets.

Okay, so maybe it was just me shoving it down my trousers. It's not the first time I've been accused of being *too* enthusiastic.

Still, that was Lesson One; make yourself blend in to your environment – by adding it to your costume, if you can. Become like the forest around you…

Colour was also a big giveaway, which is why we all carried our army-issue make-up kits. No word of a lie – we had little plastic compacts with four different shades of camouflage make-up and a mirror in the lid! Of course, this was a serious tool for confusing the enemy, so it came in a very tough-looking olive green case with military stencilling on it. And a delicate little brush to apply it with. I think they're custom-made for the British Army by Revlon.

Flashes of any kind are also a dead giveaway, which is why all the metal on our rifles was painted black and green; belt buckles were black plastic quick-releases, and smiling whilst in camouflage was strongly discouraged.

And there's one more thing that gives you away to the enemy; when the bloke crouched next to you realises that along with the long grass and ferns he's stuffed down his jacket are a goodly proportion of nettles. When he looks down at the source of his woes, stings his face on a leaf and shouts "Arrrgh! You bastard!" at the top of his voice – well, that's when the enemy snipers open fire.

So lesson two: whilst you become like the forest around you, there are some things you should avoid trying to wear. Stinging nettles are definitely one, and anything that looks like it might be excessively itchy, or attractive to things that bite. And equally, mud is ideal, but dog poo – although readily available in most forests in Britain – does absolutely no good at all when smeared all over you. Particularly when pretending to wait in ambush for several hours on a hot day.

I found endless amusement in the army's attitude towards procedure; there was one for everything, from washing in the morning to folding your underwear at night. Mostly it was designed with a large number of people in mind, to get every little detail handled in the same way every time, for the sake of efficiency.

I signed for my uniform; I signed for my beret. I signed for a hundred little bits of equipment from waterproofs to a complete suit of chemical warfare clothes lined with charcoal. Which, I have to say, is a bugger to wash off when there's eighteen of you covered head to toe in black stains, crowding a bathroom with only three sinks and less than five minutes to be dressed again ready for the pre-dinner inspection.

I signed for my gas mask, which looked like it had survived World War One. That didn't matter; there was a simple way to upgrade older gear, once you were in the field. This tip came from the guy whose brother was in the regular army, and was currently deployed in Iraq.

"If you need something, the easiest way to get hold of it is to rob it off the Americans," he told us. "They have enormous amounts of gear, it all costs a fortune, and they have no discipline at all about looking after it. My brother robbed a pair of night vision goggles worth a grand from this one bloke! And the next day the Yank reported them missing and got given another pair. My bro said it's much quicker to steal boots off them than to request another pair from our lot. That's how he got me these!"

And yes, he was wearing a brand new pair of US Army Issue Combat Boots, made by sunglasses manufacturer Oakley. They must have been worth about £250.

"There's a saying that goes, 'If the Yanks haven't got it, it's not worth stealing'!"

In the end I could hardly imagine stealing anything. I had so much stuff it filled a man-sized locker in the barracks in Taunton. Amongst the other items I'd signed for was one piece of 'red backing': a bit of cloth to be sewn onto my uniform behind my regimental badges.

It was about two inches square, and when I lost it there was so much clicking of tongues and clicking of pens that I thought Germany had decided to invade again.

I found it amusing that we didn't get a first-aid kit unless we were medics; what we had was one sealed bandage, to be placed in our top jacket pocket, designed to be applied if we got shot in combat. If I cut my finger whist putting my rifle back together I had to go and see the medic just to get a plaster – but get shot in the middle of a gun battle and I'd be expected to fix myself with my magic bandage.

At least we received careful instruction on the use of it.

"Remember this," bawled the sergeant, "if you attend a casualty, and they are bleeding out, you DO NOT use YOUR Field Dressing. Theirs will be in their top pocket, no matter what battle gear they are wearing."

"If you use your dressing on another soldier, and then you get wounded, you are asking anyone who helps you to use their dressing on you. This is asking them to put their own life in danger, and they will have orders, just like you, NOT to do it."

"You ALWAYS carry your own Field Dressing. It will save YOUR life, if you get wounded – no-one else's. Are you listening?"

"YES SERGEANT!" It was a chorus we were getting good at. For some of us, it was the only thing we were getting good at.

"WHAT are you, if you go into battle without your Field Dressing?"

"DEAD, sergeant," someone answered.

"CORRECT!"

"And your salad will taste rubbish," I commented.

A chuckle ran through the troop – but as soon as I said it, I knew I'd regret it. There was a time and a place for jokes; this was not it.

The sergeant rounded on me, eyes angry, staring up at me from somewhere near my navel.

"SLAT-AH thinks he's FUNNY! Do you SLAT-AH?"

"Yes sir."

"SERGEANT!" He bellowed.

"Yes sir, Sergeant!

"So SLATE-AH thinks he's a comedian! Do you SLATE-AH?"

"Yes sergeant!"

"And why is that then?"

"Um… because I'm a comedian."

He blinked at me. "Is that what you do for a living? In the real world?"

"Yes sir. I mean, Sergeant."

"Oh." He looked nonplussed – the only time I've ever seen that expression topping such a stern, military bearing. There were three awkward seconds of silence while his mind groped for the appropriate response to this. A fourth second ticked by. Then he flicked his eyes to the side and the mask dropped firmly into place again.

"RIGHT, well you've got nothing to smile about BUT-LAH…"

My competition with Butler was finally laid to rest in the last round of physical fitness tests. I'd always been towards the top of the pack in these, whereas he was struggling. This time I was determined to be the best – it was what had attracted me in the first place after all – so I gave it everything I'd got.

I did ninety-one push-ups in two minutes, and when the sergeant complained that I'd told him I could manage a hundred, I did the last few just to prove a point.

Then, on the run, I dug deep for reserves of strength – more mental than physical I thought, as it was my mind that wanted me to wimp out and give up – and overtook every member of the group, powering past one professional sprinter and one kick-boxing instructor to shave a full half-minute off my previous time.

As I crossed the line my vision went red.

I stumbled to a halt and collapsed on the grass, panting, dripping and shaking. I threw up in my mouth a bit and nearly choked on it, so I rolled to my knees and hung my head while I tried to synchronise coughing, spitting and panting. I felt like I would either pass out or burst, or possibly both, but at least I wouldn't be awake to clean the mess up.

"SLATER!"

A pair of suspiciously shiny boots entered my field of vision.

"…yes… sarge…ant…" I gasped.

"You've been holding out on us!"

"…no…sarge…ant…" I tried to supress a violent stomach

heave.

"That was the best fucking run I have ever seen in my life."

"Thank-you sergeant," I managed.

Then I lost control and threw up all over his boots.

"SLATER! That is the most disgusting fucking mess I have ever see in my life!"

"Sorry…sergeant."

"But well done lad. Now go drink some fucking water."

Yeah, it's safe to say, I loved being in the army.

At least the training part of it.

But you know what they say; all good things must come to an end.

And that, for now, was as far as it went.

Trialling Matters

As much fun as it was, being in the TA wasn't helping me achieve my dream of traveling the world.

I'd taken a temporary job in a summer school while I worked through my basic training, but neither of these activities were ever likely to make me rich.

I was running out of time. I had flights booked to Thailand and I'd already had to postpone them once. If I was going to afford to eat while I was there, not to mention learn to dive and have a bit of fun every now and then, I was going to have to get some money together, pronto.

So when another medical trial opened up – this time with a more reputable company – I was first in line to get involved.

I travelled down to London to be fitted with a heart-rate monitor.

"You wear it for twenty-four hours," the doctor told me, "and then you bring it back. Assuming your heart sounds in good health, we can put you on the trial."

So I submitted to the ultimate indignity; I had my chest shaved by a nursing student. Not all of it; oh no, that would be far too conventional. No, she shaved just enough space in my manly thatch of chest hair to attach a series of electrodes around my nipples. There were eight of them altogether, which meant eight separate bald patches, some of them in a curved line across my midriff. I had a nasty feeling she was enjoying her job too much; either by accident or design, she'd shaved a near-perfect smiley face into me.

I had to hope it would grow out before I found myself on the beach, or I'd tan that way too; a lasting legacy of the lengths I'd gone to just to get away.

The electrodes were attached by a series of leads to a monitor about the size of an old-school Walkman, which I wore on a special belt around my waist. It was not an endearing look, and was horribly uncomfortable; not only was I itchy as hell wherever I'd been shaved, and starting to react badly to the glue on the electrodes, but I was also starting to chafe. And to sweat profusely; something else you don't want to do after having strategic circles of body hair inexpertly removed with a razor blade.

London was on high alert at that time, with the tragedy of the bombings still in recent memory. On every tube station platform there were armed police; special Ministry of Defence officers, who looked far more fearsome than the traditional English bobby. They wore black combat fatigues, army boots and caps, and kept both hands wrapped tightly around their MP5K machine guns.

I studied the one on the end of my platform as I waited for the tube. He looked intense; eyes scanning the crowd, trigger finger laid flat along the side of his weapon, undoubtedly itchy. I looked away to avoid making eye contact; I didn't want him to catch me staring.

That's when I looked down, and saw the wires hanging out of my t-shirt.

It made my heart beat faster, I can tell you.

I froze.

The cop was turning slowly towards me.

Turning my back on his machine gun, I surreptitiously reached down and tucked the trailing wires into the waist band of my jeans.

I had to leave my hand there, holding them in place, and hope that no-one in the crowd thought I was trying to touch myself.

The cop's gaze swung back in the other direction and I dared to breathe again.

Shit, that was close! I thought.

It wouldn't do to join the army, swear to my Mum that I would never get shot, and then break that promise a week later whilst waiting for a tube-train.

Irony is made of such things.

As are tabloid headlines.

My train arrived and I moved onto it, trying to act as normally as possible. As it moved away from the station, I sighed, sank back in my seat, and tried to relax. I listened to the sound of blood coursing through my head and willed it to move more slowly. I relaxed my muscles, closed my eyes and let it all hang out.

There was a man sat opposite me, smartly dressed for a day in the office, his briefcase perched on the floor next to him.

His eyes went wide when I pulled the collection of wires out of my pants and started fiddling with them.

So I winked at him, and then held up my wrist with its plastic hospital ID bracelet on it. I'm not sure whether that made me seem more or less like a mad bomber, but he got off pretty quickly at the next station.

When I got to my hostel I lay down on my bunk, wriggled until I got comfy (takes a while when you're wearing half a Dell laptop), and crashed out to sleep for a bit.

I spent the evening looking for pizza, then settled down to watch a movie in the hostel's TV room.

It was a scary movie. The third time I jumped about three feet off my beanbag, it occurred to me that this might not make for a happy heart-rate result, so I went back to bed with the most boring book I could find.

My results turned out okay; 'although it does look like you had a series of minor heart-attacks at about ten-thirty last night,' the doctor said.

"Sorry. Watching a horror movie."

"And one about an hour after leaving here?"

"Oh, that one! Yeah, I nearly got shot as a terrorist."

The doc didn't bat an eyelid. "That's all fine then. We'll give you a call."

And not to bore you with the details, but a week later they did give me a call.

It was two weeks in hospital.

I could cope with that. Especially as they let us out occasionally, under the close supervision of a pair of nurses. It must have made an interesting sight, our line straggling through the hospital grounds, down the road and around the nearest park. Thankfully we weren't dressed in hospital-issue pyjamas, or we'd really have scared the local residents. Just for shits and giggles, one time we all went hand-in-hand, which is a testament to just how bored twenty-odd guys get in hospital together for two weeks.

We found other ways to amuse ourselves, too.

One night I was coming back from the toilet at the end of our ward, walking past a closed curtain when two hands shot out from underneath it and grabbed me by the ankles! I shrieked like a ten-year-old girl at that one, which caused the perpetrators much amusement. I gave that curtain a wide birth every night afterwards, I can tell you.

The trial I'd enrolled in was absurdly well paid.

The main reason for this was we were testing an experimental pain-killer.

And in order to test a pain-killer, there is one unavoidable requirement:

Pain.

Lots of it, ideally.

And so, for the next two weeks a crack team of doctors and nurses resolved to cause me as much pain as they possibly could – all the while monitoring my responses for signs that their drug was working.

Sounds like fun, eh?

"So, this is your torture chamber!" I said to the doctor on my first morning.

I'd been hoping for a bit of light banter to take my mind off what was coming.

But it was not to be.

"Yes," he said simply.

Oh dear.

"So, today we'll be using this," he held up a tiny syringe. "It's capsaicin, the active ingredient in chillies, and we'll be injecting it directly into your veins."

"Okay."

He at least had the decency to sound apologetic when he said the next part. "It's going to be quite unpleasant. Tests show it can rate up to ten or eleven on the Intolerable Pain Scale."

"Oh! What does the scale go up to?"

"Twelve."

Well, he was right about one thing.

It was agony.

Like having a red hot poker shoved into my arm, with the searing heat spreading further and further with every passing second.

"And how much does it hurt now?" came the question, asked calmly by the doctor sitting across from me. "On a scale of one to ten?"

"AAARRRR!" I replied.

"So, pretty bad is it?"

"AHHHRRRR! ARRRR!"

"Shall I call that a 'ten' then?"

After the pain died down, I chatted with the doctor. He had to keep asking me about my pain level for half an hour, so we had plenty of time. All I could think of was being grateful that the pain didn't last the whole time. I think I'd have passed out.

"A couple of people did pass out," the doctor confided, when I voiced my concerns.

"Really? From my group?"

"Yes! This morning. The pain was too much for them."

"Who was it?"

"Oh, I can't tell you that. But I can guess that they were on the placebo, rather than the actual drug we're testing."

"Oh really? And which am I on then?"

"I don't know. None of us know who is on what, in case it influences how we record the results. But I'll say one thing for you…"

"What's that?"

"You didn't pass out."

Great.

So either I was so used to hurting myself that I'd developed a super-high tolerance for pain – which was a proud thought, as it fit in well with the toughened adventurer I pictured myself as – or, more realistically, I was taking the pain-killer.

Which meant that next week, I'd be on the placebo…

I was glad when that trial was over.

For two reasons:

One, because the medication was making me a bit ill, even though it did its job at taking the edge off the agony; and two, because they'd paid me well for torturing me; I now had almost three thousand pounds, with which I could do absolutely anything than my heart desired.

I knew full well what my heart desired; it had been desiring it ever since my last conversation with Toby in Ecuador, almost a year ago.

Diving.

And volunteering.

In Thailand!

I couldn't help daydreaming about it as I sat clutching my cheque on the train back from London, giving not one shit for the cold stares of my fellow passengers. I'd picked a bad time to wear a t-shirt; there were puncture marks up, down and around both arms, concentrated on all the major veins, and I was sitting there cackling to myself with the excitement of being free, and being rich. Oh, and the plastic medical bracelet was still around my wrist, but I didn't notice that until I got home.

I told my Commanding Officer in the TA to put my training on hold, and that I'd be back to complete it in a couple of months.

And then I set off at last, on the adventure I'd been lusting after for so long.

The biggest adventure. The best adventure!

The adventure of a lifetime.

Thailand

Thailand, when I finally got there, was everything I had hoped it would be.

I had an absolute blast.

The END.

What? You want more? You want *details?*
But this book is already so looong!
Really?
You're not kidding?
Ah... bugger it. Okay then.
But you might want to put a jacket on.
This is where it gets messy...

More About Thailand.

Okay, so here's what happened.

The 'airport' on the southern Thai island of Koh Samui could easily have been confused with a drive-through beach bar. And not only because there were locals trying to sell me beer from their coolers as I climbed down the rickety steps from the plane.

I'd been to a few large-scale modern airports recently, and had developed a certain set of expectations; Bangkok, the Thai capital, had been bang on the money. Acres of marble floor tiles. High-end boutique shops with walls of glass. Every sign and price-tag translated into English, because everyone knows that English-speaking tourists a) have the most money, and b) are the most gullible. There are two main types of product available in these places; incredibly crap kitsch, like shoddily-made handicrafts and souvenirs, which are alarmingly expensive; and alarmingly expensive things, like Prada handbags, which are utterly insanely expensive.

That whole 'Duty Free' thing is a big fat lie. *Nothing* is cheaper in an airport.

Unless you fly to Koh Samui.

Looking around, from the single concrete runway the size of a quiet village street to the small group of thatched wooden shacks that seemed to serve as the airport itself, I had the feeling that the three grand in my bank account would probably buy the place.

The steps squeaked rhythmically as they were wheeled away from the plane by two guys in filthy jeans. I don't think they even worked there; either they were helping out because they were bored, or they were stealing the staircase; either way, no-one seemed to care.

I followed the rest of the passengers towards the largest of the huts, and tried to ignore the sight of our luggage being tossed out of a door in the side of the plane by another scruffy looking dude. A friend of his on the ground was doing his best to catch the bags, and was succeeding with about one in four.

But he did have a big trolley with him, so presumably he wasn't stealing our bags. Playing basketball with some of them perhaps, but that's all.

Sometimes, in travel books, I read phrases like 'immigration was a formality'.

Well here it wasn't even a formality; the Thai bloke who stamped my passport was barefoot, wearing shorts and a t-shirt and a big smile.

He aimed that smile straight at me as I stood in front of him – not even glancing at the passport as he stamped it – and trotted out a well-practised "Welcome to Thailand!"

And that was that – I was in.

There were no biometric scanners.

There was an x-ray machine, but no-one was bothering to use it, and anyway my rucksack was still being roughed up by the locals, so I copied the passengers who'd already been welcomed to the country – which meant waiting by a big pile of suitcases on the pavement until the next trolley-load arrived.

I'd met a cute girl on the plane, and when her luggage never arrived, I did the charitable thing and waited with her. She'd offered me a ride to Koh Pha Ngan in her boyfriend's boat the next day, but that – along with her bags – never materialised. Instead I spent the night in a rather expensive resort, woke up at 5am thinking it was time to leave, then went back to bed and slept until midday. She was gone, of course, when I dragged myself out of bed.

Never mind.

I went to order a taxi at the bar, and the barman instantly offered to take me to the ferry himself.

On his motorbike.

I'd never been on a motorbike before.

I was starting to remember what entering a new country was like for me. The first thing on the agenda was to make all those embarrassing cultural mistakes, to get them out of the way as quickly as possible so that I had plenty of time to make regular mistakes.

This time was no different.

I looked around for a helmet and saw none. I looked at the barman as he mounted his bike and tapped my head. He frowned back, then tapped his own head quite forcefully.

Had he understood my safety concerns and tried to respond in a reassuring manner? Or did he think I'd just called him a mental case?

I climbed on the back of the motorbike and instinctively clutched the barman around the waist. He froze. I froze. Then I slowly peeled my arms from around him and found a well-worn handle just behind me.

Tony James Slater

I had a feeling the price for this ride had just gone up.

Soon we were blasting through the jungle at top speed, the bike bouncing and spluttering, me gripping the handle with both hands and noticing only now that it was loose.

But it didn't matter. The strip of sky above us was flawlessly blue, the full strength of the sun was making the foliage on either side of us glow; it was beautiful, exciting and exotic.

As opposed to the road, which was just fucked.

There was more pothole than solid surface, and every time the bike bounced through another deep gouge I slid down the seat and slammed groin-first into the barman's arse.

Not on purpose I hasten to add, but due to the violence of the bike's motion; I now had an insight into why guys normally drive these things, with their girlfriends hanging off the back. It's because guys aren't built to ride on the back. My love spuds were taking such a pounding they were aching all the way up to my stomach. It was a good job I wouldn't need to use them anytime soon, as I doubted they'd be functional for a few days. It would be pretty awkward to get intimate with someone, and then have to explain to that I'd bruised my balls by slapping them too hard against a barman's buttocks.

Luckily he didn't mind. He was happy with his fare – one hundred Thai baht, which equates to about £1.80. He was happy because he knew he was ripping me off; I was happy because it was ridiculously cheap for a mini adventure which had lasted for about half an hour. You pay a lot of money for rides like that at Alton Towers.

I filled up on chicken and fried rice from a stall outside the ferry office while I waited for the boat to arrive. It was delicious, so simple and so incredibly cheap – a whole meal for less than a pound. This was more like what I was expecting, and it did bode well for my stay. My return flight to England was booked for three months hence, giving me the same amount of time here as I'd had in Ecuador. Both countries were reputedly cheap to live in, but there would be additional expenses to cope with this time around; diving, which I hadn't been able to do in Ecuador on account of living on top of a mountain, and partying which had been a rare occurrence for the same reason. Bloody mountain.

This time there would be no mountains between me and the single most vibrant party scene on the planet – and I had three whole months to take advantage of it.

I was looking forward to every single minute as I boarded the ferry to Koh Pha Ngan island.

PAC, or Phangan Animal Care, was where I'd arranged to volunteer. They had a serious mission: to help and care for the stray animals of the entire island. Anyone who's been to Thailand knows of their problem with stray dogs. They roam the cities and the beaches alike, singly or in packs, fighting over scraps and garbage. They get beaten by locals and disgusted tourists, injured through fighting, ravaged by disease and flattened by the traffic.

Even worse was the government's chosen solution; once a year a truck used to drive from one end of the island to the other, dropping poisoned meat the whole way. Strays would eat it. Pets would eat it. And whether owned or homeless they would die a hideous, agonising death and then lie rotting in the tropical sun until someone flung the remains into the forest.

PAC had been founded by a visiting vet from Hong Kong, who had been so appalled by the state of the animals and the casual cruelty shown to them that she had devoted most of her life to creating and maintaining the only centre for veterinary medicine on the island.

It was a huge success.

Since PAC had been working on Koh Pha Ngan, the poison trucks hadn't returned.

Seeing the island's coastline approaching, it didn't look like the last battleground between dog and man. It looked… like paradise.

Postcard-perfect beaches bordered deep green jungle, a blanket of dense-looking foliage that dominated the whole of the island. A mountain range rose in the centre, heavily forested, and even as we came closer there seemed to be no sign of human habitation. Only the squat concrete dock loomed into view, leading me to believe that the towns I was expecting would be buried deep in the rainforest.

It wasn't quite like that.

As the ferry docked, the chaos of the town around it came into focus. Motor scooters buzzed everywhere like killer bees on steroids, loaded up with ridiculous amounts of goods and people. A huge number of them were already queuing to catch the ferry on its return journey, revving their pipsqueak engines as though that would make the rest of us get off faster. The noise was intense.

From half a mile out it had seemed quite serene. Now that I'd arrived it sounded like the biggest hair-dryer fight in the world was taking place right around the corner.

I was met at the pier by Avril, a smiling, blonde woman in her thirties.

"Welcome to Koh Pha Ngan," she said, with a strong Irish accent.

"What do you think of Thong Sala?"

"I'm sorry?"

"This place! Thong Sala. It's our capital city."

"It's noisy! Is it all this busy?"

"This IS all of it. There's only two streets, and the docks," she made a triangle with her hands to demonstrate the layout. "But don't worry. We don't come into the city much."

She looked at the giant rucksack strapped to my back. "Will you be okay taking your bag on the back of my bike?"

I'd noticed the scooter, parked a little way behind her. But it looked like such a piece of shit that I'd assumed it was abandoned.

The bike groaned when she climbed onto it, and it took several tries before its engine coughed and spluttered into life.

"Clinic bike," she explained, rolling her eyes. "We have a trailer we attach when we go to collect dogs for treatment or surgery."

Wow. It didn't look like it would pull me, let alone a steel cage full of anxious animals. If the rest of the clinic equipment was in similar repair it was going to be a tough few months…

I climbed on the back of the bike and remembered just in time not to try clutching Avril around the waist.

Though I don't think she'd have minded.

Avril was relentlessly cheerful. She'd spent half a year as the administrator of PAC, running the day to day business and keeping up with all the paperwork. Her constant smile was contagious – between that and the bone-shaking ride through the jungle I was grinning like a maniac when she turned off the main road into the grounds of the island's high school. Behind the school lay the clinic – two buildings converted from teachers' accommodations, one for the surgery and one for the office. Avril lived above one and the full-time nurses above the other. Dogs of all sizes came running to greet us, some on three legs, all very excited.

"Get down! Boogles! Down Ploy!" Avril was the epicentre of a small canine whirlwind. "They're all very friendly," she told me. Then "Look!" she addressed the pack. "This is Tony!"

All eyes swung towards me. And the licking commenced.

Hell's Angel

After I extricated myself from the dog pile – covered in slobber – Avril gave me a quick tour. The clinic's two buildings were identical; her home and admin office was in the one on the right. The one on the left sported a tiny kitchen area and a surgery with a stainless steel operating table. There was a small dog strapped to it having things best left undescribed done to him, so I didn't try to make conversation with the pair of nurses in attendance. One was a miniature Thai lady, who Avril told me was called Por; she lived and worked here full-time, whereas the other nurse position was filled by a string of volunteers much like myself. Well, except for two things: they were all qualified vet nurses, of course; and to date, they had all been women.

A wooden staircase separated the clinic area from the kitchen, leading to two bedrooms upstairs for the nurses. It was a very compact set-up, with a series of animal pens just beyond the back door. None of the occupants looked thrilled to be there, and most of them had something quite obviously wrong with them; bandages were evident on the patients who'd been treated, and open wounds on some of those still waiting. Flies buzzed and mosquitoes whined, and the rough ground behind the clinic graduated into full jungle less than twenty metres away. To say the place was primitive was an understatement of epic proportions – but then, if they'd been stocked and equipped with the last word in veterinary technology, they probably wouldn't have been needing me.

I reckoned I could live with it.

According to Avril, a motorbike lesson was the next order of business.

She took me across to the school playing field, which had a dirt track running around the edge of it. She pushed the bike onto the track, started it up, and let me get on it alone.

All I could think of were those 'Funniest Home Videos' shows. My brain instantly conjured up the image of me twisting the throttle way too hard, causing the bike to rear up in a crazy wheelie, dumping me off before making a brief bid for freedom all on its own.

But I think that scenario is based on a somewhat more powerful vehicle.

I did twist the throttle too hard – because it was looser than my tongue – and the clinic bike, with all the power at its command, burbled a little, then stalled.

Without moving an inch.

"Ah, she's a bit temperamental all right," Avril explained. "There's a bit of a knack to it. Ye've got to treat her gentle, like."

I tried again, and managed to coax a few feet of horizontal movement before the bike conked out.

"That's grand," said Avril, applauding my efforts. "It took me most of a day to get it that far. Let's go get you a real bike."

And with that, my lesson was over.

I was now a biker.

With me on the back, Avril guided the clinic bike down the main road at top speed. Before long there was a queue of traffic built up behind us, cars taking it in turns to shoot past us violently with the drivers leaning on the horn. People pushing prams on the pavement were overtaking us. I started to feel a bit sea-sick, with the bike wobbling from side to side as Avril fought to keep it upright.

"She's not the fastest," she called back over her shoulder.

No shit, I wanted to say. But I was far too polite of course. Avril seemed like the kind of person I could say anything to, but I didn't want to push it just yet. And in any case, the clinic was her baby; maybe the bike was too.

Because otherwise it should have been skipped.

Rough buildings lined the road on both sides, concrete shells decked out as shops and in some cases houses, but with wild countryside visible behind and between them. A vast tangle of power lines followed us overhead every step of the way, almost low enough to touch in some places. The road was good though, smooth, with lines painted on it, even taking us over bridges now and then.

By the time Avril pulled in to the forecourt of the bike rental shop, I'd started to relax.

There wasn't much else to do on a ride that long. I think I'd have been quicker jogging.

We'd passed gateways to posh resorts with fancy gold signs and shanty shacks built of sticks and driftwood – often right next to one another. And we'd passed bike rental shops beyond counting. I could only assume this wasn't tourist season, and that before long I'd see all those shiny motor scooters zipping around full of holiday-makers; but for now they were lined up side by side, legions of steeds bereft of riders. It made me wonder why we'd come all the way to this rather ramshackle looking place.

I guessed Avril had her reasons.

A lean, balding bloke in his late forties emerged from the shop and fixed us with a scowl. "Oh yeah? Whaddaya want?" His gruff American accent made it sound like he was shouting at us – when in reality, all he was doing was snarling.

"Hi Yorik!" Avril said, brightly. "I've brought you another volunteer in need of some wheels!"

Yorik did not seem impressed.

"He hates women," she explained, after he swore at her and disappeared back into his shop. "Actually he hates everybody. But he gives us a good discount for clinic volunteers."

"Why?" I had to ask.

"I have absolutely no idea. Maybe he just… likes animals?"

There was no time to ponder the problem. Yorik was back, pushing a bright blue scooter. He frowned as he presented it to me. "You ever ridden one a these before?"

"Uh… yeah, sure," I lied.

"Okay. Any damage – you pay for it. Now gimmie yer passport."

I pulled the little brown book out of my back pocket and tried to smooth it back into shape. All the freedom of the world, condensed into thirty-six miniature pages. I'd grown quite protective of it.

"Will it be safe?" I asked.

He gave me a dark look.

"Okay," I said meekly, and handed it over.

Yorik snatched it off me and stormed back into the shop.

"I don't think he likes me either," I muttered.

"It's because you're with me. He's a misogynist."

"No wonder he's sick of women, if he's spent his whole life staring up vaginas."

Avril sniggered. "Not a gynaecologist!"

"Oh. Right. Is he gay then?"

"No. He's married."

"Married? To a local girl?"

"Yep. It happens a lot. Sex tourism. You know, buy yourself a sweet Thai bride?"

I looked past the desk where Yorik was rooting through a pile of keys, to spot his wife lurking in the depths of the shop. The woman weighed at least twice what Yorik did, and had a face like a lowland gorilla.

"I don't think he married her for the sex," I told Avril. "Or if he did... maybe that's why he's so pissed off?!"

Then we had to shut up, as Yorik was back with the key. "Don't lose it. You get drunk and drop it in the sea, you pay for it."

"Okay."

"Deposit's five hundred."

And just like that, I had a bike.

100cc of pure adrenaline – with a nifty wire shopping basket attached to the front. If only I owned a leather jacket...

I loved that bike.

Even though I fell off it a day later.

Next on the agenda was a place to stay.

I wobbled after Avril down a sandy track which led to a primary school, then on past it into the jungle. Less than a minute later we passed a peeling sign that read 'Liberty Bungalows', and emerged onto the beach.

A cluster of huts surrounded a raised central seating area that was covered in long cushions. It had the look of an open-air opium den. I could hear pots and pans clattering in a kitchen-shack built onto the back of it.

Avril gave a 'halloo!', and a slender Thai lady who I guessed to be about thirty came out of the kitchen to meet us.

"This Is Eieu," Avril said. "Eieu, have you got a bungalow for Tony? He's working with us at the clinic for, what? Three months?"

I nodded.

"Sorry, we full now," said Eieu.

You really have nothing?" Avril pressed.

"Ahhh... Have one, but, it not really good for... person."

I shrugged. "Can I have a look?"

The tiny wooden bungalow sat on low stilts, with rough plank steps up to a balcony at the front. Inside was a home-made double bed, with a small wardrobe built into the foot; the whole room was less than two meters square. The two windows were just framed holes in the wall, with wooden shutters on the outside, but there was an ancient fan mounted opposite the bed. A door led to an equally minute bathroom, with a cold water shower hose on the wall and a toilet with a bucket next to it for flushing.

"Have power!" the landlady said proudly, flicking a light switch.

The single bulb dangling from the ceiling flickered into life.

"I like it," I said.

The bungalow was tucked away at the edge of the jungle, on such an angle that from the balcony I looked right down the middle of the resort to the sea. The hammock, stretched perfectly across the view-side of the balcony, sealed the deal.

"It's perfect," I told Eieu.

She seemed shocked, then pleased. "I can do for you, for one-hundred-fifty *baht*. With discount."

That was less than three pounds a night.

It was good to be a volunteer here.

And now I had a home.

Things were looking up.

"I'll leave you to get settled in," Avril said. "Dunno if you're interested – a load of volunteers are leaving tomorrow, so we're throwing a party for them tonight. It's a shame really, because it'd be a great way to meet everyone, but you must be absolutely knackered."

"Yeah…"

Wait a minute – a party? Full of clinic volunteers, past and present… all of whom were women.

Suddenly I didn't feel nearly as tired.

"Yeah, I'm not too bad actually. I guess I could try and make an effort."

"Oh! That's grand! I'll come and pick you up at eight, then."

And she puttered off on the clinic bike, leaving me grinning at my luck.

I was starting to think I might like it here.

Party Time

The promised party was at the house of a previous volunteer, an English bloke who'd loved Koh Pha Ngan so much he'd decided to stay. His house was a-ways back in the jungle, with enough land to support a menagerie of broken animals; three legged dogs and cats that couldn't pee unaided, all ex-patients of the clinic that had nowhere else to go. Avril led me there, rattling along on the clinic bike, to a residence more Japanese in style than the Thai huts I was getting used to.

Drinks were already flowing, so I helped myself to a beer and a cushion on the floor, and set out to make some friends.

Two entire sides of the house were open to the outside, letting the cooler evening air and the sounds of the jungle flow in. It was like partying in Tarzan's basement.

A few hours in, almost magically, someone produced a spliff. It was passed around, some people partaking, some not – and I was eager to show off my worldliness to my new-found friends. I took a couple of puffs on the spliff and passed it on, and a few seconds later it hit me, and I was lost.

I drank, I chatted – probably nonsensical bollocks, not that I can remember any of it – and I even made flirty eye contact with a seriously hot chick who'd spent most of the party sitting in a hammock that stretched right across the middle of the room.

"That looks comfy," I said to her at one point – so she invited me in.

Lounging there in that hammock, laying back against her slender body, my shoulders pressed back against her breasts, it all fell into place. This was the kind of experience I'd been after, the kind of thing that could never happen to me back home. It wasn't England's fault – or not entirely – it was mine. I couldn't loosen up there, couldn't trust to fate and let myself go. I would never have had the courage to approach this girl there for fear of an obvious and very public rejection. But here, away from the world, where no-one knew me at all; here I could be anything. Could be anyone.

'*Who Dares, Wins,*' I thought, remembering the motto of the British SAS.

And it's true.

Even if my experience is slightly closer to 'Who Dares, Gets Severely Injured In The Process.'

The number of party-goers had dwindled as the night wore on.

Soon there was only a handful of us left, including the English guy whose house this was, and his Swedish girlfriend.

Finally the chick behind me made a move as though to get up. I was struggling to stand by this point, it must be said – something that did not go unnoticed.

"I'd better drive him home," she told our hosts, "there's no way he can drive in this state."

So she led me outside, climbed on to my bike and helped me settle behind her. I pressed my chest against her back, which felt good, and slid my hands up towards her boobs.

She noticed – but did nothing. Just kicked the bike into life and started walking it backwards, an awkward manoeuver at the best of times. I clung on, rather happily, as she pointed us towards the road and set off.

She drove; I groped; and the jungle whirled by all around us.

We reached my resort, parked the bike and staggered up the steps to my balcony.

"What now?" I slurred.

"Well, my bike is back at the house. And you're far too drunk. I shouldn't leave you alone."

And she slid past me into the bungalow, making as much body contact as is physically possible without resorting to contortion.

I couldn't believe it! All my life I'd been looking for the kind of girl that would say something like that to me. It was a line straight out of the dodgy videos I used to hide under my bed. If only I'd known; all those years of lusting in vain, when all I had to do was go to Thailand!

It was a spectacular night.

I think.

All I remember was waking, naked, curled around the equally naked form of a slender young lady. A light misting of sweat lay over both of us.

It was hot.

She was hot.

I was hot! I'd been on the island for less than twenty-four hours and already I'd gotten drunk, stoned and laid. No wonder this place had such a reputation! It was already way beyond my wildest expectations.

And at that exact moment, the hangover hit.

By mid-morning I was feeling very sorry for myself indeed.

My partner for the night had departed the island, dashing my hopes of having found true love within a day of arriving. She'd survived the night with very little discomfort, suggesting that of the pair of us I'd been the only one with severely impaired judgement. Clearly, she'd taken advantage of my inebriated state to have her wicked way with me – in point of fact, I'd been used.

That was the good news.

The bad news was, it was roasting hot, horrendously humid, and I was sweating out pure alcohol. The stink of me was only exceeded in disgustingness by two things: (1) the taste of my mouth, like the floor of a hamster's cage, and (2) the job I was doing. Which was crawling on my knees around the back of the animal clinic, scrubbing the blood, puss and vomit out of the dog kennels.

Yes, I know what you're thinking – it was a struggle not to add to the mess I was removing. I've heard people complain about the things they consider least compatible with a raging hangover – things like raw fish, more alcohol, playing badminton – or all three – but I think it's safe to say that oozing scab juice and diarrhoea takes the biscuit.

Ugh. I didn't even want to *think* about biscuits.

I tried to put on a cheery face. After all, my exploits of the previous night were already legendary. Had there been a staff of trusty lads in residence I'd have achieved borderline immortality in one day – but sadly, one night stands are one of the more obvious issues on which the genders disagree. Amongst the all-female complement of the clinic I had instead achieved notoriety, of the 'watch out for that guy – he'll get you drunk, drug you and try to shag you' variety. I felt this was rather unfair, particularly since I'd been on the opposite end of that exact equation. I'm not saying I was unhappy about it – far from it – and the only thing I'd have done differently, given the chance, was try a bit harder to remember the girl's name. My memory, which struggles enough with names when I'm sober, had done a real number on me. None of the girls at the clinic were prepared to enlighten me, and the lack of that single piece of information was cited as evidence that I was not to be trusted. Which was possibly true, but still unfair.

I would almost have believed I was on punishment detail, down on my knees in the kennels – but no. This job needed doing every morning. It was why I was here.

The rest of my job, when not out walking dogs, was to do the washing. Piles of donated towels and blankets made up the bedding which lined each cage and all of it needed changing and laundering at least once or twice daily. Surgical cloths and towels used to soak up the more unpleasant side-effects of cutting animals open were added to the pile, as were the cloths used to clean the clinic. All things considered it was a ridiculously towel-intensive operation, requiring a constant flow of clean, dry textiles into the clinic – all of which were rapidly returned soaked in some of the nastiest substances imaginable.

The clinic boasted two battered, top-loading washing machines, one either side of the kennel block. They were identical, pre-cold war Soviet Union-looking models. Both had been donated some time in the last decade by a mysterious benefactor. And neither of them worked.

It made for quite a challenge.

With a prayer and a well-placed kick, I managed to coax one more wash cycle from each machine; they alternated work like a pair of Welsh plumbers, deciding which one felt more like doing something on an hourly basis.

"We've been meaning to get them looked at," Avril told me when she stopped by to see how I was getting on.

"Any idea when?" I asked her.

"Oh, sometime soon. Before Christmas I hope, or maybe in the new year…"

It didn't sound too promising.

"If you hold the lid down on this one, and lean on it really hard when it starts, it often keeps going. But I don't know about the other one."

"One of the nurses told me to kick it."

"Yeah, why not? Might as well try it."

And with that, my training was complete.

I've never felt less like a Jedi.

One thing I could work on though, was my relationship with the rest of the staff. I felt sure they were only teasing me, sort of like an initiation. From what Avril said it had been quite a while since they'd had a bloke working at the clinic – well over a year – and my arrival was bound to cause a stir.

Well, I'd stirred all right. But if I could survive a hurricane at sea, I felt sure I could survive a bit of gossip.

I stepped into the clinic, mercifully much darker than outside, though still hotter than hell and twice as humid.

The volunteer nurse currently in residence was wiping down the examination table after their last visitor. Amanda was stocky, with short, spikey brown hair. Her only concession to girliness was a trail of paw-print tattoos across one shoulder, which disappeared down the back of her top.

"Hot work out there," I told her, hoping to elicit a response.

"Not too bad today," she replied. "I think you're suffering the effects of your rather sordid lifestyle."

I knew I shouldn't let it bother me, but it did, just a bit. I didn't want to be reliving the same joke for the next three months.

"You know, it wasn't my fault, what happened last night. I was the one who was drunk and drugged. I'm not used to that kind of partying! I was so wasted I can hardly remember what happened. If anything, I was the one who got taken advantage of."

I prepared myself for the inevitable sarcasm.

"Aww? Poor boy! It must be so hard, not being in control of yourself."

"Exactly!"

"Having a little man down there, making all the decisions for you."

"No, no! It was the booze making my decisions. In fact I didn't make a single decision last night. Not one! I was plied with drink and then kidnapped. I'm the victim here!"

"Oh, I see. Well don't worry, we can solve that problem for you. We have just the thing."

I didn't like the gleam in her eye as she said that. She was obviously messing with me, but there was a malicious delight in her as she did it. I had the feeling I might be in trouble.

"What do you weigh?" she asked.

"Um, like, twelve stone. About eighty kilos-ish."

I was braced for some staggeringly witty comment about being overpowered by tiny girls, or perhaps something more creative. Instead Amanda tapped out some numbers on a calculator sitting on the steel operating table.

"We might just have enough anaesthetic," she muttered, as though to herself. "Have we got a kit ready?"

Por, the Thai nurse, came over from the kitchen with a bundle wrapped in green cloth. "This one just finish in autoclave."

Amanda took the bundle and unrolled it on the table. It contained a large number of surgical instruments, all gleaming in the light from an overhead lamp on an adjustable arm.

"The table's a bit small," she said, slapping the metal edge, "so we'll do you on the floor."

"Eh?"

She waved her hand over the implements in front of her. "This is a castration kit. See the scalpel? That's for the incision, and these clamps —" she picked up a pair of tongs and squeezed them open and shut, "these hold you open while we go inside."

Then she picked up what can only be described as a miniature ice cream scoop. She held it at an angle and mimed guiding it delicately inside a patient. "This is what we use to take your little beans, and scoop them out like so," she gave a deft flick of the wrist, "and done. Easy peasy! You never need to worry about being taken advantage of again. We can do you right now if you want?"

"Ahhh… thanks, but I'm kind of attached to mine."

"They always are, until we separate them. It only takes one little snip!" and she brandished the scalpel in a circular motion.

"I'll pass, thanks."

"It's too bad you're not living upstairs with us," she said, as she rolled the castration kit shut. "Then we could do you while you're asleep…"

Enough was enough. "Right!" I said, changing tack. "I've scrubbed the kennels. What's the next job?"

Amanda gestured over to the kitchen table, where a pile of familiar-looking instruments lay basking on a green surgical cloth. "We need some more kits making up if you don't mind. There's a list of how many blades and how many clamps go in each one. You can start with the castration kits. We always need those the most."

Something in her expression told me this wasn't the last time I'd be hearing about this. Even being teased about it made my spuds retract defensively.

"Wrap them nice and tight," Amanda said, "and keep them clean. Don't want to go making any more mistakes now, do we?"

Meetings

As I recovered from the excitement of my first week on the island, there came an announcement that would change everything.

PAC was about to receive another volunteer.

I'm not sure what I expected, but I'd seen pictures on their website of previous volunteers and was prepared for the worst; a six-foot, shaven-headed uber-feminist, with enough piercings to suspend her from the ceiling and t-shirts that said things like 'The way to a man's heart is through his chest'.

In the last few days I'd caught a break from the Castration Crowd, but I knew it was only temporary; sooner or later I was bound to do something to rile them up again. It was in my nature.

So it was with no small amount of trepidation that I awaited the arrival of my opposite number; the second clinic assistant with whom I'd be splitting the weekly rota, a woman I'd have to work hand-in-glove with for the next three months and someone who, if she didn't like me, would really be able to make my life miserable.

It might not be obvious, but I'm not very good with women. At the best of times, they scare me. They are mysterious and complex, and quite often contradictory. I have a tendency to say the wrong thing at the wrong time, and end up labelled as insensitive, or needy, or a show-off. (All of which are true, incidentally.)

This time it was important. This time, I had to play it cool.

No piss-taking. No sarcasm. No ogling.

It was going to be tough.

I'd worked myself up to the point where I was seriously considering hiding in my bungalow until she went away again – by this time I was half expecting the antichrist.

Instead, we got Linda.

Linda was yet another savage from the distant shores of Ireland; was there no end to them? Yet she was different, a waif-like creature, small and slight, with raven-dark hair and a perfectly contrasting, gleaming white complexion.

I don't think Ireland had seen the sun in over a decade at that point.

At first glance she didn't look strong enough to survive the kind of ordeals I'd already been through, much less cope with months of heavy dog restraint.

But as it turned out, Linda had something in spades that was totally absent from me: common sense.

By way of illustrating this point, let me tell you about my first bike accident.

I was practicing by driving down the loose sandy track to Liberty Bungalows.

I rode shakily around the first corner, dipping to one side a bit like motorcyclists do in the TT. The effect was immediate; the bike swung smoothly round the bend – and I felt like a pro! Which was a little dangerous.

"Neeeeooooowwwm!" I went, as I leaned lower through the next curve. The theme tune from Mission Impossible struck up in my head, air rushed past me and I twisted the throttle. I sped towards the next corner – probably doing something approaching twenty miles an hour. The exhilaration of speed and the joy of mastering this shrieking behemoth of steel and plastic culminated in a shriek of defiance as I powered into the last bend. I leaned over as far as I dared – which was too far, apparently – and the bike slid from under me, dumping me in the dirt.

Panic kicked in immediately as I lay there in the road. I was the injured party in a high-speed collision with the ground. I'd been here less than two days. Was I badly damaged? Was this the end of my Thailand adventure already? The pain was… completely absent. This meant I was in shock. I recognised the symptoms; my injured limbs were numb, waiting for my brain to regain control before clamouring for attention. How bad were they? Could I tell? Could I move? Could I stand…?

I stood.

I dusted myself off.

I had a grazed elbow.

A bit.

Triumph flooded through my system, along with litres of unshed blood. I had done it! I had survived! My first motorbike accident, and I was walking away unharmed! A quick check of the bike showed nothing more serious than a chewed-up bit of rubber on the end of the foot rest. Oh, and the girly wire basket on the front had somehow been crushed, but I didn't count this as a loss. The rest of my machine, like me, was built of sterner stuff.

To be honest, I hadn't been driving at jet fighter speed – probably something closer to a milk float – if it was going up a steep incline. And if it was fully-laden, and the driver was being careful not to shake up his bottles of fizzy-pop.

But still, I felt like a daredevil. I felt like a legend. And I was indestructible!

All the same, I pushed the bike the rest of the way.

Linda never fell off her bike, because she never drove it more than fifteen miles an hour. Linda liked to exercise a thing called 'caution'. Now, caution to me was a concept much like trigonometry; I'd heard of it, and looked into briefly while I was at school, but could find no practical application for it. In this way Linda was a bit like an anti-me; she spent a lot of her time in Thailand trying to talk me out of doing things she considered dangerous, even though I thought of them as fun.

Come to think of it, she probably kept me alive well past my expected expiry date. She very nearly convinced me to give up my newly-discovered hobby of taxi-surfing – but not quite. Taxi surfing was way too much fun.

Our first outing together was to the Full Moon Party, which had been looming on the horizon like a storm of possibility.

"Let's not get too drunk," I suggested, remembering my last experience at a moon party.

"Yes, that's best," she agreed.

No doubt she'd heard the story herself.

So we took a taxi to the beach town of Haad Rin in the south of the island, rocking up as thousands of revellers descended on the bar-lined strip of sand.

The taxi ride itself was something of an eye-opener; between the resort I was staying at and the party capital of the island were a series of insanely steep hills, which I considered to be mountains. Somehow, no matter where I went, there was always at least one mountain. And I was destined to be on the wrong side of it.

The taxi was a covered truck, with a cab up front and two benches facing each other in the back, with a little roof of tarp to keep the worst of the weather off us. Linda held on very tightly indeed as we shuddered up the first hill, her eyes wide with fear; I wondered if anyone ever did fall out the back of these things, and go tumbling down the hillside and over the cliff edge at the bottom. From there it was a few hundred metres straight down to where the sea lashed jagged rocks at the base of the island.

I held on a little tighter too, as we crested the hill in first gear. I could tell it was first because every time the driver changed down a gear the car momentarily lost its battle with gravity and slowed almost to a stop. Whether the driver delighted in putting the shits up us, or was just fairly relaxed about this, he never seemed in a hurry to find the next gear. I swear we were starting to slip backwards a couple of times; hardly surprising given the load we were carrying.

There were ten people in the back of that taxi.

That was why, shortly afterwards, I developed the habit of riding on the roof. It was practical as well as fun; it left more room for everyone else.

So, arriving in party central and thrilled at still being alive, Linda and I headed straight for the nearest bar. Already the beach was crammed with sweaty bodies, pumping to the discordant sound of ten different bars competing for musical dominance.

We swam through the crowd and bought the same drink that everyone else was buying; a plastic bucket, such as you might buy for a child at the seaside, filled with Thai brandy, Red Bull and lemonade. A fistful of straws were shoved in the top to allow several people to share one bucket, but the price – less than two pounds – made it seem wiser to buy one each and avoid having to queue up for service again.

Together, we found a relatively empty piece of beach and shouted at each other over the deafening din of trance meets hip-hop meets Brit-pop meets *Abba*.

"Remember – not too drunk," Linda called, "it could get dangerous here!"

"Yup," I confirmed. "Not too drunk. Not this time."

And that's the last thing I remember.

I woke up draped across a large formation of boulders at the far end of the beach. The sun was high in the sky – it must have been close to midday. Linda was laying next to me, and stirred at the same time I did. We were both burnt to a bright red crisp, and mosquito-bitten to hell in every place that wasn't covered by clothing. I'd lost my shirt at some point during the night. We'd both lost our shoes. Fortunately we hadn't been robbed, so we could both afford to climb into a taxi headed back over the mountains towards Liberty.

That morning I learned that traveling those hills, combined with the terrible quality of the road and the non-existent suspension on the taxi, is not the best thing for a delicate stomach.

But I also learned that, with the vehicle pointing uphill at a ridiculous angle and me sitting right at the back corner, with only a slender metal railing between me and certain death on the road below, being sick was incredibly easy; I didn't even have to lean over.

Linda coped well with the stir we caused in the clinic, when reporting on the outcome of our first night out together.

"Of course nothing happened," she said to the assembled staff. "I mean… *really?*"

There were shrugs and murmurs of agreement at this, as though they were all admitting it was a pretty stupid thing to ask about.

Which I thought was a bit harsh.

Why was it such an unlikely prospect?

What was wrong with me?

Cheeky buggers.

In the end, I think Linda and I had made an unspoken agreement not to hit on each other, due to the trouble it would cause at work if things got complicated between us.

At least, that's what I told myself. I know *I* made an unspoken agreement for sure. I don't know if she did, because… well, we never spoke about it.

Maybe she never fancied me in the first place. Or maybe the sight of me projectile-vomiting downhill from a moving taxi was enough to put her off. Or maybe it was the stories she'd heard about me from the nurses that were putting her off?

Or maybe it was because she thought I was an idiot.

I discovered this opinion the first time I suggested it might be more fun to ride on top of the taxi.

Linda looked at me for a bit as though trying to decide if I was serious. Then she shook her head, clearly giving up. "You're an idiot," she told me.

From that point on, she felt the need to tell me it on an almost daily basis; and in fairness, I think I deserved quite a bit of it.

Although I still maintain, I'm mostly just misunderstood.

Linda and I were inseparable within a week; by the time I left Thailand, she'd become the best friend I'd ever had.

Road To Chaloklum

With Linda's arrival at PAC, I finally had time to investigate this diving lark I'd heard so much about.

Toby, my good friend in Ecuador, had apparently been very good at it – at least until he got run over by a boat and had his back broken. Because of this, I had decided to become fantastic at it; and if I could avoid breaking my back, well, that would put me ahead by several of vertebrae.

Not that I'm at all competitive, but by God I was going to prove to Toby that I was as good as he was at *something*. Because he was already better looking than me, more confident and charismatic, a world traveller with a hundred crazy stories up his sleeve; he had all the personality traits on my shopping list.

Despite being a vegetarian.

(For anyone wondering who the hell Toby is, he was my boss in the animal refuge I worked at in Ecuador, which I may have mentioned once or twice in my first book.)

And for anyone who's interested, at that moment Toby was busy doing something unspeakably heroic; he was single-handedly building a brand new animal refuge in the Ecuadorian Amazon, not far from the town of Puyo. Presumably his spare hand was lifting weights, or guiding old ladies across busy roads; all the time without putting a hair out of place. He was the real deal, that bloke.

I was sick with envy.

So I fired up my scooter for one of the scariest rides I'd yet attempted; the journey all the way across the island to Chaloklum Bay, a tiny bite out of the northern coast where the water was deep enough for boats to dock.

To say there were potholes is like saying politicians tell lies; the road to Chaloklum had more in common with the surface of the moon than with any earthly thoroughfare. It was unpaved for most of its length, after a brief, straight stretch; then it veered off, a winding, twisting ribbon of sand interspersed with holes big enough to swallow three or four amateur scooterists. More interesting were the columns. At some point in the past the government, presumably sick of all the moaning from everyone who lived at the other end of this road, had deigned to fill in the worst of the potholes. In their infinite wisdom they had done this in concrete, presumably so they wouldn't have to do it again. As soon as the rains came the packed-dirt surface of the road washed away, leaving dozens of cement stalagmites protruding from the track – proof if needed that the Thai government was as clueless as any other. In between these monolithic obstacles, new ruts and pot holes formed, creating a course that looked like it had been specifically designed to kill anyone who tried to cross it on a motorbike.

I survived the trip with only a few minor crashes, by taking it very, very slowly. It was a gorgeous drive though, cutting right through the heart of the island's rainforest blanket. At times the trees met overhead, creating a tunnel filled with dappled light. But pretty or not, I'd have to get better at it; the drive took me over an hour, which would get old real quick once I started doing it twice a day.

Chaloklum itself was hardly different from the fishing village it had grown out of. Probably because it hadn't actually grown. It had a real, sealed tarmac road, a Seven Eleven (which are so pervasive in Thailand they outnumber everything but the people) – and not a whole lot else. Oh, there was a long wooden jetty which really looked like an original feature; it was built entirely out of wood, causing me to shit myself the first time my boss drove his truck full of diving tanks along it.

It held, by some miracle, but looked like it could collapse at any given moment; the fact that it swayed in strong winds didn't help much. I never felt safe on that thing.

Especially not when driving on it.

My boss, guide and mentor in all that was diving, was an unassuming bloke called Nick. He was the image of the ex-pat Brit; middle-aged and middle-sized, with a baggy t-shirt over his perma-tan and a calmness that was only to be found on the other side of one too many parties.

His wife was Thai; he spoke Thai with a lovely English accent; and he was serious about diving.

Nick was serious about everything. Even when he was joking, he seemed serious. His voice was quiet, so that when he spoke you had to really listen. And that wasn't a bad thing. Of all the hours I spent listening to Nick, not a single second was wasted.

The first thing he told me was, "I'll only qualify you as a Divemaster if I'd be happy to employ you. I don't give out certificates to anyone who wants to pay for them. So if you'd like, we can do your Open Water course first and see if you have any aptitude."

I loved that about Nick. Not only was he open and honest, but he used words like 'aptitude' in everyday conversation without it sounding out of place. He never said as much, but I could tell he was clever; almost certainly the most intelligent form of life I had yet encountered on Koh Pha Ngan. I think Nick also believed that I was clever. Where the hell he got that idea I'll never know, but he always conversed with me as an equal. He imparted knowledge as though discussing the finer points of something I knew already, which made me want to impress him all the more. Within the first ten minutes of his opening lecture, I knew I'd come to the right place.

There were flashier schools on the island of course. I'd come to Chaloklum Diving initially because of the discount they offered me for being a PAC volunteer. A little further down the main street of Chaloklum (there was really only one street), there was another dive school; they were our main competition, and the owners of the two shops didn't talk to each other. It goes without saying that we looked down on their safety standards, teaching methods, parentage, circumstances of birth etc. – it was only much later that I realised how right we were, and how lucky I was to be with the best.

(When I say we were right, I don't mean about their parentage. They weren't bastards. Well, they were, but not in the literal sense – at least as far as I know.)

Around the corner from us was a massive dive-resort. They were the big boys of the island, and they weren't in competition with anyone. They had flashy adverts in all the guidebooks and a website that didn't look like a ten-year-old knocked it up on his lunch break. They supposedly had all the best gear, the fastest boat, the only 'training pool' on the island (it was a swimming pool), a huge customer base and a vast number of instructors and trainees. Of course, this lends itself well to a kind of diver-factory, where trainees are raised up, certified and packed off on their way with hardly a backward glance; rumour had it that the training they offered was shocking, for no other reason than they'd gotten too big; they were a business first and foremost, a money-making enterprise. I don't think they were too concerned about their instructors, or their customers, so long as they still had plenty of both.

By way of an example, I learned that all Divemaster trainees have to complete a minimum number of dives before they can qualify; I had to keep a log book and record every dive, including the maximum depth reached, the location, the duration of the dive, and any particular points of interest. My log book, given to me by Nick, had a squid on the front. Every entry in the book had to be signed by the trainee and counter-signed by the instructor who accompanied them on the dive. I needed sixty dives before I could graduate as a Divemaster, and what with working at the clinic for half the week I knew it would take a long time to achieve.

At the big dive resort they had the opposite mentality. Whereas Nick was all about careful, methodical study, the building of varied experience and careful personal appraisal, they focused on speed; the more warm bodies they had in the water, and out, and in again, the more cash they had to spend on advertising.

So their Divemaster trainees (hereafter referred to as DMT's) built their log books up by climbing into the swimming pool in full SCUBA gear, sitting on the bottom for ten minutes, then getting out and logging it as a dive. Ten minutes later, they were clear to do another one. Safety obviously wasn't much of an issue, unless someone slipped on the steps and cracked their skull on the pool edge. But the safety of future customers, taken out by these trainees after they qualified and sought employment from some unsuspecting dive school, was dubious to say the least.

And so, my diving career had begun.

In your *face*, Toby!

Ahem.

All I had to do to achieve this sought-after qualification was learn to dive, get good at diving, learn to teach the basics to others, pass a swimming test, an endurance test, study advanced first-aid, complete more than twenty modules, sit almost forty exams, and read over a thousand pages of Nick's shabby old textbooks.

And survive more than a hundred trips back and forth on the Road to Chaloklum.

It's a good job I love a challenge, I thought, as I lay in a pothole halfway home, with my bike on top of me.

Well okay, I thought something similar to that, only laced with the sort of words that people complain about reading.

Ridvanos

Linda's new boyfriend was gorgeous.

He was known as Ridvan because, well, that was his name – or most of it.

I'm pretty sure he was from Bulgaria.

She'd met him on another of our forays into the Koh Pha Ngan party scene.

Yet again we'd lost our shoes, only this time with a twist; we'd both left our brand new flip-flops at the entrance to the bar we'd been dancing in. When we came out neither of us could find a shoe for our left foot; some sadistic arsehole had stolen half a pair of flip-flops from both of us!

As an aside, I later met, then dated, a Swedish girl who confessed to this crime.

"I was so stoned," she told me, "and tripping off my head on magic mushrooms, that I thought it was a great idea! I woke up in my bungalow surrounded by about a hundred of them. I must have stolen every left-footed flip-flop on the beach!"

By that point the righteous fury had long since subsided, so I didn't bother complaining about it.

I just told her that if she'd stuck around till morning she'd have been beaten to death with right-footed flip-flops; probably one of the most amusing ways to die, if not the most profound.

So anyway. Linda had a new man in her life – who was fantastically tanned, but also slightly shorter, and slightly more elfin-built than she was.

Honestly, you could be forgiven for thinking she was dating a ten-year-old boy.

Except that Ridvan, when you got to know him, was much crazier than any ten-year-old boy.

He was like a ball of energy, vibrating at a frequency so dramatic that explosion seemed always imminent. Not in an angry way though;

he had a restless, creative vibe, as though he was constantly itching to do something important.

He honestly believed he was cool, calm and collected, and I guess he was – but not for more than three minutes at a time. Then he'd be up and off somewhere, or pacing around my balcony whilst brainstorming a new idea out loud.

My balcony wasn't built for pacing – no-one bigger than Ridvan could have managed it – and it made him seem all the more dramatic as he had to spin around after every two-and-a-half paces. I used to feel tired just watching him.

And a bit dizzy.

As for talking to him… whew!

He used to love telling me that he was the second greatest Rastafarian in the world, after Bob Marley.

"But you're not Jamaican," I pointed out. "You're… what the hell are you anyway?"

"I'm Bulgarian," he declared, shrugging away this gap in his logic, "But my spirit is Jamaican."

"You don't have dreadlocks."

"I could grow dreadlocks."

"But you don't have that big hat thingummy… Ridvan, we live in the stoner capital of the world, and you don't even smoke weed!"

"I do!" he declared. "Sometimes…"

Ridvan was far too busy to smoke weed. But despite spending almost all our free time together as best friends, neither Linda nor I had any idea what he did. Or how, or why – or where. But halfway through a meal, or whilst watching a DVD we'd rented, he would suddenly stand up. "Oh, I gotta go do this thing," he'd say. "See you guys later." And he'd be off, speeding away on his scooter and vanishing into the jungle. I used to think that he had too much energy for it to be contained by something as mundane as a meal or a movie. He vibrated from place to place in the same way his conversation rebounded between topics; I swear he could conduct four different conversations with me simultaneously, switching back and forth between them faster than I could follow. He was a force of nature, of natural, over-abundant charisma; and he was the very definition of that fine line between genius and madness.

Ridvan's spirit was certainly creative and enthusiastic – manic even – but it sure as hell wasn't Jamaican.

Ridvan had friends and contacts in every corner of the island. He talked variously about starting up a radio station, websites, magazines, a new party, and at one point (with me) a t-shirt empire!

I don't think any of it ever came to fruition, but it certainly kept him occupied.

Oh, and on top of everything else, he had a day-job; he was a freelance photographer, which meant that wherever he went and whatever he did, half his time was spent photographing it.

When my parents sent me a digital camera as an early Christmas present, together with a sarcastic note suggesting that I use it to send them some photos, I obliged by taking one of the front of my bungalow. Then I gave the thing to Ridvan, to use as a back-up when his main camera ran out of batteries.

I'm not a very photo-minded person; that was the second picture I'd taken since my arrival in Thailand, and it was also my last.

Who needs a camera when you've got your own personal photographer following you around?

Even if he does sometimes suggest you do strange things for his pictures...

It was Ridvan who suggested the three of us visit the herbal sauna, a little-known place on temple-land, not far down the road from the turn-off for Liberty.

It wasn't until we got there that we realized it was segregated; Linda was led off alone, presumably to some sun-drenched temple where near-naked nymphets rubbed each other all over with perfumed oils and wild flowers; whereas Ridvan and I sweated cheek-to-jowl with ten massively fat Thai guys in a room the size of a medieval prison cell. Seriously – there were tiled benches down both walls and a single tiny window with a grate on it. The roof was too low to permit standing, at least for me, and the 'herbal' part of the sauna came from the abundant supply of Aloe Vera which had been dumped in the steam to the point where I could taste it in the back of my throat. It tasted like a sweet, sharp acid, mixed with the sweat of ten obese rugby players after a night out on the curry. Or maybe it *was* the sweat of ten obese men; that stuff was coating so much of me by the time we got out of there that it was hard to tell.

We burst from the sauna able to stand it no longer, with tears streaming down our faces from the aloe, coughing from the heavy atmosphere and dripping with so much sweat that we knew it couldn't possibly all be ours.

There was a huge water barrel waiting, thoughtfully provided for just such a realization. We didn't hesitate to douse ourselves repeatedly, using the same kind of plastic bowl I used to flush the toilet in my bungalow.

Linda looked rather less traumatized when she emerged; we never found out where she'd been, but I guessed it had been a more relaxing experience than ours, and substantially less like endurance sumo wrestling.

I can't remember if it was Ridvan or me that suggested we get a massage from the toothless old lady who sat outside the sauna, but I'm fairly sure it was Ridvan who encouraged me to go first.

"It's not… you know, a dodgy massage?" I asked him.

"Hell no! This is a temple, man! It's healthy. It's relaxing."

"Are you going to have one?"

"Sure man, sure. But she can only do one of us at once. I can wait."

"Oh. Okay then."

What followed was not, even in the remotest sense, healthy.

Healthy means different things to different people – everything from 'an apple a day' to sleeping on a bed of nails and rising at 5am for a bowl of rice and self flagellation. The massage that I was now subjected to (and I use the word massage in its loosest possible sense) was one step removed from torture.

Now, I've never actually been tortured, so I apologise to anyone that has if by describing my experience thus I am somehow belittling theirs. But fuck me, it hurt like a bastard.

My masseuse sat on me with a distinct 'CRACK!' from my spine. She then took a hold of my arm and, with one foot on my rib cage and one foot on my neck, stretched it back in a technique I've only ever seen in wrestling matches. There was another resounding 'CRACK!'. This one I could feel coming.

Over the next hour, every joint in my body met and exceeded its design tolerance. I met and exceeded my pain threshold quite a few times, but each cry of "Oh Jesus NO! ARGH!" seemed only to spur my tiny tormentor on. She shoved her knuckles deep into my flesh, pressing with super-human strength on what I can only assume must be the pain centres of the body. It was all I could do to keep from screaming.

Maybe it's a language barrier thing. Maybe she was thinking 'Wow, he's really loving this!'. Whatever the case, she bent to her task with renewed vigour, pushing my leg up until my big toe touched the mattress above my right ear – then pushing hard on it with a sudden jerk, causing me to stub my toe on the floor and nearly break my own nose with my knee cap. At last, as I lay gasping in shock and pain, one side was pronounced done.

"Please to turn over," she told me.

So I staggered to my feet, aching in places I know aren't supposed to ache unless you're suffering from internal injuries, and waited until she turned her back to arrange some towels.

Then I ran.

Ridvan apparently got some great shots of my massage experience. "You can really see the pain in your face, man," he enthused.

Of course, he never admitted that he'd known what to expect all along. He did tell me he was glad I went first though.

And it was definitely Ridvan who came up with the idea that instead of continually buying new flip-flops, I should simply stop wearing them.

"I bet you can go barefoot for a year!" he said suddenly.

"Eh?"

"Think about it, man! It'll be amazing! And I know you can do it!"

That was what I liked most about him; he was unerringly positive. He never bet me that I couldn't do something – he bet me that I could. Of course, this made me all the keener to prove him right. Failure was not an option in a bet like this; it was not about pride, it was about pushing my boundaries, and about… oh, bollocks to it. It was about me doing something stupid, and Ridvan egging me on.

I loved it.

And I hated wearing flip-flops anyway – they made the gap between my big toe and the rest of them so sore it felt like my foot was being spilt in half.

Trust Ridvan to find an opportunity in something like that. That was the other great thing about him: he was the only person I'd ever met who had more crazy schemes than I did.

And from then on, they all involved me.

"I don't know Ridvan, a year is a long time. I'll be back in England by then."

"For as long as you're in Thailand then!"

"Erm…"

"Come on, man!" His eyes positively shining with excitement.

"Ahhhh…"

"I know you can do this man, because you're *you!*"

When we drove down to the clinic to tell Linda about it, she gave me her best 'you're an idiot' look.

"You're an idiot," she said, in case the look wasn't clear enough.

"Don't be such a downer," Ridvan told her. "No-one else could pull this off, but Tony can!"

"Tony is the only person stupid enough to try," she fired back. She fixed her gaze on Ridvan. "Are *you* going to go barefoot for a year?"

"No way man, that's crazy."

At this, Linda shook her head and went back inside.

I'd have kicked off my shoes in a symbolic act of defiance, if I'd had any shoes to kick off.

But I didn't, so instead I stared down at my bare feet; sun-burnt and filthy and covered in mosquito bites.

They didn't look like they could get much worse.

So I shook hands with Ridvan and the bet was on.

And I never again wore shoes in Thailand.

Smooth Operator

My bare feet met with mixed reactions in the clinic. Linda was disgusted with me for being so gullible; Avril was concerned, as she would have to do the paperwork if I got bitten by a snake in the back garden. No-one else cared one way or another, so long as I did my job and kept them supplied with subdued patients and an endless supply of clean towels.

At this point, some great switch in the sky was flipped, and the rains began. The Thai wet season was characterised by several intense downpours every day, though they quite often blended into one another in an unrelenting deluge of biblical proportions.

I took my time exercising the dogs, and invariably got soaked in the process, as I had to step gingerly through the long grass and dirt tracks skirting the jungle. My feet would toughen up soon enough I figured, and this way I got to spend more quality time with the animals in my care.

Plus, when I wasn't at the clinic I was spending most of my time underwater anyway – so it didn't make sense to complain about getting wet.

I was also keen to become a more useful member of PAC. This adventure wasn't only about giving my time to a worthy cause; it was about learning new skills, challenging myself and pushing the boundaries of my comfort zone.

Not that I dared tell the clinic staff this – not in so many words, at any rate. They'd delight in putting me outside my comfort zone, and probably a fair bit further than I planned on going.

Although things were much more relaxed between us now, I had no illusions about who held the power. When Avril had first explained that the entire staff of the clinic was female, and that there hadn't been a male volunteer for quite some time, visions of scantily clad nurses vying for my attention quite naturally filled my head. But the reality was rather more brutal; I was alone, in enemy territory, and I was heavily outnumbered.

Tony James Slater

I think it's fair to say there were downsides.

I'd already told the nurses I could handle watching a surgical procedure; they'd never have had any respect for me otherwise. Not that they had much now, but they weren't used to having blokes volunteering with them; I carried the honour of my entire gender on my shoulders. It was time to be a man.

So I bravely volunteered to assist in the next surgery. Never mind that I'd fainted in 'Bleeding Part One', the fifth lesson of a first aid course I'd taken in college. And never mind that I'd fainted in 'Bleeding Part Two' as well.

It would have been less embarrassing if I'd actually *been* bleeding, rather than just listening to a lecture about it, but still. I'd come a long way since college, and had spent a fair bit of time bleeding myself. Without fainting, if you must know.

I figured I could man up, tough out the surgery by not looking too closely at the icky bits, and it would be over in a flash. These girls were experts after all. It was rare for an op to take longer than fifteen minutes.

What I didn't know (and in hindsight, probably should have), was that the planned operation was a castration.

De-sexing they called it, to make it sound... more sexy? Certainly less violating. But what's in a name, eh? They were still going to cut the balls off some poor son of a bitch. I could only be glad it was a dog, although Amanda had developed a habit of smiling sweetly at me and making a snip-snip-with-scissors gesture whenever I told a bad joke. Which was pretty often.

The poor dog, sound asleep, was shaved strategically and had a green cloth draped over him. The cloth had a small square hole in it, which came to rest precisely over the nut-sack, with the balls protruding from the middle of it.

I winced when Amanda gave them a forceful prod with one finger. I reckon that would have woken me up, regardless of anaesthetic.

Deciding everything was ready, she deftly grasped one bollock between fingers and thumb, and tugged it slightly away from the body.

I nearly dropped to the floor in sympathy when she squeezed the scrotum, tightening the sack to make its delicate contents more prominent.

Then she reached out for the scalpel I was holding. She took it, raised it, aimed it and lowered it...

262

And that was as much as I could take. Something about the coldness of the razor sharp steel, the way it slid through that nut-sack like opening a zipper, affected me *deeply*. I had no choice.

I dropped my implements on the table, sprinted out of the back door and threw up in the washing machine.

Well, there are worse things to be sick into.

My stomach didn't settle, it kept jumping around inside me. I paced the patch of concrete between the kennels, trying to suppress the urge to lose more of my breakfast. I was breathing through my mouth, as the kennels had a unique fragrance to them – a mingling of wet dog, bleach, and rotting flesh – that really wasn't helping.

Up and down I walked, my guts roiling inside me. I badly needed a drink of water, but daren't risk going back inside to get one. What the hell was taking them so long? I could hear chatting and laughter from the nurses, still stitching merrily away, amused at something – yeah, no prize for guessing; that would be me. Again.

I shied away from thinking about the operation. Such thoughts were always accompanied by lurid visuals, things that once seen I could never again un-see; and the bile would rise inside me.

At last it was over.

Amanda came to the back door, a little smirk on her face, to tell me it was safe to come in. "Are you feeling better?" she asked.

"Um, yeah, a bit."

"That's good. Oh, since you're helping, chuck this in the bin for us would you?"

She threw something towards me and I caught it instinctively – then noticed her smirk widening. Por's head popped around the door, watching with interest.

This could not be good.

I opened my hand. I was holding a severed testicle.

It was a good job that washing machine was right behind me.

On The Run

I had a few days off after that, while Linda worked her shift.

There wasn't much time for fun though, as even in paradise there were chores to attend to.

First up: a visa run.

It was hard to believe, but I'd been in Thailand for a month already. My visa had run out, which meant I had to get another one. The simplest way to do this was to book a trip to Burma, to leave this country and then re-enter it. It was a crazy, almost farcical system, but for tens of thousands of ex-pats living in Thailand it was a necessary evil – and a regular one.

Nick at the dive shop had passed me a phone number for Mrs Da, the woman who arranged his monthly pilgrimage, so I borrowed the phone in the clinic to give her a call.

"Hello, Mrs Da?"

"Yes. Aha. Okay."

"Hi. My name is Tony. I need to do a visa run tomorrow, and I was told that —"

"Yes. Visa run, tomorrow, yes."

"Yes, my name is Tony."

"Yes. Aha. Okay."

"Do I need to bring anything with me? Other than my passport?"

"No worry. I do all thing."

"That's great, but do I need anything special?"

"Yes. Aha. Okay."

"Um… do we go on a bus and a boat, or just —"

"Is okay. I do all thing."

And Mrs Da hung up.

Perhaps she was a busy person.

But I didn't need to worry. The control freak in me had dozens of unanswered questions about everything from the weather in Burma to a rough idea of how long it would take, but this was one of those times when I had to let it go.

I had to leave it to the professionals.

And hope that Mrs Da really did do all thing.

I caught the night boat from the pier in Thong Sala.

If I'd have seen the thing in daylight, I probably wouldn't have gotten on it.

It was a rickety wooden effort shaped like a barge, with two narrow floors in the same amount of space as any regular boat would have one.

Inside there were two options; the upper deck, or the lower. Neither was tall enough to stand up in, so I bowed my head and shuffled down the middle of the upper deck.

Dozens of thin pads that the Thai use as mattresses were lined up on both side of the central aisle, taking up every inch of available floor space. Two numbers were scrawled on the wall by the head of each mattress, helpfully in English; these corresponded to the number on the ticket I'd bought.

I found my 'bed' mercilessly empty, though more than a little stained, and lay down quickly to get out of the way. A crush of people surged up the aisle, some dropping down into gaps between other passengers, some starting high-speed arguments when they found their allotted space was already occupied.

I had two passengers on either side of me, close enough that if I did fall asleep I'd probably end up spooning one of them; Thai to my left, Canadian to my right.

And ten minutes later, with the argument over beds heating up, the boat's engine rumbled into life, and, with a deafening din, pulled us off the docks and out into the Gulf of Thailand.

It was not a restful night.

Long after order had been restored, an angry muttering rippled up and down the rows of sleepers. Snores reverberated down the length of the boat, magnified by the enclosed wooden hull and their ridiculous proximity; I would reckon that, comfortably laden, there should have been around twenty people on that deck.

I stopped counting at sixty, when my nearest bed mate turned over to point his arse in my direction and let rip with an ear-splitting fart.

The deck was lined with windows, small square holes in the wall with no glass or screens, which helped with the odour a little. There was no way of escaping the sound though, as the dull thrum of the engine vibrated up through the boat's timbers and along its floors, so that every time I lay back on the sleeping pad, my teeth chattered.

I later discovered that the lower deck was for the lower-class passengers, who were almost exclusively locals. It was identical, except the roof was a foot lower and it didn't have any windows at all.

Seven hours, that ferry took.

If I'd have had a hammer, I'd have beaten myself over the head with it.

Sleep or death; either would have been acceptable.

From the looks of my mattress, at least one previous occupant had had the same idea.

By the time the boat docked on the mainland at dead-on five in the morning, I was ready to kill every bugger on it.

Luckily, Mrs Da was there to collect me from the cheerless grey docks before I could vent my frustration. On the gang plank (which was exactly what it sounds like – a plank), a mob of pissed-off people were fighting their way to fresh air with a desperation you can only know if you've just spent seven hours passing time by playing *guess that smell.*

Mrs Da's shop was an open fronted restaurant somewhere in the nether-regions of Surat Thani. This sprawling district was a maze of narrow streets lined with similar shops; it was the kind of place that would make town planners pee themselves in their sleep. Utter chaos of both buildings and traffic manifested itself amidst all the smoke and noise of a World War Two bombing raid.

It made me very glad indeed that I was living on a tiny island in the middle of nowhere.

Not so glad that I was looking forward to the return trip, however.

But for now we waited; three of us had been collected and brought here, to sit on plastic patio chairs in Mrs Da's restaurant and eyeball each other until something happened.

Nothing did happen.

For hours.

Around 8am, Mrs Da emerged from her kitchen at the back of the shop and ushered us all onto a waiting minibus. It had been sat there for as long as we had.

The driver followed her out from the kitchen, presumably having had a hearty breakfast in there, and fired up the minivan for the trip to Burma.

The three of us stretched out with a whole row of seats each, undreamt of luxury after the cramped night on the ferry. Then we pulled up at a petrol station and filled up with more than just fuel; eight more people were waiting for us, filling every seat and very nearly ending up with someone on my knee until the driver grudgingly allowed one of the newcomers to sit in the front with him.

After more than a few complaints about the lack of personal space, we sorted ourselves out and set off once more; and as the miles built up, the atmosphere in the car became increasingly frosty.

I've never understood this thing with air-conditioning in cars. Okay, so it's a hot country; you need to keep cool whilst driving, so you invest in a car with air-con. Surely everyone who can afford to does the same. But does this make air-con into a status symbol? So much so that it must be proved first-hand to every passenger? Traveling in the back of that van was like watching one half of a pissing contest. The dial was turned so far to the left that it ran out of numbers; the air in the car was chilled to the point where my breath began to fog in front of me. I had micro-erections in my nipples. Goose-bumps. The shivers.

No-one is comfortable in that temperature, unless they're wearing half a polar bear. Dressed for Thailand because, well, we were *in* Thailand, the eight of us froze our asses off for the whole of the four-and-a-half-hour journey.

I started to feel grateful for the crowded conditions. Quite when the huddling began was impossible to tell – but imperceptibly, by increments, we edged even closer to each other until we were all snuggling up as though we knew each other considerably better than we did. No-one mentioned it – not even when we reached our destination and struggled to unfold our frozen limbs. It was one of those unspoken agreements; we were all travellers, and we all knew that people do strange things in survival situations. Desperate things. I felt a bit sordid about it, but there it was.

What happened in that minibus, stayed in that minibus.

At least until the return trip.

We still weren't in Burma though.

First we had to queue for our Thai exit stamp. Then the taxi driver doled out a crisp US ten dollar note to each of us, the price of which had been included in Mrs Da's fee. I went to fold the note and the driver's hand shot out like a striking cobra, gripping my wrist before I could do it. He shook his head and flattened the note back into my palm.

"They won't accept it if it's got a crease in it," said one of my van buddies, revealing himself to be a Brit in the process.

"You've done this before?" I asked him.

He nodded glumly.

Through a market, and through a wall with arched openings, we came to another dock; this one under cover of a vast tin roof. Dozens of motorized canoes clogged the waterway, spurting black smog from their decrepit outdoor motors and adding to the din from the market.

Each motor had a long handle attached for steering with a motorbike-style twisting throttle on the end of it. The other end was a two-metre long scaffolding pole with a propeller fastened to it; it was this feature that earned them the nick-name 'long tails', which is a damn site more poetic than they deserved.

We filed on board a canoe and sat on the wooden planks which passed for seats. A father and son team wearing matching cut-off jeans were crewing our skinny vessel. The father kept a casual grip on the tiller while his son scampered around the canoe, collecting passports and ID documents from all of us. The kid didn't feel the need to hold on to anything.

Even the passports got stuffed in his mouth.

Once out on the river, it became a far more relaxing affair. The canoe chugged along leaving a filthy stain on the water as we passed, but it hardly mattered; the surface of the water was coated with a film of scum and oil all the way out to open water. We settled in for the long haul when a micro-island the size of a phone booth appeared. The young lad leapt over to it, waving our passports in the faces of two uniformed officials who had somehow squeezed themselves into a tiny cabin. Then the boy was back, jabbering at one of the passengers, demanding something from him and waiting expectantly. The man looked embarrassed, but dug around in his bag for a different brown book and sent that over with the boy, together with a few rumpled hundred-*baht* notes.

I had no idea if I was witnessing an official bribe, an unofficial bribe, or just part of daily business. Or all three. But it seemed best to keep quiet about it.

The same pantomime played itself out a handful of times. Every outcrop or island we passed contained a miniature garrison of bored-looking customs officials. We had to tie up outside each one while they frowned over our documents, sometimes sending the boy scurrying back to the boat with an unintelligible question for one the passengers. The third time it was my fault; I'd slipped my ten dollar bill into the back of my passport as the only alternative to sitting there holding it for the entire journey – a sure-fire way to lose it overboard at the first gust of wind. Apparently I'd committed another cardinal sin, and the check-point staff now thought I was trying to bribe them. Or maybe they thought I wasn't trying to bribe them enough? One official, resplendent in his tasselled uniform, even went so far as to leave his booth and stand on the edge of our boat, shaking the money at me as though it was evidence. I'd already learned not to antagonise customs officers, but this guy had a machine gun slung over his shoulder. There was nothing I could do or say, so I sat there, shrugging in an exaggerated manner while a queue of boats built up behind us. Most of them had a small boy aboard like some kind of scrawny mascot, all of whom climbed into our boat and out again, and across every intervening boat until they reached the check-point. After a few minutes of pointless diatribe, the officer must have considered me sufficiently chastised. Our driver revved up his outboard motor, dipped the propeller back into the water, and we chugged off again without further explanation.

Finally, after crossing a wide stretch of river out of sight of everything but a gigantic golden Buddha statue on the far shore, we motored into Burma. Both sides of the river were dominated by an entire town built on stilts over the water. Doorways opened onto ladders down to moorings and people moved back and forth on an endless series of plank bridges and gangways. It looked incredibly cool and scary at the same time; these were rough, shanty-town buildings, made of scraps and scavenged materials. It seemed audacious of the people to build so many structures, such a complex and interlocking series of buildings, without a shred of solid land beneath them; but these were poor people and this river was their livelihood. Hundreds of canoes identical to ours plied up and down across this stretch of water, and dozens more were tied to every ramshackle pier and jetty in town. The romance of a life over water gave way, in my mind, to the incessant noise of diesel engines and the awful quality of the buildings they lived in. The whole town seemed ready to collapse at any moment.

Again I was glad for my little log bungalow, simple yet robust; never before had I thought of it as posh, but compared to these dwellings it was the height of luxury.

It brought it home to me that, rustic as it appeared, Thailand was not a poor country. At least in the touristy areas I was used to, Thailand was relatively affluent.

Burma, and more than ninety percent of the Burmese population, were destitute.

By a massive 'Welcome to The Republic of Myanmar' sign, our driver cut the engine and let the canoe drift under a dangling ladder. One by one we climbed the ladder onto a huge steel bridge, whilst the boy held the boat steady underneath it; and now, at long last, we were in Burma.

We stayed there nearly six minutes.

Our passports were stamped in a cabin at the far end of the bridge and redistributed to us by the boy. He had a fair bit of responsibility this lad, and seemed to handle it well.

The other children of the town were gathered at the far end of the jetty just beyond the check-point. They swarmed towards us selling cigarettes and whisky, shouting "Hey mister!" and "Very cheap, very cheap!"

I told one of the older boys I wasn't interested, as he seemed keen on following me up and down the rusty iron bridge while I waited for my passport to come back. I could tell the stuff he was offering was very cheap. Most of it didn't even have labels.

"Hello my friend, where you from?"

"England," I said. He was the persistent type, but that was no reason to be rude to the lad.

"Where you from, in England?"

"Manchester." I'd lived all over, and Manchester was one place everyone had heard of.

"Ah! Manchester United! You know?"

"Ah, not personally, no."

"Ha! Manchester! Hey, you want Viagra?"

"Eh? Um, no, thank-you very much. No Viagra."

"Okay. You want Viagra for woman?" he asked.

"Eh? I didn't know they made Viagra for women?"

"Yes!" He dug a tiny brown bottle out of his pocket and dangled it in front of me. "Viagra for woman! Same as for man. But you pour it in her drink."

It was the best joke I'd heard in weeks. At least, I hoped it was a joke.

So, the Thai had stamped me out of their country.

Now the Burmese had stamped me in to theirs.

Then there was the matter of the ten dollar note. It was examined minutely for defects, before being tucked away in a wooden desk drawer crammed full of them. I later learned that anyone showing up without the cash was made to buy one out of the drawer – at a ridiculously extortionate rate – and then hand it back, for inspection and eventual return to the stash.

No wonder they were checking the notes so carefully. The slightest defect, and they could sell me one of theirs, presumably pocketing a healthy commission into the bargain.

It made me smile – when I was a safe distance away from the border guards. They obviously didn't give a stuff who I was – I hadn't even been in the room when they'd checked my passport. But the almighty dollar was all-powerful, even half a world away from where it was born. Every government is corrupt to some degree, but these guys were the pros. They were so blatant it was funny – yet armed to the teeth and deadly serious all the while.

Overall it was quite an assault, and I was glad to drop down the ladder back into the boat. I'm sure I'm doing Burma an injustice by judging it based on this one border town (called Kawthaung) – but to be honest, six minutes there was five minutes too long.

As we huddled miserably in the boat, a few flecks of rain fell from the lead-grey sky. And then we made the exact same journey – every passport-stamping, bone chilling, achingly boring stage of it – in reverse.

Except that this time it was pissing it down the whole way.

Linda picked me up from the Thong Sala pier at 10pm.

I couldn't get my own bike back until I returned my passport to Yorik.

I was starving hungry, soaking wet, exhausted in both body and soul, and so dehydrated that my head was pounding in time to the throb of the ferry's engine. I was aching and cramped and my feet were killing me – though it could be said that that was my own fault, for making the entire journey with nothing on them.

I'd been gone from Koh Pha Ngan for twenty-two hours exactly.

I can't say I'd hated every minute of it, but I was bloody glad to be back.

And already, I was dreading having to leave again.

Because I'd had two options, when first planning my trip to Thailand; to apply in advance for a visa, which would have been valid for three months, or to ignore that in favour of getting a one-month visa on arrival. Predictably I'd chosen the latter – not because I was lazy or disorganized (though both are generally true of me) – but because reading about visa runs on a travel advice website had made them sound like an adventure.

"I'll have a bit of that," I'd said to myself.

But they'd neglected to mention that afterwards you were left feeling like you'd been flattened by a train.

Never mind. I would have plenty of opportunity to relive this feeling; from now on I would have to make a visa run every thirty days, for as long as I wanted to remain in Thailand.

I don't want to spoil the story or anything, but so far I've done ten of them.

And you know what?

They get worse every time.

You Win Some, You Lose Some

Phangan Animal Care was run entirely on donations. The volunteers didn't pay for the privilege of mopping up poo and vomit on a daily basis, and the few paying Thai customers had very limited means to cover even our meagre bills. So when cash was running low, we headed over the hills to Haad Rin, to hit the streets! Well, the street – there really was only the one.

We deployed our forces at a strategic location – in the shelter of a café whose owner was a long-time supporter of PAC – and set our traps for the unsuspecting public.

Koh Pha Ngan was mercilessly free of charity muggers. You know the ones? They dominate the flow of traffic through any pedestrianized area in the UK, whilst trying to raise money to save starving whales in Africa.

"Have you got a minute?" they ask, with carefully practiced cheer. But they don't want a minute. You know they don't want a minute. They want you to sign a form allowing them to take money from your bank account every month for all eternity.

And by the time you've politely refused, or mumbled something about already saving starving whales, the next one is on to you, wanting a minute to talk about orangutans with AIDS.

Now I love charities, especially animal ones. I support loads of them. But I hate having to run the gauntlet of those professional guilt-trippers, all of whom earn more than I do, anytime I venture near an urban area.

Yet another reason to escape to a tiny island in the middle of nowhere.

Now, having said all that, we set ourselves up to do exactly the same. Only we didn't want bank details and a reoccurring pound of flesh; just a few coins, a handful of *baht*, to keep food on the table for the poor creatures unlucky enough to need our care.

And anyway, we were way better than the pros!

Not only because we genuinely cared about our cause, rather than spouting spiel memorized for the charity of the day, but because we had

two distinct advantages:
    1) most of our audience were already drunk, and
    2) we had kittens.

Oh, yes! We recruited the tiniest, cutest little bundles of fluff from around the clinic – there were always plenty of homeless kittens and puppies in residence – and prepared to unleash some serious emotional blackmail.

It was a simple concept. I'd approach a clutch of partygoers on their way down to the beach and thrust a minute kitten at them. Any women in the group were immediately entranced, leaving them and their attached friends or partners sitting ducks for my tales of triumph and woe.

It worked like a charm!

Even people with no English could recognize a collection tin, and get a rough idea of what we were up to. And who can resist the charms of a two-month old puppy? They're all belly and ears at that age, regardless of breed – with furiously wagging tails for added delight.

By the end of the evening our various mascots were totally played out, and curled up asleep on our table. It was getting too dark for passers-by to see our large 'before' and 'after' style posters featuring animals the clinic had rescued and treated. As the crowd around us became progressively drunker my sales pitch had simplified, from trying to explain the individual case histories to just pointing at the table full of baby animals and saying "Give us money or they'll all die!"

Eventually Avril called us off. We'd been very lucky with the weather, and the streets had been packed with partygoers. We had collection boxes stuffed with notes and heavy with coins. Some tourists had parted with the price of a beer – about 30p in loose change – and some had been swayed to a greater degree, leaving us with large denomination notes and promises to come and visit us at work.

They never came. But they had done their part, as had we. I was amazed by how much money we counted out when we got back to the clinic. And secretly, I knew the evening had gone even better than expected. There were obvious benefits to being laden with kittens whilst attempting to chat to women. It was a tactic I'd never really considered – for ethical reasons I assure you, rather than because it had never actually occurred to me. But it had worked, and worked well. For some reason, along with their cash, several of the girls I'd talked to had felt compelled to donate their phone numbers! I had a pocketful of scraps of paper, each one bearing a name and those sacred digits…

I decided not to share this trifling detail with the rest of the clinic staff. We'd all been working hard, and in our own time, to transport the whole circus to and from Haad Rin, and we'd all thrown our personal embarrassment to the wind for long enough to make the fundraiser work.

Surely no-one would begrudge me a little benefit on the side?

The clinic was in the money again, and I was eagerly anticipating romance.

Everyone's a winner, baby!

Except that, now I needed a phone. No way I was going to borrow the landline in the clinic's kitchen to make these calls.

I'd brought one with me from England of course, but it had survived less than a week.

I blamed it on the Thai humidity, though in fact it was moisture of a different kind which had seen the end of yet another device; it had fallen into a bucket of booze in the middle of a night out, when I'd rather cleverly tried to swat a fly with it.

"There's only the one phone shop on the island." Avril told me. "Everyone goes there. Likely some of the phones are stolen, but hey, what can you do? And it's the only place to get a bargain."

On her advice I checked out the shop, a single unit in the middle of Thong Sala's main street just down from the market. They had a few dummy phones on the wall to represent the new ones which came with a contract – not an option for me, with my foreign bank account – and a pair of glass cases at the front of the shop, with second-hand phones laid out in neat rows. There wasn't a lot to choose from. Several of them bore battle scars; bashed corners and chipped edges from where they'd fallen, presumably to be scooped up by a willing pair of hands and sold on to the shop. Or perhaps that was just my imagination, working overtime after Avril's advice.

In the end I opted for the cheapest phone on display, a cheery blue Nokia that was hardly worth the effort of stealing. Anyone trying to trace it could have it – it only cost me three-hundred *baht*. Plus an extra hundred and fifty for a pay-as-you-go SIM card, and that was that. The missing pieces of my life all came together. It was like I'd made a proper home here, and having a phone cemented that feeling. It took me a week to figure out the menus as they were all in Thai, but really – what do you expect for a fiver?

But I never rang any of the numbers I'd been given that night.

Would you? I mean, what was I going to say? "Hi, I'm that guy from the other night, with the puppies…" Actually, now I say it, that sounds quite good.

Ah well.

Truth be told, I chickened out.

The rest of the week was back to normal at the clinic.

Linda and I took turns doing the washing, walking the dogs, feeding the kittens and cleaning out cages. There was never any shortage of stuff to do, and for days at a time we followed our simple, regular routine. The biggest drama in our lives was trying to dry as many towels as we could in the gaps between rainstorms.

Life could be monotonous right up until it wasn't.

Like when a local man skidded to a halt outside our front door. In the back of his truck his dog was dying – poisoned by a neighbour he'd annoyed once too often. Emergency stations!

Immediately the entire crew sprang into action, sprinting around the clinic for supplies whilst calling measurements and drug names across the room to one another. I could do nothing but hold the terrified dog as a charcoal solution was mixed and fed to her to induce vomiting, injections were administered and tubes inserted. The nurses whirled around me like soldiers on manoeuvre, precisely and efficiently deploying every treatment in their arsenal.

I don't even remember the name of that dog.

Everyone in the clinic knew it was too late within minutes of her arrival. But that didn't stop them trying, desperately grabbing for any technique, any remote possibility that might prove lucky and somehow save her life.

The dog died in my arms about three quarters of an hour later. I held her as she thrashed, shuddered, then merely trembled until she was finally still.

The owner was distraught. He'd stayed off to one side, watching every stage of the process, every frantic effort the nurses made, with clenched fists and tears in his eyes. Then, when it was over, there was nothing we could do but hand her back to him, so he could take her home to let his family say goodbye. He thanked the nurses, quietly, and left the same way.

You win some, you lose some. And we won more than most.

I cried myself to sleep that night.

Holy Cow

Racing through the jungle on Por's battered motor scooter was enormous fun. Being on the back while Por drove was an even greater delight, as she was from the Tony Slater school of driving – pedal to the metal, weaving to avoid potholes, and if you leaned the wrong way into a curve you'd be lying in the road wondering what happened. Being a passenger allowed me to fully appreciate the lush tropical terrain we were ploughing through. Stick-built bungalows were scattered here and there along the route, their dogs coming out to bark at us as we passed.

Por called out to them; she'd treated most of the owned animals on the island at some point or other, and they all seemed to know her and respect her.

This thrilling, high speed adventure race was Por's favourite part of the job. As the only Thai speaker on the staff, she had a fairly tough deal, handling the bulk of the customers, taking medical histories for new patients and translating everything from drug labels to grocery shopping lists for the rest of us. On top of that she was the only permanent vet nurse, ultimately responsible for everything medical that happened at the clinic.

But the upside? She got to make all the house calls.

Occasionally she needed a little help. Whilst most of her trips involved repeat visits to ex-patients, giving injections or wound dressings to dogs and cats that had already been treated by PAC, there were times when something a little bigger reared its head.

Today was one of those days.

Today wasn't a house call.

It was a temple call.

"I hope him not too big for you to handle," she called back, as we turned in past a pair of vine-clad stone gateposts.

"That depends. How big is big?"

"Oh, not so big as you, I think!"

Por had a delightfully sarcastic sense of humour. One of her favourite jokes was to feign complete ignorance when I was recounting my party exploits, and then by asking seemingly innocent questions, to get me to completely incriminate or embarrass myself (often both) in front of everyone.

Typically, it would go something like this:

"Who was girl I see you with last night at party?"

"Oh, um…"

"And who was other girl I see you with later?"

"Oh! Ah…"

"Where you go, with first girl, for so long?"

"Weeell… er…"

"And why she look so pissed at you when she come back?"

(Cue raucous laughter.)

Por had a heart of gold, but in spite of her compassionate nature she had some steel in her soul – no animal, no matter how pissed off, would willingly cross her. Her 'Bad Dog!' look would freeze a Velociraptor at a hundred paces.

We stood in a clearing close to the carved wooden outbuildings of the temple, eyeing up our morning's work. The buffalo stared back nervously – all nine-hundred pounds of him. He'd been badly abused by his previous owners, so he wasn't overly fond of people. Only his eventual rescuer, an orange-robed teenager built like a coat hanger, could get close enough to hold his lead rope. The young monk and the massive beast had become inseparable, with the lad treating a nasty wound on the animal's flank – but without an injection of antibiotics it was sure to get infected. The jungle was hot and humid, and full of insects; this remote temple was beautiful, but poor. Life out here was dirty for both man and beast. If the buffalo was to survive it had to have some protection from its environment.

Por wasn't fazed in the least. Chatting to the monks who emerged to watch us, she quickly came up with a scheme for restraining the massive creature.

The young lad threw his buffalo's lead rope over the branch of a sturdy tree just beyond the temple complex. With the bulk of the tree between us, I could approach and snag the end of the rope, and slowly pull it taut to coax the buffalo closer.

All good so far – but this was where the plan got difficult.

It went like this: I was to haul on the rope, hoisting the buffalo's front legs off the ground. This would hopefully immobilise him long enough for Por to run in and administer the jab. But the beast was agitated. His sole guardian had been called away to a safe distance, leaving him alone and wary, with the scent of humans in his nostrils.

There wasn't much we could do apart from follow the plan.

An elderly monk stepped in to give me a hand, and as Por poised herself for the run, we hauled on the rope with all our might.

Nothing happened.

The combined weight of two people was nowhere near enough to counterbalance even a quarter of this beast. Especially not if one of the guys was an ancient Thai monk – I think his robes weighed more than he did.

The buffalo, annoyed now, twitched his head, nearly pulling my arms from their sockets as he did so. The rope burned through my hands and I let it go slack; it was either that, or end up dangling from the tree in place of the buffalo.

We needed reinforcements.

To her credit, Por made a run anyway, but the buffalo unrestrained proved impossible to corner. All she got for her trouble was a jab in the finger from her own needle!

Another two guys were drafted in; local farmers from the looks of them. They took the end of the rope from the monk, though neither of them looked particularly enthusiastic about it.

Take Two was dramatically more successful. As the buffalo took a threatening step forward all three of us threw ourselves onto the rope – and it was just enough to hoist his forequarters off the ground.

He gave a bellow of dismay, which Por took as her cue. She darted in, syringe in hand, just as the buffalo began to swing...

He was trotting towards us on his hind legs, while his front hooves made the same running motion in fresh air. He was swinging right at us, as heavy objects in suspension tend to.

What the hell were we going to do?

If we dropped the rope and ran for it, we'd never be able to try again – he was already way too spooked by this unnatural treatment. So we hung on, scrabbling frantically around to the other side of the tree. We fell over each other in our desperation to keep solid wood between those horns and our fragile bodies. Suddenly, I needed to pee really badly.

And the buffalo kept coming!

We held on for grim death, but the Thai guys were yelling at each other in fear. In a few seconds either the buffalo was going to swing into us, or we'd all end up twined around the tree like ribbons on a maypole…

Closer! All of us were full-on dangling from the rope now, one tangle of terrified humans versus one seriously pissed off cow. A Thai forehead bounced off my shoulder and for a second I thought the beast had reached me.

Then Por gave a yell of triumph! She'd braved the flailing hooves – and the very real danger of us letting go and dropping half a tonne of angry cow on her – and delivered the drugs.

We backed away, easing off on the rope, and hoping the buffalo's first move once he regained his freedom wouldn't be to charge straight over the top of us.

No. He'd had enough.

He retreated from the group, not at high speed but more of a tactical withdrawal, reversing warily all the way to what he considered safety.

His young handler walked over, tut-tutting at him under his breath, and laid a comforting hand on the beast's back.

And that was that! Por bowed to the monks and we climbed aboard the aging scooter, speeding back through the jungle towards the clinic.

"You never expect to do that huh?" Por sounded exultant after her heroics.

"No… never…" I could hardly believe what I'd just been involved in.

"Hopefully him be okay now," Por explained, "the young monk tell me if him still sick, but I think him get better."

We paused at a junction and she turned in the saddle to give me a cheeky grin. "If not, we do same thing next week, eh?"

Miscalculation

It was another miserable day in Thailand.

The rain had been falling consistently for more than two months at this point, and it was driving people to despair. The streets were empty when I cruised through them on the way to work, and I was the only customer the diving school had had in weeks.

At Liberty we spent our evenings huddled in the central restaurant area, watching the same collection of DVD's endlessly. Optimistic young backpackers still arrived regularly, laughing at the rain and settling in to enjoy their holidays. There was always a movie they hadn't seen, so it went on the screen without complaint. Ninety-nine point nine percent of the time, they wanted to watch *The Beach*. The long-term crowd had seen all our movies at least a dozen times by this point, and that one in particular more than any of them, so we sat there drinking, smoking, chatting, generally trying to bring some cheer into the monotony of a life so restricted. Most of the new arrivals left after a few days, citing as their reasons the weather, their boredom, and being forced to watch *The Beach* again every time someone new showed up.

Somehow, we toughed it out.

It helped that we had jobs; there was always something going on at the clinic, and life for the animals of the island didn't stop just because most of the humans did. The work was also quite monotonous, but in a comforting way; it made me feel domesticated, as though I'd settled in and become part of the local population, with my chores to do regardless of the season.

I also had friends.

Good friends.

Even more important than my fleeting adventures with the opposite sex was my relationship with the small group of individuals centred around the clinic. We had in common a love for the animals in our care and a deep concern for those that weren't; we also shared a sense of adventure sufficient to bring us all together, here on this tiny island thousands of miles from where we lived. And we were all good people.

Even though some of us threw testicles at each other.

It occurred to me one day, as I wondered yet again if the rains were going to stop, that I didn't really care; of course I wanted to experience the freedom of blue skies, the bustle of a town without deluge and the delight of exploring for its own sake again. But none of that mattered as much as the community which had formed, and which I very much felt a part of.

I might be the token male, the standing joke, the person that the whole group loved to take the piss out of, but that was a role I was well used to. I could cope with that.

These people were now close friends, people who knew me only as the person I'd become since my arrival on Koh Pha Ngan, and they were (or seemed to be) happy to know me.

I'd finally found what I'd been looking for all this time, a sense of belonging that I hadn't felt since the end of my stint in Ecuador. I had a purpose, albeit a small and comparatively insignificant one, as a part of the clinic team – and, alongside that, I had friendship, and I had love.

Not sexual love – at least, not at the moment – but there was plenty of time for that.

I didn't really care about the rain.

I was happy.

And I didn't want to go home.

So I didn't.

Of course, I say it like that for dramatic emphasis, but that's not exactly how it happened. I love to imply that I'm the kind of decisive, follow-my-instincts sort of guy, who would make a snap decision on something as important as this and stick to it no matter what.

In fact I'm a second-guessing, indecisive, over-analysing bundle of neuroses when it comes to these kinds of situations. I hate decisions. I've never been a big fan of responsibility – which is part of the reason I'd travelled halfway around the world to party hard and poke dogs instead of getting a real job.

So when a situation like this arises – should I stay or should I go – or, should I return home to the safety of my parent's house in England while I regroup and plan my next adventure, or should I blow off several hundred pound's worth of return ticket and trust the rest of my life to Fate and the tides… well, I had a lot of thinking to do.

Normally, I weigh up the odds, I make lists of the pros and cons,

I meditate on the possibilities resulting from each course of action, I ask my friends, I ask strangers, I pretend to decide so I can see how I feel about the decision, then I second-guess that decision and the associated emotions in case my subconscious was lying to me because it knew I hadn't really decided yet…

I become a mess. Usually until I have no choice but to make the decision immediately, or the decision gets made for me.

But this time, none of that happened.

Not because my love of Thailand and my new friends was enough to quash all objections. Not because the choice to stay was blindingly, obviously, the right one.

Oh no.

What happened was, I was chilling out in my hammock, listening to the sound of rain on the tin roof of my bungalow. Linda and Ridvan were there too, and none of us doing a whole lot of anything – just appreciating this place, this life, this friendship.

Okay, so we were bored shitless, a little damp and slightly stoned.

And eating cheesy chips.

Ridvan had just come up with the idea of going away for New Year, to some part of Thailand that wasn't still stuck in the middle of a monsoon.

"No way I'm staying here for New Year if it's as wet as this," he said.

Oh yeah – I should probably mention – it was Christmas Day.

"We should go to Green Spirit, man," Ridvan continued, "it's a trance music festival in Krabi. It's on the other side of the country! No way it'll be raining over there. We could go for a week, spend some time on the beach…"

He was really selling this idea to us. After our planned Christmas bonfire on the beach had been called off due to the weather, forcing us to spend the day huddled on my balcony doing very little, he didn't have to try very hard.

I think he had us at 'not raining'.

"Yeah," I said, "it's not a bad idea, that."

"But aren't you going home soon?" Linda asked me. "Will you still be here long enough?"

That surprised me. I hadn't given a moment's thought to my departure, which suddenly seemed a bit slack of me.

"I dunno," I told her, "I'll check."

So I rooted through my rucksack and found the little plastic wallet where I kept the few important bits of paper I had with me. My printed e-ticket was in there, the paper slightly soft with the all-penetrating moisture. I came out onto the balcony to read it.

"Oh," I said to Linda after a moment. "Oh, shit."

"What is it? When do you fly?"

"Tomorrow."

"Oh SHIT! Where from?"

"Bangkok."

"But… you'll never make it! Even if you flew from Koh Samui… even if you could get to Samui… even if…"

"Yup," I said, climbing back into the hammock and stretching out. "No chance at all. No ferries running. No planes. No buses. And it takes a day to get to Bangkok no matter what you do. I wouldn't have made it even if I'd left yesterday…"

"So you're staying then?" Linda seemed excited by the prospect, which was encouraging.

"I guess I am."

"And you're coming to Green Spirit with us?" Ridvan was positively vibrating with enthusiasm, which was not unlike him.

"I… uh, I guess so. Why not?"

"We still have to talk about that," Linda pointed out. She was already wary of Ridvan's spur-of-the-moment schemes.

"Ah, what's to talk about?" he replied. "It'll be crazy fun, man! It's got to be better than staying here. No way we want to spend New Year sitting on a soggy balcony."

He made a good point.

We all sat in silence for a few moments. I tried to wrap my head around the idea of not going home. Of never going home. Of staying here permanently… it wasn't hard to adjust to.

I'd never missed a flight before. Especially not one that was still almost a day away… I thought about the frantic effort I should be putting in, swearing and flinging clothes into my bag, making desperate phone calls and credit card transactions and booking ferries and buses. It made my head hurt. In contrast I could lie here, watching the patterns made by the rain on the ocean, and feel it all slipping away. The urgency, the worry, the guilt; there wasn't anything I could reasonably expect to do about it all. Not now. So why let it bother me?

"Are you going to ring your mum?" Linda asked me. "And tell her you're not coming home?"

I thought about that for a minute. It would be one hell of a conversation.

Not least because I'd have to ask her to explain the situation to my commanding officer in the TA. That wouldn't be much fun.

"Yeah, I guess I should. I've been meaning to ring home for a couple of months, actually. After all, it *is* Christmas…"

Krabi Weather

Even in Krabi, the rain continued to dog us.

Green Spirit was a shambles.

As a result of the unexpectedly drawn-out wet season, the site chosen by the festival organisers had turned into a swamp. Signs drooped; scruffy-looking hippie types grooved away in the ankle-deep mud, so hooked on the music – and doubtless a wide variety of other substances – that they were oblivious to the rather feeble image they cast.

"What a shit-hole," Linda said.

"Doesn't look like much fun," I agreed.

"But guys, it's about the music!" Ridvan, said. "Can't you *feel* the music?"

Neither I, nor Linda, could feel the music.

All we felt is repulsed by the squalid quagmire – and Ridvan, tugging on our arms like an over-enthusiastic six-year-old.

He could feel the music.

So we left him to it.

With a cold day on the beach only marginally more appealing than sludge-dancing, we set off to see what there was to do in the town.

We ate at McDonalds, which was amongst the most delicious things I'd ever tasted. Thai food was all well and good, as was the *Farang* (foreign) food served by most of the bars in Koh Pha Ngan, but I still craved western-style fast food.

With lunch done, Linda thought we might kill an hour by getting a massage. They were cheaper here than almost anywhere else in the world, though my mistake at the herbal sauna had very nearly put me off for life.

I voiced my fears to Linda, and we talked about the disastrous potential for getting a massage in the wrong place, but then we came across a parlour that just had to be decent. It was right in the middle of the main shopping street for one, and it looked clean and tidy inside.

The sign had flowers on it and the walls were tastefully decorated with large posters of tranquil islands and rainforests and diagrams of Chinese acupuncture points. Incense wafted through the air; if there was a safe place to get a massage in Krabi, this had to be it.

I hoped it would be a more enjoyable experience than my last one.

My masseuse was a proper swamp-donkey. I was a bit annoyed because there was a much prettier lady on duty, but straight away she had picked Linda.

Damn it.

"Relax," I told myself. Surely, that is the point of a massage? It was probably for the best, too – unless you count the agonizing brutality of the old woman at the herbal sauna, I'd never had a massage before, and I was a little concerned about the reaction my body would have to being rubbed all over with oil. At least this way I was unlikely to become aroused.

There was a brief moment of awkwardness as we were led into a curtained off area and told to strip. Apparently we were both being done together in the same cubicle. I respectfully turned my back and hoped Linda was doing the same. A couple of large towels handed in at an opportune moment salvaged the situation – and there we were, lying face down, stark naked on twin beds about a hand-span apart. "Relax…" I reminded myself.

I was already feeling a bit embarrassed, so I avoided looking at my masseuse as much as possible. The more attractive woman appeared through the curtain and got straight to work on Linda's shoulders. I closed my eyes, ignored her, and lay still.

Thirty seconds later my eyes shot open. The towel had been removed from my left buttock, though it was left strategically draped across the right for no immediately apparent reason. The first move in the massage was a long, slow glide up my left leg, terminating in a rather intimate cupping of my arse cheek. This however, was not the main cause of alarm. Being naked, and a guy, lying down involves certain… logistical considerations. Without putting too fine a point on it, 'it' has to lie somewhere – up, or down, to the left or right. Mine was down… and left. Which meant that, with each powerful stroke up my left leg, as the heel of her hands dug into the soft muscle tissue of my upper thigh – her trailing fingertips just grazed the end of my willy.

Relax…

Well, why fight it? There was nothing I could do. I sighed with relief as she switched legs and slid the towel across, then remembered that Linda was still lying right next to me. Too much sighing might be misconstrued…

I was finally starting to relax when the she finished on my legs – and started on my buttocks.

It was a shock for sure to feel the towel pulled away completely, but that was nothing. She had a particularly invasive technique reserved for my bum cheeks – I mean, she was really getting *in there*. If she'd been cleaning my bathroom I'd have been impressed with her thoroughness. Mid-massage, I just felt violated.

But what can you do? And it wasn't all bad… in fact it felt altogether too good. As time to turn over approached I realised that this was no longer a possibility for me – not without creating an interesting towel-sculpture in the process. The more I thought about it, the more of a problem it became. *Jesus*, I thought, "*if I turn over too quickly it might smack her in the face!*"

No choice. I rolled onto my back and resettled the towel. The masseuse looked at it, then pointedly at me. I closed my eyes and hid from her. I heard her chuckle to her friend, who responded in kind. Then to my horror an answering snigger came from Linda!

Oh my God, I thought, *I'll NEVER live this down! Damn her for cheating and taking a peek…*

And then my thoughts weren't on Linda anymore. Because the masseuse had taken hold of my leg. With one firm hand she was squeezing and massaging my ankle.

Her other hand was doing the same to my cock.

For the next half an hour I was treated to an amazing display of ambidexterity. Whichever side of me she was working on, her spare hand kept a constant rhythm on my willy – up and down, up and down, up and down. She was clearly quite experienced at this. I gritted my teeth and concentrated on anything other than what was happening to my penis. Imagine the mess I'd make… it didn't bear thinking about. Not with Linda well within splattering range. How was this happening? And why? And OH MY GOD! I gritted my teeth and thought of home, of the sea, of the ache starting to develop in my stomach from all this rough handling. *Please don't, please don't*, I prayed silently. Surely we were nearly finished?

I know I was.

I felt her breath in my ear before I heard the whisper. "You want stay for two-hour massage?"

Oh shit. I was already getting sore. If she carried on like this, in another hour she'd have snapped the thing off!

"No, thank-you," I managed, sounding more like I'd been running very fast up a bloody steep hill than lying on a soft mattress.

"So, finish!" she proclaimed. There was irony in that. And tears in my eyes. I struggled to my feet, dragging the towel tightly round me.

"Bathroom?" she asked perceptively, and pointed to the back of the shop.

I bolted through the curtains before Linda could sit up and make eye contact. I felt a powerful urge to be alone just then.

But it was not to be. The bathroom door had hardly closed behind me when my masseuse slipped in and put her arms around me. "Go across main road, there is car park," she told me. "If you want, I meet you there!"

How romantic.

And so I fled. I legged it outside as quickly as possible, muttering something about coming back later to appease the girl. In fact I just wanted to put as much distance between myself and her dubious massage parlour as possible.

Linda caught up with me outside.

One look at her face told me she already knew far too much. I staggered at the thought of it. And of course, my legs were still quite shaky. I gave up trying to outrun Linda's grin, and leaned back on a convenient wall, breathing hard.

"Are you okay?" Linda asked. She seemed genuinely concerned for a few seconds, before the mischief returned to her eyes.

"Yeah, sure," I lied. "I just need to catch my breath. That was... that was a..." I found I didn't even have the words to describe it. "Interesting," I finally managed.

"What's wrong? You're in a proper state!" she wasn't going to let it drop.

"I'm fine! Just... tender."

"Aww! Are you all embarrassed?" The mocking had started already.

"I don't want to talk about it."

"Don't worry, we can make it our little secret!"

"Bloody hell! I can't believe you looked. It's, like, the first rule of a massage – keep your eyes shut at all times!"

"Ah, come on, I didn't see anything. I kept my eyes closed."

"Bullshit. You know bloody well what was going on!"

That wiped the smile off Linda's face. "Eh? What? Tony, what happened?"

"Really? You didn't see... what she was doing?"

"No! Why? What was she doing?"

"Well, it was pretty, um, invasive… to say the least. It was, ah…"

I gave her a brief account.

Linda was blown away. "WHAT?! I can't believe it! Actually *playing* with your… Holy shit!"

It wasn't the reaction I'd been expecting from her.

"But I thought you knew! I could hear you giggling to yourself for half the massage!"

"No, I didn't look at all. No, really!" she saw the disbelief in my expression, "I swear I had my eyes closed the whole time. I could hear them giggling and I wondered what was going on, but I didn't dare look."

"So what the hell were you laughing at then?"

At this her grin reappeared magically. "Oh, Tone! You really didn't know, did you?"

"Know what?"

"I was just laughing because the one doing you was a man."

Full Moon

I was understandably quite keen to get away from Krabi.

I'd managed to elicit a promise from Linda that she would never tell anyone about what had happened there.

And as far as I know, she mostly kept it.

Mostly.

With our New Year's holiday quite literally a wash out, we'd agreed to return to Koh Pha Ngan as soon as possible. And as if to reward our loyalty, we were greeted on arrival by clear blue skies with not a cloud in sight.

I'd been declaring the rainy season over every time we had a dry day, and until now I'd always been punished for tempting fate when the heavens opened for another deluge.

But this was different.

This time it felt *right*.

I hardly dared say it, but maybe – just maybe – the rainy season really *was* over.

And it was just in time for the Full Moon, which had to be some sort of sign.

You know what they say: after the rain, comes the flood; in this case, of people.

We'd been penned up for too long, and the next Moon Party promised to be an epic affair. It also marked the official end of my stint of volunteering with PAC; it was hard to believe, but I'd been a clinic assistant for three months already. All the staff were looking to let off some steam, and this seemed like the perfect excuse – even though I couldn't see anything changing in the immediate future. I was still part of the clinic crew, and I wasn't going anywhere.

Well, other than to Haad Rin, for the party of my life!

On a Party night it wasn't advisable to hit the beach much before midnight. That was one of the tricks we'd learned, as veterans of the scene; being fashionably late was a survival mechanism more than anything else.

On a Full Moon Party night you got there when you could, sometimes waiting up to an hour for a taxi with enough room left in the back to contort into. You fought your way through the crowds to the beach, and from there to the nearest bar; and from then on, very little remained in your control.

You see, there is no party on earth quite like it. Nothing prepares you for the onslaught of twenty thousand people mobbing a strip of beach not much wider than a tennis court.

The booze is insanely cheap, dangerously drinkable and ridiculously potent; less than two pounds (or three dollars) buying you the infamous plastic bucket containing close to half a bottle of your chosen spirit. Vodka, whisky, brandy – the harsh taste of cheap liquor is covered with a couple of cans of coke, and then laced with an energy drink so concentrated it's banned in pretty much every country other than Thailand.

The straws, ostensibly to promote sharing, also made the liquor easier to drink. You didn't even need to stop dancing while you did it. And if the worst happened and you dropped a bucket – hell, join the club! There were dozens of the things rolling around the beach, and the concrete dance floors were slick with spillage. Dig deep – find another couple of quid – and buy another one…

People came from all over the world, thinking they were ready for the party to end all parties. Most of them were wrong.

The buckets seemed so innocent, so emblematic of Thailand, and they were so damn *delicious!*

The hard-core party-going fraternity of the world rocked up in their droves, at roughly the same time they would expect to start a night out back home.

They bought their first buckets at 9pm. Their second around 10pm.

Spurred on by the amphetamines in the energy drink, they would boogie harder than they'd ever known they could boogie; perhaps knocking back a couple of beers or the odd vodka-Red Bull in the process.

Somewhere between midnight and 2am it generally went squiffy, and around the time they'd normally be heading home to spend the night throwing up in the loo, the party was just getting going for those of us in the know.

At five-thirty, dawn hit, throwing the remaining revellers into stark relief. Up and down the beach as far as the eye could see, the sand was littered with motionless figures; face-up, face-down, in various states of dress and undress, the party-addicts of the previous night were this morning's casualties.

And moving between the unconscious forms were nimble-fingered locals, individually or in groups, calmly, methodically, robbing every single one of them.

It looked like they were looting the corpses on some ancient battlefield, except they didn't stop to slit the throats of the wounded.

For some of those unlucky customers, awaking half blind in the full light of day, with the worst hangover they'd ever known and a vicious sunburn to match, missing their watches, wallets, phones and jewellery – and sometimes most of their clothing – it might have been a mercy.

None of us had ever passed out on the beach, not since that first night when Linda and I found ourselves quite literally on the rocks.

We partied hard, but relatively responsibly; roughly halfway through each night, when I reached the point where I started slurring my words, Linda would ask to borrow my keys. I always fell for it, never having the presence of mind to wonder what she needed them for. Then, when time came to leave and I made my usual declaration that I could ride my scooter home and save the taxi fare to buy another drink, Linda would remind me that she had confiscated my keys, and that I'd have to come back for the bike after I'd sobered up.

Bless her, she had my best interests at heart, although I rarely appreciated it at the time.

I'd long since learned not to go out with anything I couldn't risk losing. I was always barefoot of course, but on Haad Rin nights I left my bungalow with exactly three items: my jeans, my keys, and a five-hundred *baht* note.

Underwear had been deemed a hindrance; likewise a shirt, which would only get lost anyway as it was impossible to keep the thing on whilst jumping through fire hoops and rolling around on the beach.

I was 2-1 down for shirts, after losing three but making up for it one night when a random t-shirt came sailing out of the darkness and landed on my head.

It fit me a treat, and I still wear it with pride.

Fire was the punctuation of every moon party. It was everywhere on the beach, from the incredibly talented fire dancers, whose lightening-fast stick-twirling was utterly mesmerising, to the flaming jump-ropes and limbo dancing contests, burning torches and blazing signage.

I got quite good at leaping through the hoops, suspended in the air by two Thai guys stood on bar stools. Of course, everyone thinks they're a ninja when they're drunk; I had my mishaps alongside my triumphs, including one time where I managed to set my hair alight. I saw plenty of people come off a lot worse though; enough booze makes anyone think they can fly, and one slightly larger lady paid for her indulgence when she made a pathetic hop, barely leaving the sand, and then pitched forward right on top of the burning hoop. The attached ropes dragged the Thai guys off their stools onto her, and by the time her friends had extricated her from the pile her clothes were charred to ash, as was quite a bit of the skin underneath. It wasn't the first time I saw someone stretchered off the beach, nor was it the last.

We usually danced in the Drop Inn – a dingy beachfront bar that played the cheesiest music around. In fact they played exactly the same cheesy music, night after night. I can tell you every song they played; if I think hard enough, I could probably tell you what order they were in too.

They had a DJ in a booth to maintain a professional image, but we all knew he had the entire night's musical repertoire stored as one playlist on his iPod.

The dance floor was packed; sweaty, energetic westerners mingled with locals – insanely hot women for the most part, all on the look out for a rich foreign date.

Or, customer, to be more accurate.

I had a rule about Thai women, formulated in my first few days in Thailand.

Actually, I had two rules. The first was to stay away from them completely. Especially on party nights. It was easy to tell which ones were hookers, because they all were; 'nice' Thai girls didn't go trolling bars for foreign boyfriends, no matter how pretty they were. They stayed at home with their families, dressed modestly and married nice Thai boys.

To show even a hint of interest in one of the scantily-clad Thai chicks at the Drop Inn bar would have been considered an instant invitation; they'd be all over you like a rash, and were harder to get rid of than a fart in a space-suit.

The other rule was less obvious.

Sure, if a Thai girl is talking to you, or dancing with you, she's a prostitute. But if she's out of your league – like way, way, out – stratospherically, orgasmically, smoking hot; then she's a man.

Some pretty girls became hookers, but not many.

The ones bumping and grinding on the dance floor, skinny as rails with flawless coffee-coloured skin, wearing one microscopically thin strip of Lycra around their bust and another around their hips, and absolutely *nothing* else – those were the infamous Thai lady-boys.

And they were absolutely stunning, to a man.

No pun intended.

Most of the hookers gyrated in the crowd, and it never took long for them to draw plenty of attention. We avoided getting caught in the crossfire by jumping straight up onto the stage, where we could bust out our worst moves for the appreciation of the whole bar.

I was loving the energy that night, feeding off it – and off the two buckets of strong alcohol swimming around my system.

I was bopping away with exactly one item of clothing on – my jeans – when the music reached a crescendo, and suddenly it all became clear.

The jeans were only hampering my freedom.

Constraining my movement and stopping me from being noticed.

Well, no more!

It was the work of seconds to drop them off me and fling them into the crowd.

When Linda found out, she was less than impressed of course.

Probably because she was dancing right next to me at the time.

She'd only turned away for a couple of heartbeats, to bust a few hand-jives in the opposite direction. Then she turned around and I was naked; tackle swinging freely (and quite energetically) to the rhythm of *La Bamba*.

I think she had a mild heart-attack.

She turned as though to go, visibly horrified, perhaps reacting to some primitive urge to flee – except that, dancing on the other side of her was Ridvan.

In one of those delightful moments of synchronicity, he'd come to exactly the same conclusion as I had, whipped his pants off and was also standing there stark bollock naked. Well, he was jiggling there, rather than standing.

Linda looked left. Linda looked right. Cock and balls flapped in both directions. There was panic in her expression. She could see no way out. The crowd cheered us on, surging up to the front of the stage. There was no escape!

Ridvan and I, dancing hard, suddenly realised that our audience wanted more. What more could we give them, naked as we already were? The excitement was palpable. A hundred pairs of eyes were fixed on these two naked fools, wondering what they could possibly do next –

So we did the only thing we could.

We made Linda the filling in a naked manwich.

Her shriek was audible despite us being less than three feet from the main speakers.

Phones and cameras flashed, lighting up our world – in that moment I finally knew what it was like to be a celebrity!

It's a damn good job I'm not easily embarrassed, I thought.

And such a pity that Linda is.

I had a feeling she might not forgive me for this one. Not quickly.

Things got chaotic after that.

We fled the crush as more people surged onto the stage, and found ourselves in the alley outside the Drop Inn. It was a rare space with room to stop and breathe, to regroup – only, we weren't a group any longer. I'd recovered my jeans – only to discover that my phone, which had been in the pocket, was gone.

Stupid!

Fun, but still, stupid!

Ridvan had last been seen running naked along the water's edge, his business flapping in the breeze, as he tried to find the bugger who had stolen his entire outfit.

Inwardly cursing the loss of yet another phone – I *was* cursed where technology was concerned – I volunteered to find Ridvan, hoping that I wouldn't have to spend the rest of the night with him in the nude.

I needn't have worried.

Finding anyone at a Full Moon Party was an exercise in futility. The press of bodies, the endless expanse of dancing figures covering the sand for as far as the eye could see, it made finding a needle in a haystack sound comparatively easy. That was why, against all my instincts, I'd brought my phone out with me. I searched the crowds for an age, before it occurred to me that I could take my quest to higher ground.

There was a door in the Drop Inn that led to a little-known staircase. That in turn led to a balcony where DJ's sometimes sat, but it was closed for the Full Moon because of the danger of drunken idiots jumping off it.

I'd always wanted to do that.

The balcony led over a narrow bridge, above the alley I'd just come from, to the balcony of the techno club next door. And from the bridge I had the best view it was possible to get, the one all the photographers used to get their postcard pictures of the Full Moon spectacle.

I still couldn't find him.

But then I heard a familiar voice. Clear as a bell, Linda said my name. I span around, expecting to find her behind me, and braced myself for a good telling off for being up here in the first place.

But Linda wasn't there.

Yet I could still hear her...

Beneath me.

I looked down and noticed Linda, Avril, Por and the rest of our group gathered in a circle directly below me. They were scanning the crowd in all directions, much as I'd just been doing – only from their height they had even less chance of success.

"I've no idea where Ridvan's gone, but now Tony's vanished too!" Linda sounded annoyed. I guess that shouldn't have been a surprise.

"I thought Tony went looking for Ridvan?" Avril said.

"He did. And now God knows where he is."

It was too tempting for me to resist. I leapt over the safety rail and jumped down off the bridge, landing with a massive 'SLAP!' – dead centre in the middle of the group.

"I'm here!" I yelled, right into their shocked faces.

"JESUS!" Avril shrieked.

"No, no, only me." I grinned around at them all.

"You were up there the whole time?"

"Only some of it. I was looking for Ridvan. But he's nowhere."

"You gave me a fright! We were just trying to find you. We're going to get a drink. Are you coming?"

"I'll catch up," I told her, and Avril led the others back into the blaring noise of the Drop Inn.

Only Linda stayed behind, and she waited until the others had gone before asking, "Are you okay?"

"No," I admitted. I let my grin fade, and clenched my teeth against the pain shooting up my right leg.

"Did you hurt yourself?"

"Yes, a bit. I think I've broken something."

"Oh, Tone! What am I going to do with you?"

"I've done my foot in. I don't think I can walk. Can you… get me a drink?"

"Oh God! Of course I can. Wait here."

"Thanks Linda."

"Yeah, right. You know what you are?"

"Um… magic?"

"You're an idiot."

And for once, I agreed with her.

Monkey Business

My foot wasn't broken.

It felt like it for a long time, but there wasn't much I could do about that.

The hospital on Koh Pha Ngan didn't have an x-ray machine, and there was no way I was going to spend hours on a ferry just to be told to rest the thing.

So I rested it.

My phone, however, was gone for good, which meant a trip into Thong Sala to replace it. On the up side, this was a good time to buy; funnily enough, the choice of second hand phones on offer increased dramatically just after the full moon. It wasn't hard to imagine why – with only one phone shop on the island, any handset that was 'found' by one of the locals was bound to end up there sooner or later.

In fact, as I stood there browsing the possibilities, a familiar phone caught my eye.

"That one?" I asked, tapping the glass display case.

The shop owner obliged, handing me the phone which, until yesterday, had been mine. I turned it on; it still had charge. Sadly the SIM had been removed and all my numbers wiped from the memory. Not that I was hoping to prove ownership of course – good luck to anyone trying that tack! But it did mean I had the gruelling task of reacquiring phone numbers from everyone I knew on the island. Punishment, I guess, for being dumb enough to take my phone out during full moon. In addition to the three-hundred *baht* price tag, which might as well be considered a fine. Or maybe an idiot tax? It certainly wasn't a mistake I'd be repeating.

I swung by the clinic to see Linda, then headed for home to work on that foot resting business. It was time to relax, and maybe do some thinking.

One of the things I loved most about my job was the sense of identity it gave me. Back home I was no-one in particular (and what with all this gallivanting off around the world, I was likely to stay that way), but here I was 'That Guy That Works At The Animal Place'. Everyone recognised me, regardless of whether or not I recognised them. It was a bit spooky at times, when random Thai people would just start chatting to me as though I knew them. Maybe I'd held their dog while it got its jabs, or come to collect a sick cat from their resort. But the strangest occurrences were when someone had an animal problem and came straight to me.

Later that afternoon I was stretched out in my hammock when Eieu came rushing up. "Tony, need help at next-door! Have... ah... monkey!" she told me urgently.

Technically I no longer worked at the clinic; my three months' indentured labour had come to an end and I was now diving for a living. But I still kept a weather eye on PAC, helping out on odd days and doing little chores for them when I could.

So with an urgent problem occurring right next-door and the clinic typically up to their eyes in sick animals, I had to check it out.

Eieu led me around the line of coconut trees separating her resort from the next one over. "There! In restaurant!" she pointed.

A truly massive monkey sat on a table glaring belligerently at the customers. He was a macaque – the kind kept by coconut farmers for climbing trees – with a protruding snout, a bulbous nose, reddish-grey fur and long, heavily muscled arms. A length of thick chain hung from a leather collar around his neck.

Interspersed with the customers now hovering around the restaurant entrance was a fairly hefty number of cops. With Koh Pha Ngan being such a tiny island, the six or seven uniformed officers in attendance must have comprised at least half the force. Yet they seemed to be having a spectacular lack of effect on the situation. Some lounged against palm trees. The rest were filming the monkey on their phones, or sending text messages. Probably telling the other half of the force to come and have a look.

The resort owner spotted me and hurried over. "Help!" she said. "He escape from somewhere... go crazy in restaurant! He throw things, break things... scare everyone. Him not happy!"

Contrary to this assessment, the monkey now seemed to be picking his toe nails.

I gave the owner a reassuring smile and walked into the restaurant. Everyone had panicked, I figured, when the monkey landed in their midst and started flinging things. Their panic had probably made him worse, and there was no doubt that in a bad mood he was capable of demolishing the place.

His long, muscular arms were used to hauling him to the top of the giant palm trees at a speed that was dizzying to behold. Once up there he had to wrench the coconuts free from their stems and toss them down onto nets laid out below.

It was the kind of job that kept a monkey in good shape.

And the kind of job I couldn't fault him for escaping from.

At some point his lead chain had gotten caught under the leg of the table he was sitting on, which had probably driven him wild – certainly enough to persuade anyone still sitting in the area to get the hell out.

But he was used to being chained up. By now, having sat around long enough for Pha Ngan's finest to make YouTube clips of him, he'd calmed down quite a bit.

Or at least, I hoped so.

I looked down at the floor as I approached his table, lifting my eyes occasionally but without making eye contact.

I'm not a threat to you, I thought. Just in case he was telepathic.

As I hoped, he completely ignored me.

When I was stood next to him I reached down and freed the chain. I crooned and hummed under my breath, a low murmur of sound that I hoped would communicate my desire for friendship. Where this idea first came from I have no idea – it's just something I've always done around animals. Mostly it seems to work.

Then without warning the monkey grabbed my arm – and hauled himself upright. He looked at me as if to say, "Let's go."

So we went. Chain in hand I led him calmly out of the restaurant, and into the shade of a nearby palm tree.

All around me people stared with open mouths. This must be what Jesus felt like after a quick stroll on Lake Galilee, I mused. We sat together on the sand, the monkey and I; he busied himself with a spot of personal grooming while I wondered what the bloody hell I was going to do with a three-foot monkey now that I had one.

Neither of us gave much concern to our surroundings, until a tourist from the resort edged a bit too close with his camera. Suddenly my monkey friend bounded forward with a deep growl. He pounded the ground and bared his teeth at the guy, who must have realised just how much damage those inch-long canines could do to his soft pink body. He went a bit pale at the thought and edged slowly backwards.

And the monkey went back to hunting lice.

Now what?

People had been calling me Monkey Man for quite some time now, but I'd always assumed it was because I'm damn ugly.

Yet here again was proof of some sort of bonding with these animals, an understanding between species perhaps. Or maybe I'm just a few million years of evolution behind everyone else. My eyebrows alone could be considered proof of this.

Whatever. Musing on my affinity for primates wasn't going to get me out of this situation. What the hell was I supposed to do with this bloody great big hairy monkey?

He may well have been asking himself the same question.

Our dilemma was solved by a very small boy. To my western eyes he looked about six, which meant he was probably approaching his teens. The resort owner brought him over and held him at a safe distance while she called to me, "Him know! Him know from where monkey!"

Well now! This was good news. Moving slowly and calmly, I got to my feet and led the monkey out of the resort. The boy stayed far enough ahead of us, and a small crowd of cops and holiday-makers followed behind.

The monkey seemed quite content to go for a stroll down the sandy lane, and I encouraged him now and then with a gentle tug on the chain.

A bike approached, the droning of its engine preceding it, and I moved to one side to let it pass. The monkey had other ideas though, and leapt towards it shrieking and clawing. The rider wobbled and slewed off the path into the undergrowth, finally regaining the road a bit further along.

"Mind yer fucking monkey!" he bellowed back at us.

"It's NOT my monkey," I retaliated.

But quietly, just in case I upset the big fella.

I kept him a little closer after that.

Before long our strange procession turned onto the main road, and the boy led us towards the scattering of shops surrounding the Liberty junction.

Yorik was sitting on the forecourt as we passed his bike shop. "Huh. Nice monkey you got there," he grunted.

"It's not my monkey," I told him. "It's escaped from somewhere. I'm walking him home."

"He belong to that guy from behind here?"

"Err... I dunno? Yeah, I guess so. This boy thinks he knows."

"Okay. Give him here."

"Oh? Well..."

And before I could say another word, Yorik reached out and took the end of the chain off me. He stared down at the monkey as though making sure it appreciated the switch in power.

"How's the bike?" he asked.

"It's... good, yeah. Thanks." I was a little thrown by the sudden change of tack.

"You crashed it again, huh?"

"Ah, no. Not yet."

"Uh-huh. You will."

"I, um, hope not."

"Right." Then he tugged on the chain, and the monkey, who'd sat down on the curb for a rest, climbed obediently to his feet.

"Okay. See ya," said Yorik.

And just like that, he strode off with the monkey in tow. As though it was the most natural thing in the world.

I never did figure that guy out.

And then my phone rang. I'd only given the new number to two people.

It was Linda.

"I hear you've got yourself a monkey?"

Wow. Word spread fast around here.

"No. Not any more. I had a monkey. Now I don't have a monkey."

"Did you *lose* your monkey? Were you spanking it too much?" I could tell from the tone in her voice she was taking the piss out of me.

"It's not *my* monkey! It belongs to some guy who lives behind Yorik."

"That's a shame, because I know you've been kind of lonely lately... and I heard you like 'em hairy!"

"Oi! Watch it!"

"Sorry Tone. Only messing. Was it a male? Or a female?"

"Err... I dunno."

"Oh, that's right! I forgot, you have trouble telling the difference."

"Hey! You said —"

"Sorry, sorry! I couldn't help it. I'll be serious now. What kind of monkey was it?"

"A bloody great big ugly bugger."

"I see. I wonder…"

"Eh? You wonder what?"

"I wonder… are you sure you haven't found your soul mate?"

.

Shift Change

I was having one of those dull weeks when I wasn't doing much of anything.

After finishing her volunteering stint, Linda had asked if she could replace Avril, who had come to the end of her year as administrator. Unfortunately for me, being the boss was keeping Linda much busier than being a humble clinic assistant had. I still called around most days to see if there was something I could do to help out, but they had a full complement of volunteers again, and more often than not all I could do was drive into town and fetch them some lunch.

Occasionally there would be a suitably manly task that required my attention; like burying a less fortunate patient, or pulling the ticks off dogs – or like when a gigantic centipede was discovered mooching around Linda's living room and needed removing. Those things were seriously poisonous, with one bite causing agony in humans and quite often death to cats and dogs. So it had to go, and none of the staff wanted to tackle it. Oh, sure, they could cut the balls off anything that moved, but show them a real fight and they went and hid in the corner!

Which was a mistake, as that's where the centipede was hanging out.

A somewhat panicked Linda offered me first a brush, then a butter-knife, then a hammer, by way of a weapon.

I'd bought a machete from the market a few months back – for the clinic of course, not for me – but that seemed like overkill; eventually I settled on a sizeable kitchen knife and attacked the beast with that.

I lost that first fight, discovering that the knife was blunt in the process, and retreated to the bedroom where I was seriously reconsidering the use of Linda's hammer.

In the end a second, even more vicious-looking kitchen knife spelled the end for the beast, though the little bugger kept trying to bite me long after I'd cut him in half. It seemed to be the season for them; a few days later Nick discovered one in his bed. But not before it bit him on the bum cheek.

One side of his arse swelled up like an inflatable armband, and (apparently) went a bright blue-ish black – though I took his word for this part of the story.

It was a full week before he could walk, let alone take me diving again.

Ridvan had buggered off to Bangkok on some mysterious errand; I only knew this because he'd asked me for a lift to the ferry.

"When I come back, I'm totally gonna bring those t-shirts, man!" he promised.

It was his latest scheme to stay on the island permanently; designing and printing witty slogan t-shirts to sell to tourists, and eventually, to tourist shops.

It was a crap idea, born of one too many whiskies back when the rain was penning us inside day and night.

Unfortunately it was also my idea, so Ridvan had built me into his plans in spite of my objections.

Realistically, there was no way in hell we were going to become t-shirt entrepreneurs. But trying to tell Ridvan that was like trying to tell Gandhi that we'd given peace a go, but it wasn't really working for us.

And so, not only was I without my friend and wingman for a week – when he returned it would be with boxes of shitty t-shirts that he expected me to help him sell.

Luckily, I hadn't been left entirely alone. The founder of PAC, a delightful Irish lady called Shevaun, had returned to the island for a spell to oversee the running of the clinic. She was a vet herself, living in Hong Kong, but she spent as much time as she could on Koh Pha Ngan, nurturing the clinic as though it was her baby.

Which in a way it was. Her devotion to PAC was absolute, bordering on obsession; there was no other way really, as the whole organisation was held together by the twin forces of her love and her willpower.

Shevaun and I had taken to hanging out together quite a bit, as we both enjoyed exploring the island. She was a workaholic of course – it went with the territory – but she also embraced the lifestyle of the island and its relaxed, stress-free vibe.

That was why she'd chosen Koh Pha Ngan, of all places, to found her clinic.

Well, that, and the sheer number of stray dogs that needed their balls cutting off. Once, she described her personal philosophy to me: "I want to spent the rest of my life with sunglasses on my head," she'd said.

It was a sentiment I could well understand.

The only problems I had with declaring myself an expat and settling down on Koh Pha Ngan forever were 1) the money, of which there never seemed to be enough, and 2) the visa runs, which I loathed.

Especially as I was due to set off on the next one in about three hours' time.

While I waited, the pair of us were relaxing in Shevaun's rented bungalow. One entire wall of the place was made of roll-up blinds which we'd left open to the cool evening air.

She was telling me about the toughest part of running the clinic; not chasing donations or organising medicine shipments or dealing with labyrinthine Thai legislation. In truth it was always hardest to get, and to keep, good staff.

There'd been a constant flow of volunteers through the clinic since I'd finished my official stint. Some had been better than others, but recently we'd had one girl whose uselessness was only matched by her beauty.

She was called Lauren, and she'd made fantastic eye-candy.

And that morning, Shevaun had had to fire her.

"It's an odd thing," she said, "to have to fire a volunteer. But to be honest, she was so rarely at the clinic that it will hardly make a difference."

Lauren had showed up for a shift now and then, often days since the last time anyone had seen her. Her excuse was always the same – she'd gone out to a party and lost all track of time. Really.

Lost track of time? She'd been missing for up to a week!

The first few times we'd come close to calling the police. The only thing that stopped us was the knowledge that the police, if informed, would do absolutely sod all about it anyway.

At first our little social crowd had been the apologetic ones when she suddenly resurfaced, having missed several shifts at the clinic. I thought perhaps it was our fault, for leading her into a lifestyle that was clearly too much for her to cope with.

Then, as it happened again and again – and again – we came to the only conclusion we could: that Lauren was a brainless party bimbo with no intention whatsoever of helping out at PAC.

Personally I found such a dereliction of duty unthinkable, but Lauren just didn't care. She seemed to drift through life, not paying much attention to anyone or anything; all that mattered to her was the next party. She was so busy going out to them that she frequently met herself coming back. What happened to her during those long periods of absence we never did find out. With anyone else I would have imagined them locked in a bungalow, devouring a new sexual partner (or partners) in a week-long orgy of drink-and-drug-induced debauchery. But Lauren? She seemed too… *ditsy*, for that. She was very pretty, and had a smokin' hot body, yet she somehow lacked enough presence to be a sexual being. Even when she was there, she wasn't – her sing-song voice and vague manner always made me think she was off with the fairies.

She didn't seemed grounded enough to crave a good rooting.

Eventually Shevaun called it – she had 'the chat' with Lauren, and they came to a mutual understanding. Both women agreed completely, that Lauren was utterly useless as a clinic assistant.

So Shevaun asked me to step in until a replacement volunteer showed up.

I didn't mind one bit.

"Did you ask her what happened, when she went off partying and didn't come back for days?" I asked. I had to know.

"Yes."

"And?"

"I half expected she'd have some sob story about being drugged up or date-raped, or she'd admit to a serious addiction to something."

"And?"

"Nothing. I asked her what happened, and all she said was, 'Ohhh! Mmm. I don't know, really…'!"

"Wow."

"That's what I thought."

"Do you think she's nuts? Like, properly crazy?"

"I'm having thoughts that way, absolutely. It's funny – remember, we named that crazy white poodle after her? Silly-Lorrie! Because that's how we always thought of her – pretty, but a bit nuts. But then she got crazier and crazier by the minute. It's almost like she's got…"

And Shevaun trailed off.

I sat in silence, wondering what she'd been about to say. I have a bad habit of anticipating the ends of people's sentences, and saying them before they do – to let them know I'm paying attention. Something had just changed though, a sudden cooling of the air. I looked at Shevaun for a clue as to what had cut off her train of thought.

Her face was white. Whiter than normal, I mean. The blood had drained away in shock.

"You okay?" I put a joke in my voice, recalling the subject of our conversation.

She didn't take the bait.

"That poodle," she breathed. "She got madder and madder, until she died."

"I know. I wrapped her up and buried her this morning."

Shevaun turned to look at me, and there was real fear in her eyes. "She could have died of rabies."

Then it was my turn to go pale.

Rabies… one of the most dreaded diseases on the planet.

Incurable. Utterly deadly.

And highly contagious.

I'd been immunised of course. It was recommended for all PAC staff. But the immunisation for rabies worked a little differently from most of them. It couldn't stop you getting the disease – nothing could, really. Instead it gave you roughly 24 hours – if symptoms developed – to get to a major medical centre, where doctors could race against the odds to try and save your life.

Any later than that, and you were gone.

The enormity of what Shevaun had just realized flooded into my brain. How many volunteers had been through the clinic in the last few weeks? Stuffing tubes down that dog's throat, nurses taking blood, clinic assistants scrubbing up her piss and shit… all of them from different countries. Most of them safely on their way home to various parts of the world.

And this afternoon that dog had died, as mad as a straw hat.

Had we just started a global epidemic?

Oh God. I really hoped not.

Partial Delivery

Action stations.

I took our rusty shovel and exhumed the body.

Now there's a sentence I never thought I'd write!

It was a definite first for me.

I'd buried quite a few animals in my time here, but I'd never had occasion to dig one up again.

Then Shevaun enlisted the help of the new nurse, a volunteer who'd only arrived this afternoon and probably hadn't even unpacked yet. While she readied the operating table, we hunted behind the clinic for old coolers, the polystyrene boxes that were used to transport donated medicines to PAC from the mainland.

"Ugh! This one's full of spiders!"

"Don't worry. I'll sort them out."

The dog had to go to a major veterinary clinic for testing, because PAC didn't have anything like the required technology. Hell, we didn't even have a microscope, and most kids get one of those before they turn ten.

So after Shevaun made a few frantic phone calls, the ladies started to prepare the dog for transit.

I stood at the sink, scrubbing dirt out of the polystyrene box. It had been sitting outside the clinic for a few weeks, and was starting to become a miniature ecosystem in its own right.

It was quite a small ecosystem though.

I decided to voice my concerns before it was too late.

"You know what, guys, I don't think she's going to fit in this..."

Then I froze.

The scene which had presented itself as I turned around was not one I'll be forgetting in a hurry.

Poised over the corpse of the dog, the nurse was wielding two instruments. In one hand a scalpel, dripping blood; in the other, yet to be bloodied – never to be bloodied I hoped – was a saw.

"I..."

Shevaun saw the look on my face and beckoned me over to the table. "We're about ready to start," she explained.

"But what are you doing?"

"I told you – we need to send it to the mainland for testing."

"But.. but why…?"

"Oh, I see!" Understanding dawned in her eyes. "We don't need the whole dog!"

Of course not! Silly me. Why send the whole dog, when you can just chop a piece off and send that?

"So you're going to…" I couldn't take my eyes off the shine of the saw. It didn't look like it had ever been used.

"Rabies lodges in the brain stem. That's what they need to do the tests on."

"So…"

"We're sending the head," Shevaun said.

"Riiight…"

"Are you going to stand there gawping, or are you going to come and help?"

That was a very good question.

To which there could only really be one answer.

Be a man, Tony. Be a man.

"Yeah, sure. What do you need me to do?"

"Come and hold her head."

Right. I could do that. I'd been restraining dogs at the clinic on a daily basis, and I'd heard that request plenty of times.

But this was the first time the head was going to come off in my hands.

I took position opposite the new nurse, noticing as I did that she was kind of cute. Slim and delicate, with high cheekbones and grey-green eyes behind her glasses.

I made a mental note to introduce myself, though ideally under better circumstances.

In one hand she was brandishing the shiny steel saw, making practise cuts in the fresh air above our patient.

I curled my fingers through Silly-Lorrie's fringe and made a fist to hold her steady.

Then the nurse made the first cut with the saw. Blood didn't spray; it just splattered.

And suddenly that nurse didn't look so cute anymore.

She leaned in to put her weight behind the blade, and the vibrations of each cut transmitted through the dog into my hands, up my arms, and back down into the pit of my stomach.

But I didn't throw up.

I was past all that.

She was mostly through the bone when Shevaun handed me a thick black bin liner rescued from the kitchen drawer. I took the bag, shook it open and held it with both hands beneath the dog's head.

Just in time. There was a little crack, and a tearing sound, and a last stroke of the saw sent the head into free-fall.

It landed in the bag with a sickening thud.

I don't know what I expected, but it was surprisingly heavy. You know, for a severed head.

But then, my experience with them is fairly limited.

Wrapped in the black bin bag, the head was far less disturbing. It could almost be anything…

Except it wasn't.

It was the decapitated head of a dog, shortly to be placed in a now spider-free polystyrene box.

"Won't it start to smell after a bit," I asked.

Shevaun nodded. "Don't worry, I've thought of that."

"Good. So?"

"Would you mind nipping down to the Seven-Eleven and getting a bag of ice?"

Such an innocent request. I was almost grateful.

"Yeah, sure. No problem. Do you… does anyone want anything?"

"I fancy a can of Coke, actually," said Shevaun.

"I wouldn't mind one too," said the nurse.

"Right then. Coke, and ice. At least I'll look like a normal customer."

I made for the door.

"Oh, and Tony?" Shevaun called.

"Yeah?"

"Better get some duct tape."

By the time I returned with the corpse disposal kit, the head was wrapped in several layers of plastic. Shevaun held the thing while I cocooned it in duct tape, and together we placed it gingerly into the cooler full of ice. More ice was poured over the top, and then the lid was fastened on and sealed with more tape. From the outside it looked like any other package; some flowers perhaps, or a delivery of medicine such had originally graced the box.

Only the three of us knew the secret.

Oh, and Linda. Because bike-ninja though I was, I couldn't carry the thing and steer at the same time; Linda was going to have to come with me.

Now, Linda and I had a long-standing disagreement about the driving of motorbikes.

I was of the opinion that they should be driven fast enough to remain upright, the better to avoid falling off; she felt that they should be driven slowly enough that you wouldn't hurt yourself even if you did fall off.

Okay, so she would say that I was a speed freak. Admittedly one of my main aims in life was to get my bike up to 100kmph – an almost impossible feat on a 100cc bike and with most of the roads pockmarked with craters.

And I'll also admit that terrifying Linda was a hobby of mine, because it was fun, and easy, and the only damage was psychological.

Unfortunately, she'd yet to master the art of riding two-up with a passenger on the back. Which meant that not only did she have to put up with my driving – she had to carry the box.

When she left me at the ferry I carried the box on board, being careful to place it so it would be wedged upright in the baggage area. The usual ordeal of scuffling over beds was over quickly and the boat pulled away into the night.

I'd only just made it; call me disorganised if you like, but I hadn't left much room in my schedule for decapitation.

Now, it was all over, and I could relax. Nothing much could go wrong – unless one of the other passengers had a similar cooler full of soft drinks, and opened up the wrong one by mistake.

I'd developed a habit, over the last few visa runs, of escaping the sleeping area as soon as we were at sea. To do this I squeezed out of one of the windows and sat on a narrow ledge, barely a hand-span wide, that ran around the outside of the boat at deck level. Discovering those eight inches of private accommodation had been one of the happiest moments of my life. After worming my way out of the window I folded myself up like a gargoyle, and perched with my heels on the ledge while the Gulf of Thailand churned away a couple of meters beneath my toes. And there I could be alone with my thoughts, to dream of the future, of a life lived in Thailand, of maintaining my little circle of friends through many more adventures, and on and on until the end of time.

I was utterly content here. I was happy.

Then a scruffy head poked through the window, and I braced myself for a bollocking.

"Mind if I join you?" said the man.

"Why not?" I replied.

So he climbed out and sat on the ledge, sparking up a spliff he'd brought for the occasion.

"Can't sleep otherwise," he explained.

We sat in companionable silence for a few minutes.

Then I said to him, "I bet I've got stranger luggage than you."

The stranger considered this, puffing on his joint. "Okay. What have you got?"

"You first. My bet."

"Fair enough." He took another drag while he thought about it. "I've got weed, of course. And my guitar. And some mini-bongos, made from coconuts. Oh, and see this?" he swung his head, revealing a dreadlock on the other side. "Fake – but it's real hair."

"Not bad," I told him. "Not bad at all."

"And what about you then?"

"I have the severed head of a dog in a polystyrene box."

Mrs Da met me at the docks as usual. 5am never looked any prettier in Surat Thani.

While we waited for the rest of her customers to show, I asked about the vet who had agreed to meet us.

"I call him now," Mrs Da said. "He come to my shop."

"Okay then. This is what he wants." I indicated the box on the ground between us.

"Yes, aha, okay. I put in back, for when he come."

"That's good. But it's probably best not to touch it."

"Aha. What is?"

"Head. Of dog." A night on the ferry had sapped even my desire for comedy.

"Is safe?" she queried.

"Well, it won't bite you," I said.

But then I thought about this. Was it safe?

The only answer I could arrive at was no. This thing was not safe. Not in the least.

It was a biological hazard of apocalyptic proportions. She'd have been safer stashing an atomic bomb in the back of her shop.

And that's when it hit me: Mrs Da's shop wasn't a shop.

It was a restaurant.

And the back of it, quite obviously, was the kitchen.

"Ah, Mrs Da? This, ah, not good to keep in kitchen."

"Eh?"

"This," I said, placing my hands on the box, "NOT in kitchen.

Okay?"

"Not in Kitchen. In shop?"

There weren't many places to hide in a typical Thai three-sided concrete cube.

There was the added problem of the ice; I'd bought it from the Seven-Eleven nearly ten hours ago, and already the day was starting to get hot. It goes without saying that it wouldn't last forever. At some point in the not-too-distant future, this innocent little box would start to smell like someone had stuffed a dead dog's head in there.

I mulled it over.

Then I had an idea. "In bathroom?"

I'd had the occasion to visit Mrs Da's bathroom several times on previous visa runs. It wasn't something I relished. The place was a potential source for contagion only marginally less worrying than the dog's head itself.

"Okay. I put in bathroom."

That was better. Then, if all went according to plan and the vet showed up on schedule, the head would be out of her way long before Mrs Da was properly open for business.

And if not? Well at least this way, if it started to smell, she could always blame the toilet.

By the time I got back from Burma, we knew we were in the clear. Silly-Lorrie had indeed died of a degenerative brain disease, but not one that was going to kick-start the zombie apocalypse.

Shevaun was intensely relieved – and she was also on her way back to Hong Kong.

But Ridvan was there at the docks to meet me, grinning like a maniac.

He was wearing a huge black t-shirt that engulfed his scrawny frame. On the front was printed:

My other t-shirt is cooler than this one.

Oh, crap, I thought. *Should have stayed in Burma.*

Cash Flow; Or Lack Thereof

Bike repairs.

Bloody bike repairs!

Was there no end to them?

I put this question to Yorik, as he relieved me of the last of the cash I owed him.

"You'll stop paying for it when you stop crashing my bikes," he grumbled.

Which I guess was a valid point.

In spite of myself I was starting to like Yorik. Or maybe like is too strong a word; I was starting to *get* him.

At least I felt comfortable arguing with him now and then.

"Can you just not put the bloody basket back on? The damn things are made of tin-foil. I swear, I only need to look at it and it's wrecked."

"Can't have you driving round looking like a bad advert for my bikes," he said.

How much did I want to say, 'I'm a bad advert for your bikes? Look in the mirror mate!'

But I didn't. There was no reason to let it get personal.

I'd had two major crashes in the last few months – one had been my fault, and one had not.

The first time I'd been speeding down an unlit hill on the far side of the island, carrying a very precious cargo of peach iced teas in my basket. Because the baskets were stupid, stupid things, the ice teas filling mine obscured my single headlight. Which meant I didn't see the humongous pothole at the bottom of the hill, and my bike slammed into it so hard that any chance of having children was gone for good. Then it bounced out the other side, and at that moment the rough treatment proved too much for the iced-teas, so they tried to escape.

As the teas went airborne, I instinctively reached out to catch them – and in the process lost control of my bike.

It slid out from under me, landed on top of me, then dragged me down the road for a hundred metres still underneath it.

A local woman rushed out from a house nearby – the only house in fact, as I was fairly deep in the jungle – and she doused my wounds with antiseptic from a tiny yellow bottle.

I rode the rest of the way home in shock and arrived at Liberty quite the worse for wear. My friends at the time took one look at my face – and another at my back – and nearly called an ambulance.

I healed. Eventually. I'd lost most of the skin on my back, giving it the colour and consistency of raw steak, and it was a few weeks before I could do anything more strenuous than hang around the resort eating Eieu's delicious cooking and running up a sizeable tab on booze.

The bike had lost all the bodywork on its right side, all the rubber on the grips and pegs, and needed a good few bits of metal beating back into shape before it was road-worthy again.

Oh – and it needed a new basket.

Bloody baskets.

The next accident had been over a month later ("you see?" I'd told Yorik afterwards, "I don't crash your bike *all* the time.")

I'd been moving out to overtake a scooter with one guy and two skinny Thai chicks on it, when they'd decided to pull up at one of the 'lady bars'.

The one on the other side of the road.

Without warning, and certainly without looking, their bike had turned right across my front wheel, stopping it much more efficiently than my brakes ever could have. Broadsided, they fell flat, whereas I was on the receiving end of all the momentum my bike had been building up.

I flew off my bike, over theirs, and landed a good way down the road – luckily enough on my head, which is the part of me least susceptible to damage.

Well, people are always telling me I must have been dropped on my head at birth. What was one more knock going to do to me?

The police were called to that one, by the owner of the Lady bar. An officer showed up promptly, while three people were still trying to stop my bleeding.

He spoke English, which was an immediate relief.

Somewhat woozily I explained the whole situation to him. There had been no warning – no indication of any kind. The keys were still in the ignition of the other bike. It was still turned on. If the indicator had been flashing at the time of the accident, it would still have been doing so now.

The policeman relayed this accusation to the Thai man who'd been driving the scooter, and in response he grabbed his handlebar and angrily yanked the stem up and down. His indicators didn't work, he explained, which apparently absolved him from all responsibility.

Then the officer told me that according to Thai law, whoever was behind was at fault. Although I'd landed quite a way in front, my bike had been to the rear at the time of the accident.

Which meant that this time I'd had to pay for my repairs *and* some of theirs. After the driver followed me to hospital to demand a ridiculous fee, I bargained with him until he settled for a more sensible amount, and that was the end of it.

Then I took my bike back to Yorik and showed him the mess I'd made of it.

"But this time it wasn't my fault!" I said.

"So who paid for the other guy's bike?"

"Um… that would be me."

"And who's gonna pay for yours?"

"That… would also be me."

"Hm. Figured."

I could tell he didn't believe me.

But there wasn't much I could do about it, apart from leave my bike with him, wait for the bill to arrive, and visit Linda in her bungalow to bitch about what a pain in the arse Yorik was.

And you know what? He replaced the basket first.

I swear he was doing it on purpose.

Partially because of all this, I was coming to the end of my money. I blamed the diving too; the course itself was the single biggest expense I'd incurred, and then Nick had recommended that I start to acquire some equipment of my own. I was super-keen on diving as I'd passed a whole slew of exams with flying colours, so I went a bit overboard (no pun intended) and bought all kinds of random bits.

Fins. Snorkel. Dive slate. Safety Sausage.

Yup! The big stuff I got him to order for me, with the promise that I'd figure out how to pay for it when it all arrived.

And no, I'm not telling you what a Safety Sausage is for. You'll just have to look that up for yourself.

So, between repairs and impulse buying and the mounting cost of partying – plus little incidental expenses like, you know, food and rent – my original three grand had dwindled to the point where I was starting to worry.

A smarter person might have started to worry when they got down to the last third of their money, but I'd embraced the laid-back culture of the island completely over the last few months.

So I didn't start to worry until I was down to my last ten quid.

Then I did panic a little, and my first thought was to call Gill.

I figured she would know how my parents were feeling at the moment, and whether or not this would be a good time to ring them and beg for money.

She was more excited than I expected, when I got through to her.

"Tony! Mum and Dad have been trying to get hold of you for weeks!"

"Oh? Right. Yeah, well I was thinking of calling them, but… I dunno. Busy, really."

"Busy drinking you mean?"

"No! Well, yes, but also no. Busy diving and… stuff."

"Stuff, huh?"

"Yup. Stuff."

"Well they're really worried about you. Apparently Mum got an email from you saying you were 'okay, and not to worry' – which obviously made her worry. What's wrong?"

"Oh, nothing! I had an accident is all, fell of my bike and made a bit of a mess."

"Oh, bloody hell! I *knew* you were going to do that. Mum thought you were in prison for drugs, or had caught something incurable from a twelve-year-old prostitute."

"WHAT? Hey! Shit dude, I'm not that bad! Thanks for the vote of confidence."

"Yeah, but you know she worries, like, 500 times worse than anyone else ever…"

"Yeah…"

"and you have been known to do some fairly stupid things."

I started to protest, then realised I was utterly broke and stranded on the opposite side of the world. I was sitting on a bike I'd crashed so many times that I couldn't afford the repairs.

And I still wasn't wearing any shoes.

"Yes, that is true," I admitted.

"So you should probably call her. And stop sending cryptic emails."

"Ah. Okay."

"And one other thing – she keeps getting phone calls from some army dude, she says he sounds really pissed off that you're not here."

"Oh… shit. Yeah. I guess she'd better tell him that I'm not coming back…"

"Really? Well you can tell her that yourself, and good luck with it!"

"Ouch. I don't know who'll be more pissed off – Mum, or the army!"

"At least you know Mum's not going to shoot you as a deserter."

"Shit, do they still do that?"

"I don't know! Why are you asking me? You're the army dude."

"Yeah. Not so much, any more. Ah well. I guess if I stay out of England for long enough, they'll forget about me?"

"Ha! Maybe. Anyway, do you want to hear some good news?"

"Good news? Of course I do!"

"We're in the money, dude! Mum and Dad have re-mortgaged Treorchy so they can use the 'profit' on another house – and they've given us our share!"

"What? No way! That's awesome news!"

"Yeah, pretty sweet isn't it? We've got two grand each. I'm going to use mine to visit Roo in Australia."

"Wow… that sounds pretty cool."

"Yeah, I can't wait! I'll be going as soon as I can find a decent flight. I thought I might swing through Thailand and visit you!"

"Yeah, that'd be great."

"So what do you want doing with your money? Put it in the bank?"

Sister or not, if I could have reached through the phone and kissed her, I would have. But I didn't want her to know how desperate I was.

"Yeah, might as well put it in the bank. It'd be nice to have a bit in reserve, just in case…"

"Right. In the bank it'll go. Tomorrow in fact."

"Thanks dude."

"You're welcome. Just don't spend it all on booze and hookers."

And she hung up before I could swear at her.

Family, eh? I was copping shit from every angle.

But none of that mattered, because once again I was in the money.

Time to call Linda and tell her she'd better steal my keys.

Because tonight was going to be party night.

Again…

Oh yes, life was good.

Basket or no basket.

In Too Deep

I'd taken to diving like a fish to water, if you'll excuse the expression.

It was the perfect hangover cure. Or rather, the cylinder of emergency oxygen on the dive boat was the perfect hangover cure!

Pure oxygen was kept on board as part of the first aid equipment. In the extremely unlikely event of a diver getting 'the bends', it would help to stabilize them until they could be taken to a decompression chamber. Without getting too technical on you, the bends results from too much nitrogen in the body. Nitrogen is in the air and we breathe it in and out all the time, but it does funny things under pressure – which is one reason why all divers need a minimum level of training before they're allowed to do it.

It goes without saying that no-one had ever gotten the bends on Nick's boat – never in the whole history of Chaloklum Divers. But Nick was ever a cautious fellow, and kept the oxygen cylinder on hand at all times.

Breathing from it was pure magic.

Instant and complete cure for even the worst hangover.

But we were under strict instructions not to do it.

So I, um, didn't.

At all.

Ahem.

My typical diving day started at 6am, when I woke up and rang the shop to see if I had any customers.

If not, then it was back to bed.

But if I did have someone booked in I'd leap up energetically, full of enthusiasm for the day ahead.

The icy water from my cold-tap-only shower served to blunt a bit of that enthusiasm, which was for the best as my next task involved negotiating that lethal dirt track all the way to Chaloklum.

I know I bitch about it, but it really was a magnificent start to the day; blasting through the jungle at top speed, the early morning sun on my face, wind whipping past me as I swerved back and forth to avoid the craters in the road.

And the concrete stalagmites.

I always arrived in a fantastic mood, and spent an hour transferring all the dive gear from the shop to the boat, by way of our next-door neighbour's pick-up truck.

Two tanks per customer. Two tanks for each of us, the guides and professionals who would be accompanying them. And a couple of spares just in case; we had over sixty tanks at the shop, each weighing about eighteen kilos when full.

We rarely needed more than forty of them.

So, one by one we'd pass the tanks up to whoever was standing in the back of the pick-up. That person would lay them down and stack them. Then we'd load up the crates filled with dive gear, wetsuits, snorkels, buoyancy jackets and the like. And then we'd drive the truck fifty metres to the pier, another fifty down it, and repeat the whole process in reverse.

Only this time we were lifting the tanks from truck to dock, and then from dock to boat – which was a drop of about two and a half metres.

Suffice to say, I was developing muscles in places I never knew had muscles.

My arms, for example.

This particular morning I was feeling pretty crappy, on account of not having been to bed yet. I'd been partying so hard I'd had no choice but to slap myself sober and come straight to the shop – a fact which hadn't escaped anyone.

Consequently it was me who ended up stood on the side of the boat, hands stretched over my head, waiting for the next tank to be passed down to me. Lowering the heavy metal cylinders from above head-height all the way to the deck below – where another pair of hands waited to carry them to the storage racks – *forty* times – was by far the worst part of my morning.

Until my sunglasses slid down my nose, off my face and disappeared into the murk beneath the pier.

"SHIT!" I shouted, venting my frustration in the only way possible with eighteen kilos of pressurised aluminium in my hands.

"Don't worry, I saw where they went," said Nick.

"Well that's no bloody good is it? They're in the water!"

"So they are. And you're on a dive boat. Go on then – get your gear on."

"Oh, you've got to be shitting me…"

Dive boats weren't the only vessels that moored up at this pier. Every morning whilst loading tanks, we fought for space with the trucks unloading Chaloklum's sizable fishing fleet. Their boats were out all night, every night, lowering booms covered in hundreds of light bulbs to just above the surface of the water. Squid were attracted to the lights and were netted in vast numbers by this trick – and as we struggled to get our gear down to the boat, the fishermen were hauling their slimy, stinking cargo of freshly caught squid out past us.

They weren't too careful about it either, which made for a very slippery, very unappealing texture on the surface of the docks. As for the water beneath them – also clouded with oil and diesel from the aging fleet's engines – let's just say, there are patches of water in the world that I'd rather dive into.

Especially as I'd just bought a brand-new wetsuit.

"Don't wear it then," was Nick's answer to that one.

So into the hideous mire I went, naked apart from my shorts, with just a facemask and snorkel, and located the sunglasses sitting in a pile of entrails that had built up around something even less pleasant.

For the rest of the day, I stank.

Squid guts and oil, in case you've ever wondered, does not make people like you.

The boat trip out to the dive site was usually glorious – especially once the nightmarish hangover had been taken care of. Which, um, it never had been. Honest.

Customers relaxed and sunbathed – as far away from me as possible – while I held my own nose and planned our dives. As always we did two dives, separated by a bowl of delicious curry that Nick's wife made fresh for us every day. I had a habit of spending the lunch break trying to do somersaults into the water from the top deck of the boat, but on this occasion I was content to swim laps around it, hoping that enough exposure to salt water would wash the stench away.

Diving was out of this world. The sensation of weightlessness; drifting above crazy formations of plants and coral that looked like they belonged on some alien landscape; rising and sinking a tiny fraction with every intake of breath… I loved it.

I'd learned the best places to find huge batfish and tiny clown loach (aka. Nemo in Finding Nemo). Vast schools of barracuda streamed by overhead, as we descended through a coral-lined tube in the reef known locally as Sail Rock.

It was one of the finest dive sites in the Gulf of Thailand.

On the way home, all anyone wanted to do was talk about their experience. Out came Nick's prized fish-ID books (all carefully waterproofed) and he'd spend the rest of the afternoon sharing his knowledge with the customers.

After unloading the empty tanks and washing all the customers' gear, I climbed onto my scooter for the return trip to Liberty. More than anything, I wanted to sleep.

But there was some kind of party going on outside the dive shop down the street, so I stopped the bike to have a quick look.

"Hey, it's the competition," one of the guys slurred. "Wanna beer mate? Wolf's buying!"

Five pairs of fists beat the table as the staff chanted "Wolf, Wolf, Wolf, WOLF!"

"Nah, I'm good, thanks. Got to get home. Just wondered what was going on."

"Ha! We should let Wolf tell you! Go on Wolf!"

Another round of drumming and chanting broke out.

Wolf didn't seem keen to volunteer any information, so his mate took up the tale.

"At Sail Rock today *two* of Wolf's divers ran out of air! His beer fine is fuckin' *massive!* How many beers do you still owe us, Wolf?"

Cat-calls and jeers rang out again.

"Wow, that's… pretty unlucky," I told him. Inwardly I was reeling. *Two…?*

"Well guys, I'm off. Have a good one. Wolf, try not to kill anyone, eh."

"Fuck you," he replied, sounding bored.

I fired up the bike and trundled off through the village. Soon I was roaring through the jungle, feeling very much like Tom Cruise in Top Gun.

Two divers out of air? My mind kept circling back to it, not quite able to grasp the magnitude of the cock-up.

For a diver to run low on air on a dive spoke of bad planning. For one to run low enough to have to alter the dive plan by surfacing early meant a combination cock-up – either forgetting to check their tanks beforehand, or pushing far too deep or too hard for their ability – and that was *in addition to* their Divemaster's almost criminal inattention. Nick would have fired me on the spot for that one, but I was way too good at my job to let it happen.

But for a diver to *run out* of air? It was unheard of. It had never happened to Nick in over thirty years of diving with multiple customers almost every day.

It would never happen to me – never. It was like a bungee jumping instructor forgetting to tie off the other end of his customer's rope. Any Divemaster that happened to… well, it goes without saying they'd never work again. Or so I'd thought.

For it to happen twice – in one dive – was absolutely terrifying.

Almost as terrifying as the shop having an established beer-fine as punishment for it. It made me wonder if they had a beer-fine for actually killing someone. What would it be? Three cases?

I couldn't help but imagine the scene:

'Hey, is my girlfriend back yet? She went out diving with you guys?'

'Ah, sorry mate, we lost her at Sail Rock. One minute she was there, the next – who knows? Don't worry though, the body usually washes up somewhere. You want a beer? Wolf's buying!'

I made damn sure no-one I knew ever dived with them.

Gill Imminent

I'd been keeping in touch with Gill as she planned her Australian adventure, partially because I was a little jealous. I loved Koh Pha Ngan, loved my friends, loved diving, loved my life in fact. And yet… there has always been a tiny part of me that wonders if I'm missing out. If the next party over the hill is that little bit wilder, or if the next country I visited could hold the ultimate adventure…

Well, if I wasn't careful I'd be finding out. Gill was constantly trying to convince me to come with her, and her planned stop-over in Thailand would obviously be spent trying to persuade me in person.

I was quite looking forward to seeing her.

So I booked a super-posh hotel in Bangkok and bought a bus ticket up there, intending to meet her at the airport and bring her back to my island paradise myself. I wanted to be there when she first saw the place, and say to her, "See! This is why I didn't come home!"

I felt sure she'd understand.

"Surely you're going to wear shoes in Bangkok," said Linda.

"Nope," I replied.

"Oh, Tone! You know what your sister is going to say?"

"That I'm an idiot?"

"If she does, will you believe her?"

"Linda, I never doubted you in the first place. I just love to hear you say it."

"Well I won't. But… be careful, okay?"

"I'm always careful!"

She let the rolling of her eyes do the talking for that one.

The long trip north, on a huge double-decker coach, was uneventful except for one thing. We stopped for food in the equivalent of a motorway service station, somewhere in the middle of the country. There was a vast, empty gravel car park with a toilet block and a restaurant grouped close enough together at one end that the smell from one of them overpowered the other. I'll leave it to your imagination which way round that was.

All I'd eaten in the last ten hours was a Mars Bar, a parting gift from Linda who knew me well enough to predict that I'd forget to bring food with me.

I made sure I was one of the first off the bus, as nothing makes a public toilet experience less pleasant than using it directly after fifty-plus other people have dropped their guts in there.

After that, we had half an hour to get some grub.

As this was an overnight bus it was somewhere around midnight; darkness stretched impenetrably in all directions, and the solitary beacon of light was the restaurant next to the toilet. So, that was the dinner spot chosen then.

I was famished. I queued up with everyone else, and was given a choice from three vats of brightly-coloured curry. The signage was all in Thai, but the options were blood-red, piss-yellow and poo-brown.

"What's this?" I enquired, jabbing a finger at the glass.

"This?" the server's finger hovered over the poo-brown.

"Yes."

"Is chicken."

Oh. That sounded palatable. More so than it looked, at any rate.

"And this?" I pointed at the yellow pot next to it.

"Is chicken."

Hm. Okay. So, chicken was definitely featuring on the menu. Well that was okay, as it was the safest thing to eat anyway. Not much can go wrong with chicken, to my way of thinking. Unless I'm cooking it.

"And this?" I gestured towards the bubbling pot of blood. It really did look like there should be a severed limb floating in it.

"This chicken," came the reply.

I probably should have seen that coming.

Well there was no point in trying to ask what else was in them; I didn't need language skills to guess what the signs said. The Thai are not particularly inventive when it comes to naming their dishes. Had I bothered to enquire, it's possible she would have had enough English to tell me the names of the meals on display; red curry; yellow curry; and diarrhoea. No, sorry – I mean 'normal curry'. It just looked like… well, suffice to say I had no intention of eating it.

The queue was backing up behind me while I had these musings, so I pointed at the yellow stuff again and said, "Chicken, please!"

The woman ladled some yellow out, slopped it onto a plate of rice, and thrust it towards me. The way she did it, I could tell I was getting a reprimand.

Nosey foreigners eh, always wanting to know what they're eating!

I took my plate and sat down at one of the stackable plastic tables.

Almost every shop or restaurant in Thailand seemed temporary, as though they were waiting for the building work to be completed before buying proper furniture; it was an endemic situation, apparently. I'd never been to a place that had proper furniture. Or had finished the building work, for that matter.

I looked down at the bright yellow, almost luminous goop, and had a moment of apprehension. This wasn't the cleanest of places, and I'd already visited the toilet on the bus more times than I wanted to (which was never). That toilet was no cleaner than the ones outside, and they hadn't seen a bottle of bleach since they were built.

Why couldn't the bus just stop at McDonalds? I thought.

But perhaps I should have been grateful; there were over sixty passengers on our bus, and less than half of them had been served before the red and the yellow ran out. *It could always be worse,* I reminded myself, watching the counter lady serve up a ladleful of brown.

So I braced myself for the worst, and tucked into my yellow.

It wasn't that bad, actually.

But it wasn't chicken.

The meat was the right colour, which was disturbing. What do they say about chicken? That it tastes like everything else? Well, put a healthy dollop of yellow on it and it certainly solves that problem. But this meat was... different. Stringier, somehow. And it had fat on it – not loads, but enough to be recognisable, a sort of rind almost like bacon – and lots, and lots, of gristle.

I was only a couple of mouthfuls in when I made the following connection. There is no fat on white meat. At least, not on chicken, and it seemed unlikely they were serving me swan. Not at these prices.

Neither should there be those hard, chewy nodules that meant a joint had previously been connected there. No, whatever it was, it wasn't fowl. Foul perhaps... but not beef, either. Or pork. Those were premium meats in Thailand, and would have been proudly advertised as such. And anyway the texture was all wrong.

There was only one thing I could think of, and given the look of the place, it made more sense the more I thought about it.

This had to be *cat*.

Cat curry.

It wasn't half bad.

I cleaned my plate, but drew the line at going back for seconds. Because if the yellow really *was* cat... God only knows what the hell was in the brown.

I'd booked a posh hotel for Gills arrival, figuring that neither of us were ever likely to afford the five-star treatment anywhere else. Also, I'd been away from home for more than half a year at that point, and I was quite looking forward to seeing her. Might as well surprise her while I was at it.

But there was no point in going overboard.

Even in Bangkok, hotels cost money, and while they were unbelievably good value for a rich westerner on holiday, I was living like a local now; earning my wages by taking people diving, and trying to stretch them out to cover rent on my bungalow, food and booze, and executive coach travel including all-you-can-eat feline.

So I'd booked the hotel for two nights, to give Gill a treat – but while I waited for her to arrive, I was staying in a backpackers hostel.

I'd feel more at home there anyway.

So I ditched my needlessly outsized rucksack – containing one book, one t-shirt, one water bottle and a Mars Bar wrapper – in the hostel dorm, and headed out to explore. Or rather, to get away from the smell; it was rather fragrant in there, and I was going to have to sleep in it as it was. There was no point in torturing myself needlessly.

In almost any city you visit, the backpacker district is where all the bars are.

In Bangkok, there are two types of bar: those with entertainment, and those without. I was looking for one of the latter, but I'd hardly left the hostel when a gorgeous Thai chick grabbed me by the arm and steered me into the bar behind her.

I got about ten feet inside when my eyes adjusted to the gloom, and I realized I was staring at a naked woman. No – I was staring at a reflection of a naked woman. There was a giant mirror on the floor and above it, on a ceiling of solid glass, this chick was gyrating for all she was worth.

Deciding this wasn't quite my kind of place I beat a hasty retreat – not without a backward glance I must admit, but then I'm only human.

But the hooker wasn't going to let me go as easily as that.

"No, stop!" she called to me. "No can go! No have shoes!"

I looked down at my bare feet. They were filthy.

Should I explain to her that almost six months ago, having had my shoes stolen for the third time in a week and frustrated with the general crappiness of flip-flops, I'd made a bet with a friend that I could go barefoot for as long as I lived here?

No. She'd never understand.

So I just smiled at her and said, "indeed."

And left.

I was waiting to cross the junction at the bottom of the road when I head a slap-slap, slap-slap, gaining in speed and volume behind me.

Just when it sounded like I was about to be flattened by an overly enthusiastic sea lion, I turned around to find the hooker wheezing right behind me.

"Take, take!" she panted, and held something out to me.

It was a bright pink pair of flip-flops.

So concerned with the health of my feet was she, she'd run back into her bar, grabbed the first pair of shoes available and chased me all the way down the road with them.

"Um, thanks?" I said as I took the plastic shoes. Given her profession, I was grateful she'd offered me tat instead of tit.

"No pwobwem!" she lisped, giving me a smile to melt hearts, then skipped merrily away up the road with her good deed for the day done. It made me feel a lot better about hookers. They weren't bad people, particularly here where it was considered a profession much like any other; it was their clientele that had to be avoided.

The flip-flops, though pink and rather sparkly, actually looked like they might fit me. *Jeez, that hooker must have big feet*, I thought.

Which meant, of course, that she was a man.

I should have known – all the prettiest ones were.

But where the hell had she managed to buy these things?

Then I realised that that, too, was a stupid question.

If there was anywhere in the world that made sparkly pink flip-flops in a man's size nine, it was a safe bet it was Thailand.

I stood bemused at the crossroads, wondering what to do with my new footwear. I didn't want to carry them around all day – anyone not noticing they were the size of table tennis bats might think I was a child molester.

The traffic lights changed and people began crossing the road. I made eye contact with a girl coming the other way and stretched out the shoes to her as she passed.

"Want these?" I asked.

"Oh! Ah, okay?"

And she took them.

She gained the other side of the road and turned to stare at me in confusion.

    I looked back and caught her eyes.

    I waved at her.

    She held up the flip-flops and waved back with them.

    "Now shoo!" I said.

Lady and the Tramp

The next morning I had to get out of the hostel and all the way across town to Sukhumvit, where most of the posh hotels nestled together like a clutch of Fabergé eggs.

The simplest way was to take a tuk-tuk; the ubiquitous motorbike taxis which varied from sleek, purpose-built three-wheelers to a scooter with a home-made wooden trailer. Somewhere in between those extremes fell this one, which looked like a large pram super-glued to the back of a trail bike.

Because I'd made precisely zero effort to learn the Thai language, I had no chance of convincing the driver I wasn't a tourist. So despite a lengthy period of haggling before I got in, I still got taken to his cousin's carpet shop for a drink. And then to his other cousin's cut-price diamond warehouse.

I seem to attract carpet salesmen wherever I go. I have no idea why. Unless it's a magic carpet, and can be used as the sole means of transportation for both me and my giant rucksack, I have about as much use for it as a monk has for condoms.

And as for the jewellery? Part of me wished I had learned Thai, just so I could ask my driver if anyone had ever made a purchase from his cousin the diamond merchant. I mean really – would the kind of person who could afford designer jewellery – even at half price – ever get into a tuk-tuk?

No. Not a chance.

And I was barefoot, for God's sake! Even the hookers were taking pity on me. I had to admire the guy's optimism, but there comes a point where it crosses the line into blatant stupidity. If I was disguising my wealth, I was doing a damn good job of it.

But I had a nice drink, a frustrating two hours in Bangkok's infamous traffic jams, and saw some lovely carpets.

No magic ones though.

I barely had time to check in at the posh hotel, and had to invest in a proper taxi if I was to have any chance of getting to the airport before Gill did. Hell, I'd have been lucky to make it if we'd left at the same time – and she was coming from London.

So if you ever feel the urge to moan about your rush-hour commute, think of the thousands of poor sods trying to get anywhere, at any time of day, in Bangkok.

If it's anything less than five miles, you're honestly faster walking.

I reached the arrivals terminal only minutes before her plane landed.

Then I waited two hours whilst she cleared customs; the speed of the traffic in Thailand being second only to the speed of their bureaucracy.

Still, it gave me time to think about the surprise I had planned for her. She'd probably assume I'd found cheap beds in a hostel for us, as that was my usual style; instead I was going to blow her away with the kind of opulent luxury she'd never even dreamed of! For two nights. Then we were catching the train back towards Koh Pha Ngan, and Eieu's cosy little bungalows.

I was grinning with sheer anticipation. What would she say when I told her? How would she react? She'd think I was joking perhaps. But I'd tell her the truth; I'd done it for her. Because she was my sister, and she was worth it.

Then the doors hissed open and Gill emerged, pushing her backpack on a trolley.

She made it through the press of taxi drivers holding their little signs, passed through the opening in the crowd control barriers, and caught site of me leaning nonchalantly against a column.

She took one look at me and stopped dead, eyes wide with shock.

"Oh my God, Tony! Are you okay? What's wrong?"

It wasn't exactly the greeting I'd expected.

"I'm fine, thanks. How are you? Nice flight?"

"Um, it was okay, yeah… Tony, are you sure you're okay?" There was genuine concern in her eyes. " 'cause dude, you look like shit!"

I looked down at myself, feeling a bit defensive. Okay, so I was barefoot; itself a strange enough phenomenon in the gleaming white-tiled airport, but then I'd been barefoot all day. Indeed for quite a lot longer than that, as the state of my feet could attest; they were black, utterly, disgustingly filthy, and cut and scabbed in dozens of places. My jeans were ripped, because… all my jeans were ripped. I've no idea why. It seemed to be an endemic problem in my life. They were also blood-stained, baggy and rolled up at the bottom to reveal the full glory of my feet.

I was wearing a sleeveless top – as in, a regular top which I'd cut the sleeves off with a kitchen knife. The frayed edges and sweat rings (it was very hot and humid outside) didn't do much to help my image.

But to top it off, I'd planned on shaving at the hotel but had run out of time. It had taken me so long to get there that I'd had to check in and then leg it to the airport. I had several days' growth of beard, my hair hadn't been cut since I left England and the impossibility of sleep in a Bangkok backpacker's hostel contributed a lovely pair of dark bags, like bruises beneath my eyes.

Filthy, skinny and dressed in rags; it's fair to say I looked like a homeless person.

"I'll carry my own bag, thanks," Gill said when I reached out to grab it from the trolley. "Don't want anyone to think you're trying to rob me!"

"Hey! I'm not that bad."

"Dude seriously, all you need is a dog on a piece of string. And a bit of cardboard that says 'This Dog Is Hungry' on it. You could make a fortune."

"Well, I meant to have a shave, but…"

"A shave? Dude, you look like you're a heroin addict! Please tell me you don't have your razorblades in your pocket."

"No. They're back at the hotel."

"I can't believe security let you into the airport!"

Gill had a point.

I hadn't felt at all self-conscious when I'd checked into an executive suite in the Royal Parkview Hotel. Now, as I padded across the opulent marble-clad foyer, I did wonder why I hadn't been thrown out on sight.

It didn't help that Gill had been taking the piss out of me since we left the airport. She'd stopped for ages outside the underground station, peering in all directions. When I'd asked what she was doing, she told me she was wondering where I'd parked my shopping trolley.

Fortunately the desk clerk at the hotel didn't bat an eyelid as I shuffled past into the plush-carpeted lift. Maybe the colour of my credit card had impressed him, too.

Safe in the lounge of our cavernous suite, we could finally relax.

Gill said that three things amazed her: how tired she was, how expensive our room looked – and how I'd managed to check in to it without being arrested.

"There's worse off people here in Thailand," I told her. "That's why they need people like me here. And I fit right in, amongst the hippies and the long lost backpackers."

Gill cast a weary eye over me one last time before retreating to her bedroom.

"The only thing I've seen around here that looks worse than you is the dogs," she said.

Which I guess was true.

And that was also why I was here.

Our day in Bangkok flew by. We took the monorail to a gigantic shopping centre, walked all round it, and bought nothing. Gill took one look at the crush of motor scooters thronging our road and told me she was amazed that I was still alive. I showed her my accident scars, now fading, and she decided that she wasn't going to go anywhere near a bike. Which was going to make getting back from the pier tricky, as that's where I'd parked ready for our triumphant return, but never mind. She'd ease up.

We took a tuk-tuk ride purely so that Gill could have the experience, and inevitably ended up at a 'cousin's' shop – where they tried to sell me a tailored three-piece suit! We got quite a giggle out of that. Back in the tuk-tuk Gill treated me to a shaky rendition of 'What a Difference A Shave Makes...'

Then we retreated back to the serenity of the hotel, to luxuriate in the spa and goggle at the sheer grandeur on offer. It didn't seem likely that we'd get to stay in a place like this again – short of winning the lottery – so we consoled ourselves by stealing everything that wasn't nailed down.

No, only kidding! But I did take a couple of towels. Because, well, hotels expect that, and mine had been out on the dive boat with me every day; it was in such poor condition that Gill suggested I donate it to the clinic for the mopping up of unpleasant bodily fluids.

I won't tell you what she suggested I do with my jeans, but I think it required holy water.

And then we had to leave the lap of luxury, and ride the underground back to the station.

It was with childish delight that we discovered the underground signs were in English. Gill cackled like mad and dug for her camera, while I praised her for being clever enough to have one. I would have been gutted to miss this shot. Signs hanging from the roof directed passengers to their platforms, indicated by the station at the furthest end of the line. We were going 'To Bangkok' – just like most of the people around us. Which was far less interesting than the station at the other end of the line.

So we legged it around to the other platform, where Gill snapped a great pic of the sign hanging from the roof.

'To Bang Sue', it read.

We were left with just enough time to nip back to the ticket office, where I asked the man behind the desk, "How much to Bang Sue?"

I couldn't help myself.

Apparently it's only fifty baht, which seemed like a bargain.

I bet they could sell dozens of tickets to Bang Sue at that price.

I don't know how Sue would feel about it though.

Now, I love my sister more than almost anyone else in the world – we share the same shockingly immature sense of humour (see above!) – but I feel honour-bound to share this titbit of information with you: she is the only person I've ever known who is a) clumsier than me, and b) almost as likely to say something stupid.

Maybe that's why I love her so much; not only does she provide a constant source of comedy, she sometimes takes the heat off me for a while.

Anyway, she amply demonstrated both traits in Bangkok train station, where we were hoping to find a train down to Surat Thani.

She expressed her clumsiness by falling down the main staircase, from top to bottom; she simply stood at the top, her bulging rucksack strapped firmly to her back, and stepped out into nothingness.

Gravity did the rest.

Quite what she expected from the staircase I don't know, but I honestly thought she was old enough by now to have figured out how they worked.

She tumbled down head over heels, and landed in a heap on the landing in the middle. By itself this would have been more concerning than amusing, and I was already rushing to help her when she tottered to her feet, took a second mis-step sideways, and fell all the way down the second flight too.

After that, there was nothing I could do but laugh.

Saying something stupid is perhaps a more subtle art; after all, one man's genius is another man's fool, as is proved to me every time I get an email that accuses me of being a genius. It doesn't happen all that often, but those poor, deluded souls are out there.

Amongst the finest examples of Gill's work was her creation, as part of a discussion about three reoccurring problems, of the phrase 'Vicious Triangle'.

Verily, there is no shape in all of geometry as feared as this; sharp-toothed, sharp-edged and all evil; beware, you students of maths, beware you pizza-slicers, beware all you designers and drawers of technical shapes; for you know not when the Vicious Triangle shall strike!

She was also responsible for a masterpiece of prose wherein she decided to describe an eerie forest on a dark and spooky night. Whilst groping around for suitable descriptions she lit upon the image of an owl, hidden in the darkness, and wrote the now infamous sentence 'in the distance, an owl honked.'

That phrase nearly killed me as I was eating when she read it out, and I came closer to choking on a mouthful of Cornflakes than I ever did to being eaten in Ecuador.

I could just picture this rather smelly old owl, wafting its wings a little and causing all the other owls nearby to fall of their perches when the stink hit them.

Ah, good times!

In Bangkok her turn of phrase was even more subtle, and could have been put down to simple inexperience were it not for the fact that she'd already spent one entire day in the capital city of Thailand. We'd arrived at the train station ready to catch the night train back to Surat Thani, only to be informed that all the tickets were sold out – except for the last few seats in Third Class.

"Third Class can't be *that* bad," Gill said.

She was wrong, of course.

Why Third Class Is Not Good

Third class was unbelievably bad. To help you understand just how far down the train hierarchy we'd fallen, I should point out that it doesn't start at first class – it starts with *Farang*, or 'F' class. These are the carriages considered suitable for foreigners, those soft, touristy type people who require such decadent luxuries as beds and access to a buffet car.

Then there was First Class, which also contained beds; folding bunks with ceiling fans mounted above them, or even air-con if you paid a little extra. This was still a fairly comfortable place to spend the journey.

After First of course came Second Class, with seats like you'd find in many of the world's railway carriages. They were upholstered, albeit garishly, and offered a slight degree of recline-ability. Or they should have done; bitter experience had taught me that they were all broken. Not ideal, given the length of the trip, but they'd do in a pinch.

Then, right at the bottom of the heap, came Third Class. This was designed to accommodate the poorest strata of Thai society, and consisted of unpadded bench seats with low backs, like the kind you get on a really shitty old minibus.

There was no air-conditioning, because there was no glass in the windows; just wide holes through which a frantic mob of hands appeared every time we stopped at a station, all competing with each other to sell us food.

Now this I could live with – at least it kept our dinner options interesting.

What I could have lived without was being seated directly opposite the toilet.

Anyone who's been to Asia will have fond memories of the toilets; that delightfully simple system of two foot-plates to stand on and squat, coupled with a hole below to do your business through. In this case it was literally a hole cut in the bottom of the train, through which the tracks were visible – and if that's all that was visible, it might not have been so bad.

Unfortunately this toilet cubicle also had no door.

So not only were we treated to the sight of each customer shuffling past on their way to the toilet, we were also privy to the sight of them actually *going*.

Along with the full range of appropriate sound effects.

For some reason that put me off the banana curry which was handed in to me through the window.

If only it put everyone else on the train off it too, there might have been fewer trips to the loo on the next leg – but no.

Sat opposite a family of six squeezing onto a bench built for three close friends, we got to watch every one of them eating the gloop, revelling in every gelatinous mouthful; and then two hours later we watched them take it in turns to shit it all back out again.

About the only people I felt sorrier for than me and Gill at that moment, were the people living alongside these tracks, which we now liberally splattered with second-hand banana curry.

Of course, there was always the danger they were just scraping it up and selling it back to us further down the track…

The carriage smelled so bad anyway, they could almost have gotten away with it.

This is another reason that most toilet cubicles have doors.

I'd convinced Gill to buy a small bottle of vodka before boarding, by way of anaesthetic; even then I'd been under no illusions that third class would be a cake-walk. Now we drained the bottle dry and tried to laugh, because sleeping was impossible; not only were we three feet away from the busiest open sewer in the country, we were sitting bolt upright on a plank of wood with a half-height metal railing for a back rest.

And it was broken.

The bench had sagged away from its brackets at one end and was tilting forwards; I had to keep a firm pressure on my feet just to stop myself sliding off the damn thing. And if there was one place I really didn't want to be, in third class this close to the toilet – it was the floor.

That journey took eleven hours.

It felt longer.

But at least we got to see the countryside.

"Might buy a better ticket for the way back," Gill mumbled as we got off in Surat Thani.

"Or a bigger bottle of vodka?" I suggested.

"Some ear plugs…"

"Or butt-plugs for the other passengers?!"

"And a raincoat…"

"A raincoat? Why a raincoat?"

Gill shook herself before replying. "You know that when you smell something, it's because you're breathing tiny bits of it in, right?"

After that, all either of us could think about was getting home for a shower.

She was too tired to protest as I helped her onto the back of my scooter. We did a lightening-fast trip to the clinic, where I introduced her to the staff and the dogs, and then I showed her to the bungalow I'd rented for her next door to mine.

And then, at last, we slept.

Gill was lucky enough to have arrived just before Songkran – the Thai new year, which is celebrated by a country-wide water-fight. In preparation I'd bought us a pair of super-soakers, a whole bag of water balloons, and had cable-tied two squeezy bottles to the handle bars of my bike.

We were going out locked and loaded, baby!

Of course, it's hard to compete when the first truck you pass has a sixty-litre water barrel in the back and six people that are emptying it over you a bucket at a time! And it wasn't until we were approaching the strip of road lined with lady-bars that I noticed some of the girls were aiming a fire hose…

I nearly had more accidents in one morning than I'd had in the last six months.

Town was rammed with traffic; cars, trucks, taxis, bikes; all loaded to the max with water-pistol toting westerners and resort staff with buckets. Running battles were being fought between every building, and no-one was safe; not the police (who were also armed with water pistols) and certainly not our clothes, as brightly-coloured talcum powder was being mixed into a paste by the locals and smeared on anyone they could get their hands on.

We spent the day alternating between ice-cold dousings in a series of vicious street fights, and hiding (and drinking) in a wide variety of bars. It was a combination that cried out for trouble, and yet we made it through the day with hardly a scratch. I did get a nasty burn on my foot from my scooter's exhaust pipe, something that apparently happens to most tourists within their first few days of riding the things. Somehow I'd avoided it without even knowing it was an issue, until the need arose for a high-speed dismounting in the face of stiff opposition from a truck full of Thai hookers armed with water balloons. Those girls lived for Songkran, and they got plenty of practice in, year after year. Their favourite targets, unsurprisingly, were tourists; they were taking a small measure of revenge on their potential clientele for the year ahead.

Swearing at the pain of my injury and cursing my decision to ride barefoot, I hobbled into the nearest bar, making it just in time to avoid another drenching.

Gill wasn't so lucky, taking a water-bomb straight to the face. The force of the hit nearly knocked the poor girl off her feet, lending strength to my theory that the women in that truck weren't really women at all.

Gill staggered into the bar, pulling bits of shredded balloon from her hair. She looked like she'd just been baptised by Mike Tyson.

"Damn those whores can aim," she said.

There had, however, been one regrettable casualty.

Songkran had been so much fun and so chaotic that I'd never even noticed my phone was gone until I needed it to call Linda the next morning. Bloody phones! They were a plague. Now not only would I have the expense of buying another one, yet again I would have to go around collecting numbers from all my friends. I was starting to think I was cursed.

Cops and Robbers

The mess on the streets the next day was horrendous. Talcum powder and body paint congealed in doorways; litter floated in puddles and bits of sodden clothing were draped over walls and sign posts. It looked like the apocalypse had come and gone while we were asleep.

Mounted on the back of my scooter, Gill gazed around us at the clean-up effort in progress. I knew Thong Sala would be relatively devoid of tourists, as most of them were nursing epic hangovers in their resorts. This made it the perfect time to run a particularly irritating errand.

We approached the main junction and followed the stream of traffic smoothly around to the right.

Mistake!

As soon as I rounded the corner I saw him waiting for me; one of Koh Pha Ngan's finest, mounted on a shiny scooter of the latest model. It even said 'Police' on it in English, especially for the tourists.

He waved me in and I pulled up just behind him. I knew instantly what my crime was, but I couldn't believe I was being singled out for it. Koh Pha Ngan had exactly one set of traffic lights – on the junction just behind me. They'd stopped working a couple of weeks after I'd arrived on the island, and had remained non-functional ever since. Last week I'd nearly had a heart-attack when I saw them change as I approached them! After six months of being merely decorative, suddenly they were traffic signals again, and had to be obeyed as such.

Oops.

In my defence I'd like to point out that, although the lights were clearly on red, nothing else had stopped for them either. I'd followed a whole row of cars and bikes through, all presumably being driven by honest, law-abiding Thai nationals. But us foreigners? We were a menace, and we had to be punished.

"Don't argue," I said to Gill through gritted teeth. "Just follow my lead. Say what I say."

I felt the bike rock slightly as she nodded. My heart thumped as the cop swaggered towards us, pulling out his notebook.

"G' morning," he opened. "You, uh, see light?"

"Yes sir. I thought it was broken."

"NO! Not broken. Is red!"

"Yes sir."

"You from where?"

"England."

"Both from England?"

"Yes sir."

"You name?"

"Toby. Toby Cannon," I lied.

"An her?"

"My sister."

"Sarah… Cannon," Gill added.

"Have passpor'?"

"I gave it to the man who rented me this bike. We both did – we both have rented bikes."

"Where you get, ah, motor-bikes?"

It was hardly a secret. I pointed at the bright yellow lettering running down both sides of my bike. 'PHANGAN DIVE CLUB' it read – actually the name of Yorik's long defunct dive school. Not a highly original title. Maybe that's why it had gone bust years ago.

"Where you stay?"

I was ready for this one. "Rainbow bungalows in Haad Rin. This is our first time on this side of the island."

"Ah." I could see him weighing it up: the effort involved in a trip to Haad Rin was substantial. I'd played it deliberately vague; no simple tourist would have contact details for his resort or bike rental shop on hand, making it extra difficult to check up on them. There was a silver lining, I guess; had this happened on any other day I'd have had both Yorik and Eieu on speed dial in the phone in my back pocket. That would have been hard to disguise.

"You have ah, mobile phone?"

"Sorry sir!" I shook my head. "Only in England." I stood up off the saddle to display the absence of a square bulge in any of my pockets.

"Okay. Number?"

I gave him the direct dialling code for the UK, and then spouted a long list of random numbers, pausing every three or four digits until he seemed satisfied. He wrote it all down, indecipherably, in his little book.

"Have ID?"

"No sir. Only our passports…"

"Okay. I give you fine, because you go through red light. Okay? Have money?"

"Erm…" I dug in my front pocket and pulled out a couple of crumpled notes. It was my standard strategy for dealing with beggars, to have only a few low-denomination notes in each pocket so I could give them something without having to sort through a big wad of cash in front of them.

"I just have enough for petrol. For gas, I mean." I offered him the notes. I think there was about fifty baht there – just less than a pound.

The cop looked deflated as he waved away the notes.

"Have bank card? For bank? Can get money?"

"I have my bank card back in my bungalow… in Haad Rin."

Now he was scowling at me. I did my best to look upset and scared, in case he was on a power trip. Most of the cops around here were.

"Here is fine." He presented me with a piece of official-looking paper. "Here, the amount – five-hundred baht, okay? You go to police station to pay!" He sounded more belligerent as he gave his last command. I responded appropriately – as any frightened, cowed tourist would.

"Yes sir! Sorry sir, so sorry. I'll go to police station. I pay straight away!"

And that was that. He went back to his ingenious stake-out; literally sitting at the scene of a crime, waiting for it to happen. The lights had changed several times during our chat, but the traffic had continued to flow in complete disregard of them. Several tourist-laden bikes had passed us, their rider's eyes wide with fear (or occasionally sympathy) as they realised just how close to sharing our predicament they'd come.

Better me than you, I'd thought at them as they sped on their way. I didn't mind, really, once the initial shock had worn off. I'd been here too long not to know how this game was played.

"You okay Sarah?" I shot back at Gill. I caught her answering grin as I studied the traffic over my shoulder. I guided the bike into a gap in the flow, and we were off again, free and happy, with the varied smells of Thong Sala in our nostrils and the open road ahead of us.

I do believe I still have that fine ticket somewhere. I think I glued it into one of my journals as a souvenir. I didn't pay it, of course; why on earth would I? That kind of money would buy us a damn good night out in Haad Rin.

Unfortunately, I already had a use for that cash.

After the encounter with the traffic cop we made a long, slow circuit of Thong Sala, and once I was sure we were out of danger I parked us up outside the phone shop.

A lot of things were changing on the island, of which the traffic lights were an obvious symptom; big construction was coming to Koh Pha Ngan, and new shops were springing up daily – but as far as I knew this was still the only place to buy a cheap phone.

"You never know," Linda had joked, "you might find yours has been 'handed in' again!"

"Ha! Yeah… well, I might as well have a look."

And bloody hell! If it wasn't there, that same battered blue phone, looking for all the world like it could have been anybody's. But it wasn't. It was mine. Or it would be. Again.

"Three-hundred and fifty *baht*?" I complained to the guy in the shop. "It was only three-hundred last time! You're telling me my phone has actually appreciated in value?"

He didn't get the joke, but he was keen enough to take the money.

I guessed that the price of phones increased with the supply – and consequently the demand – immediately after each of the big tourist events on the island.

Sneaky buggers.

"I tell you what," I said to Gill, "that is absolutely the last time I am buying that frigging phone from that same damn shop."

She didn't comment. Gill was wise enough to know that whenever I tempted Fate in this way, Fate had a habit of biting me on the arse.

I was right though. Never again was I stupid enough to lose that phone.

I drove my bike over it, dropped it out of a second storey window and finally killed it by taking it swimming with me – but I never lost it again.

Sister Act

Although Gill had relented on her scooter embargo when she saw my bright blue machine waiting for us at the docks, I knew she'd have second thoughts when she saw the Haad Rin hills.

In fairness, it had been months before I'd felt confident enough to tackle them on a bike, and Linda never had; luckily she had Ridvan to drive her, and she clung to him like a drowning woman clutching a life-belt as he powered up the ridiculous inclines, sparing not a single glance for the panoramic view of the coastline spread out below.

I loved that view.

It was my second favourite on the whole island, and could only really be appreciated in the open back of a taxi on the way to Haad Rin, or as the passenger on a scooter on the way back. I sneaked the occasional glance while I was driving, but to stare long enough to fully absorb the majesty of the waves crashing against the jagged rocks was to lose control of your bike and end up getting a much closer look at them than anyone wanted.

But I didn't bother telling Gill any of that – I thought I'd surprise her.

And I did, when my bike drove slower and slower, crawling up the hill barely fast enough to stay upright. In the end I had to ask her to get off and walk the last hundred metres!

Poor girl. It wasn't quite the triumph I had in mind, but my bike simply didn't have the power to haul two people up that slope.

"How come Ridvan managed it with Linda on the back?" Gill enquired, as she re-mounted for the run down the other side. "Is he a better rider than you?"

"Hell no!" I declared.

Although he was.

"No, Ridvan just has a more powerful bike. Mine's only 100cc – his is a 125."

"So why don't you get a 125?"

"Well, I did try. I asked the guy who rents me this one. He's a bit odd, but he's okay in small doses. Anyway, he told me he'd sooner let Linda rent a 125 – because even though she drives like a woman, at least she wouldn't kill herself."

"So he doesn't think you can handle it?"

"Guess not."

"But why?"

"Gill, I have no idea what Yorik thinks. No-one does. He's a strange, strange man."

I left out the part about having had three major accidents, all of which had required Yorik to make extensive repairs to my bike.

There are some things it's best for a little sister not to know.

Especially when she's the first bike passenger you've ever taken up the Haad Rin hills.

No point in scaring her unnecessarily.

It goes without saying that we were headed to Haad Rin for a night out. I couldn't exactly bring my sister to the party capital of the world, and then keep her away from them, could I? Even if, in hindsight, it might have been advisable…

I managed to keep the fire dancers at arms length, though. They were all locals, and had two skills at which they were so practiced they could quite literally do them blindfold; spinning flaming sticks at such incredible speeds that it hypnotised everyone who saw it; and seducing drunken white chicks afterwards.

If you look up 'Cool' in the dictionary, I guarantee you'll see a picture of one of these guys.

And he will NOT be wrapped around my little sister.

I've always considered it my job to protect her from the evils of this world. My method for this is to identify said evils, partake of them for long enough to understand what they're all about, and then decide whether or not they are a threat to her child-like innocence.

Well, how else am I supposed to know?

So I deemed the alcohol an acceptable risk, in moderation. My opinion of moderation may have gotten a little skewed over the last few months, but I checked regularly to make sure she was still standing.

Unfortunately, while she could stand she could dance – and my sister, like me, loves to dance.

We're both crap at it, but that's beside the point.

Gill boogied her way through the entire night, literally from dusk till dawn – barefoot to match me, on the rough concrete floor of the Drop Inn bar.

I'd sustained dozens of injures in exactly this manner, from slicing my feet on broken glass bottles to inadvertently stubbing out a cigarette someone had dropped by grinding my heel into it. It served me right for choosing the path of the shoeless, so I tried to avoid complaining about it too much.

Especially as Linda was the only person I could complain to, and her opinion of my barefoot bet hadn't improved much.

Gill's feet, untoughened by months of such abuse, weren't ready for the harsh realities of a night on the Drop Inn floor. When she woke up the next morning, the worst hangover she's ever experienced paled in comparison to the agony she was in from her feet. Dancing all night had abraded the bottom surfaces to the point where there was no skin left at all – just raw, bleeding mess.

Needless to say, she wore shoes from then on.

Well, when she could walk again, she did.

In the meantime she lay in my hammock, petting Peto, a gorgeous German Shepherd that had lived at Liberty for as long as anyone there could remember. Like all street dogs he was incredibly smart, and bore small scars here and there from a lifetime of proving who was boss. But Peto also had a deep serenity about him, as though he'd been there, done that, and most likely eaten the t-shirt. He was gorgeous, a fantastic specimen of an Alsatian in his prime.

"He's amazing," Gill said, offering him another biscuit. "He just looks at me, as though asking permission, then strolls over and takes it with a nod. It's like he's acknowledging the favour."

"He's an incredible dog," I agreed. "You know, one time this girl who was staying here had been followed home from a Full Moon Party by two Thai guys. They'd been pressuring her for sex and she'd been too drunk to fight them off, but when they'd forced their way into her bungalow they didn't manage to close the door in time. Peto went in there and bit the shit out of them! They both legged it, missing a few chunks, and then Peto slept on the girl's balcony until the next morning in case they came back. He's the kind of dog they write TV shows about."

Gill offered another biscuit and the wonder dog sighed, as if he was embarrassed by all this attention.

He took the biscuit though.

"Is that story true?" Gill asked.

"As far as I know. Everyone has a story about him, about something amazing he's done. We saw him in Haad Rin once, on a night out. I think he was keeping an eye on some of the newcomers."

"No way!"

"Yup. But I'll tell you one thing he does, which is really cute – if a girl goes to walk from here to the Seven Eleven on her own, if Peto is around, he'll go with her. Everyone knows that. Not that there's a huge amount of danger between here and there – just a dirt track through the jungle – but it's like he knows they'd appreciate the reassurance."

"Wow. And he's so pretty!"

That was too much for Peto; he loped down the balcony steps and went in search of someone with a less patronising attitude.

I honestly think he was that clever.

That night we ate with Linda, Ridvan, Avril and Por, at the all-you-can-eat Korean buffet. Or, as we called it, 'Hot Pan Hot Pan', because that's what it said on the sign. I don't think the person who wrote it had a strong grasp of English.

Comedy signs were everywhere on Koh Pha Ngan, and Gill stopped to take pictures of most of them for her collection. Her favourite since arriving on the island was outside a fairly typical wooden bungalow on the road to Thong Sala. Obviously one of the occupants was qualified in herbal massage, and was running her business from home. She'd had a lovely yellow sign made up in English, to advertise it to passing tourists – presumably without asking around the local ex-pat community first.

I don't know if she got many customers or not, but it never sounded very appealing to me.

'HOT POO MASSAGE' read the sign.

Gill nearly fell off the bike laughing.

Our days we spent touring the island, visiting waterfalls and temples, watching the giant monkeys hard at work fetching coconuts and eating snacks at every roadside stall we came across.

And we spent the lazy evenings on my balcony, feeding the tiny geckos that lived in the eaves by flicking the light on just long enough to attract a swarm of flying insects. With impressive speed the lizards scooted out of the shadows and pounced – which always amazed me, given that they did it all upside-down.

It was an idyllic life I showed her, and I think she was starting to understand the depth of feeling I had for my home amidst the palm trees.

We also took a trip around the island in one of the 'long tail' motorized canoes, the sole legacy of which was a sunburn so bad that the next day we both looked like we'd contracted leprosy. It was called the 'Reggae

Boat Trip' and was run by a local bloke I knew vaguely through the clinic. There were dozens of identical trips run by one and two man outfits up and down the beach, all with the same rough itinerary of stopping at tiny deserted beaches up and down the coast, all with equally unlikely monikers. What made this a 'reggae' boat trip? Why, Mr Bob Marley himself was painted on one side of the boat.

And to celebrate that fact, they gave out free spliffs to all the passengers every time we stopped.

Which I guess is why no-one complained about the sun burn.

On Gill's last day on the island, I took her to see my number one favourite view. It was part of a route I didn't get to travel much, as it led around the top of the island, eventually to Chaloklum. It was a much better road, but took twice as long as the direct route through the jungle, even accounting for pothole-avoidance time.

The view was from atop another hill, albeit a much gentler gradient, and it faced the west so that every night around 6pm, the sun seemed to sink into the ocean, setting the water aflame as it did so. The slope down to the coast was steep and covered in foliage – and it was for sale.

"One day," I told her, wistfully.

"But you can't stay here forever," she replied. "Aren't you going to come with me to Australia?"

"I'll think about it dude, honestly I will. But you've seen the kind of life I have here. You've met my friends. I can't imagine anywhere in the world where I would be happier."

"You're right, but then so am I. You *can't* stay here forever. You'll get bored of this lifestyle eventually, or else everyone else will leave, and at some point you'll wish you'd moved on while it was still so perfect."

"Yeah… I know."

And the next day she left, bound for Australia via one ferry, one minibus, one taxi and an international flight that had eaten up a goodly amount of her profits from the sale of Treorchy. But then I couldn't talk; most of mine was gone already.

I did relish being so remote though, as the difficulty of reaching the outside world from here worked both ways; what went on out there didn't seem to matter here much at all.

Gill could have Australia, and all the excitement that the place inspired. No matter how alluring it was, it still represented civilisation; the real world, encroaching just for a moment on my private dream of paradise.

I worked hard, after that, to make it go away again.
But for some reason, it just kept coming back.

Bad News

I never had another bike accident on Koh Pha Ngan.

I had a few scary moments though, because no matter how carefully you drive, it's what the other people do that ultimately screws you.

And yet, the most scared I ever got in Thailand had a far more mundane, quite depressing reason.

I went to the bank to draw out some cash, only to find that there wasn't any.

Panic.

Had I really spent everything? I'd known it would happen eventually, as my earnings from diving could never keep me in the style to which I'd become accustomed – but now? So soon… and so suddenly! I should have checked my account more recently – or at all – but to be honest I'd been too scared to do so.

Well that had to end now – I leapt back on my bike and roared around to the internet café. I still had some cash in my bungalow, but not enough to last. A week maybe, or two at a push? And by a push, I meant by not eating anything…

The online account statement was even more of a shock.

Someone had been withdrawing funds from my account at regular intervals. The rogue transactions, each for the maximum amount that could be withdrawn from an ATM, were dated two months ago, and spaced a few days apart – and there were six of them.

SHIT!

I'd been robbed.

How? I had no idea, other than the fact that this was Thailand. If there was a scam, if it were possible to steal money right out of a cash machine, then this is where it would happen. I'd only remained unrobbed so far because I looked so poor. The lack of shoes really seemed to bother the Thai; combined with a few days' stubble growth and the fact that my clothes were mostly comprised of holes, it made me look like the kind of person you felt the urge to give money to, rather than the other way around.

So what to do?

I rang my bank in England.

"Did you give your card to anybody?" The woman on the other end of the phone wanted to know.

"Well, yeah," I told her.

"What? Why?" It clearly wasn't the answer she'd expected.

"You have to, don't you, when you pay for things?"

"Oh yes, but other than that?"

"No, of course not. But then, this *is* Thailand."

"Yes. I see your point."

Things ran smoothly from then on. First Ridvan, then Linda, stepped in with offers of support. I borrowed from them and discovered a remarkable thing; at some time or other I'd done favours for almost everyone I knew.

When word got around that I was unexpectedly broke due to some asshole defrauding me, people went out of their way to help me out – they bought me food and drinks, hung out with me when I couldn't afford to go out, and took me out with them when I really wanted to go.

It felt good. I don't think I've ever enjoyed being penniless quite so much!

And it meant I could horde my last bit of money to pay my rent and food bill at Liberty. They'd been good to me there, and the last thing I wanted to do was cheat them.

The full moon loomed large, and Linda and Ridvan took me out to cheer me up. Not that I was unhappy by that stage, but I was still fairly stressed about the whole situation. Because it couldn't go on forever; none of my friends were what you'd call wealthy, and I couldn't expect them to pay my way forever.

Gill had been in touch, and she'd reacted to my news by offering me a free place to stay with Krista's family in Australia. She was already living there after all, and she said they wouldn't mind having one extra mouth to feed.

And then I'd be able to get a proper job…

Understandably, that option became my absolute last resort.

Then, returning from the Full Moon Party, I discovered that my bungalow had been broken into and the last of my cash had been taken.

It smacked of an inside job; I'd never been overly cautious about hiding my money, and there were a few local workers who could have spotted me taking notes from the stash under my pillow. The door had been locked, and remained so; they could only have come in through the window, which due to the bungalow being on stilts, would have required a ladder. Nothing else was taken, and no other bungalows were raided that night. All the evidence seemed to suggest that someone in the know had snuck up through the jungle behind my place and gone straight for the thing they were after: my last £50 in all the world.

"What I don't get is how they managed to get in and out without anyone hearing them," I told Linda. We were sitting on my balcony; I was lamenting the loss of my money and she was trying to convince me it would all be okay.

"You're right," she said. "the dogs go crazy every time I arrive after dark, and they all know me. Imagine the noise they'd make if someone showed up with a ladder!"

"Yeah, that's a good point. I haven't seen Peto since…" And then a sick feeling began to develop in the pit of my stomach.

"I haven't seen him since before the full moon."

"Oh…" said Linda. "Oh no."

We never found Peto. We looked for a whole week, spending every scrap of free time combing the jungle around Liberty, scanning the beach for an hour in both directions… all to no avail. Peto had always been a wanderer, coming and going as he wished; he'd been sighted as far north as Thong Sala and as far south as Haad Rin. But he'd never been gone from Liberty for longer than a couple of days, and usually when he returned we could figure out why he'd been gone; more often than not he'd been out looking for someone who hadn't come home from a party, and he showed up again not long after they did.

Okay, so maybe that's a bit of a leap, but we'd all seen him on escort duty, protecting drunken residents on their excursions here and there. As incredible as it seems we had no problem believing he was actively on a mission to protect the humans he shared his home with.

We scoured the surrounding terrain more in fear than in hope. Enough dogs had been poisoned in our time that we knew how they behaved. They tended to crawl off somewhere and hide, until they either got better or died. In all our searching we found the remains of a few different animals, but never anything that could have been Peto.

We asked at every resort within a couple of miles, and we were stunned to hear that all of them knew him. Quite a few places had stories of times when he'd helped people out, or chased off troublemakers, or raised the alarm when something was amiss. Peto, it turned out, was known by a different name in every resort along the beach, and all of them held him in high regard.

But none of them had seen him more recently than we had.

I'd like to think that he took off, deciding it was time to spread his wings a bit; or even that he'd been stolen and sold to a new owner, as dog kidnapping was quite common on the island, particularly for dogs in such great condition. But then again, I can't imagine the person that could successfully kidnap that dog. He was smarter than I was for one thing, and a whole lot more intimidating.

Realistically, as time wore on with no sighting, we had to face the likelihood that he'd been killed by whoever had robbed my bungalow; most likely someone he knew, perhaps even one of the locals who worked at Liberty from time to time. He'd probably crawled away to die in the undergrowth, and what was left of him would have been long gone before we ever found it.

It was an unfair ending for so noble a protector, such a beautiful, powerful, intelligent animal.

We missed him a lot.

All Better Now

The gears of bureaucracy meshed and turned. I received forms to fill out detailing the rogue transactions and made an official statement saying the same thing I'd said on the phone – I couldn't possibly have taken that money out. All the transactions were listed at a bank I'd never heard of, at a branch in Surat Thani on the mainland – at least five hours by boat from Koh Pha Ngan. Had I lived in London, it would be like having the money taken out of an ATM in Dublin.

The gears turned slowly but surely, and a few weeks after my shocking discovery, the money was back in my account.

Banks, eh! Some people love 'em, some hate 'em. So far, for me, they've been bloody fantastic.

Another of my serious problems reached a happy conclusion that week.

Around the same time my bank account was refilling with cash, I was lying in my hammock nursing the most painful injury I could ever remember having.

It had started as a cut, deep but relatively clean, caused by some coral on an aborted attempt to do a night dive.

I loved being underwater after dark; the calmness seemed creepy, the marine life more active and scary as a result. And always, niggling away at the back of my mind, there was the threat of disappearing into the bottomless gloom never to be seen again. Even thinking about it sends a shiver of excitement down my spine!

Unfortunately, on this occasion the sea had been a bit rougher than we'd anticipated. Whilst picking our way delicately through the shallows, walking out towards deeper water where we could float while we strapped on our fins, we'd been buffeted by wave after wave. Eventually we'd given it up as too dangerous, but not before I'd sliced my foot on a razor-sharp chunk of pretty pink coral.

The cut had become infected within days.

I'd tried everything to keep it clean, and when it got darker and more swollen I'd forced myself to be a man and sliced the thing open with a razor blade from the clinic. The pain of cutting through the skin was nothing compared to the relief I got once all the ickyness inside the wound had been squeezed out. I'd considered asking Por to stitch me up, but in the end I settled for a load of dressing pads and bandages, and had spent a couple of days off my foot, resting.

Then I'd gone diving again and the wound had gone right back to being a swollen, puss-filled mess.

"It's the water," Nick had told me. "There's nothing you can do about it. The temperature of water in the UK is so low that sea water helps to clean a wound, but here the water is warm. Bacteria thrive in it, so any cut you take underwater is guaranteed to be infected by the time you get out. The only thing to do is take a week off and let it heal completely before you get back in the water."

As always, Nick knew his stuff. I wasn't happy to be off diving for a week, and even less so for such a stupid reason.

One tiny little cut… but it hurt like hell to touch it.

Once at the clinic one of the dogs had got close enough to stand on it, and I'd come close to passing out from the pain.

So, pathetic or not, this cut needed resting, and I was doing exactly that, under Captain's Orders.

I trusted Nick way more than any doctor on the island.

Ridvan was taking the opportunity to discuss his latest t-shirt designs, and Linda, in a rare day off from the clinic, had popped round to see how I was getting on.

"It's itchy as hell," I moaned, wriggling my feet around in the hammock.

"Don't scratch it! Bad Tony!" said Linda.

"Easy for you to say. I can't help it!"

"If you would only start wearing shoes again, this sort of thing wouldn't happen."

"Leave him alone," said Ridvan, "he's doing great!"

I twitched again.

"Oh, scratch your damn foot," said Ridvan, "it's driving me crazy! I'll scratch it for you. Then maybe we can get some work done."

And then the wound didn't need scratching anymore, because it burst.

A sour smell drifted out from it and the edges of the cut began to move.

"Holy fucking shit, man!" yelled Ridvan. He was looking right at the thing when an army of tiny white spiders began to spill out of it, darting across my foot and vanishing between my toes.

"Jesus Tone, they're alive!" Linda screeched.

I scrambled out of the hammock and grabbed a cloth to press against my foot. It came away soaked with nastiness, and with a few more of the microscopic critters clinging to its surface.

"Holy shit man, did that just happen?"

All three of us craned our necks to study the wound.

"Well, whatever they were, they're gone now," I said.

I never found out what they were, because I never wanted to know. Even now, writing this, the memory of it makes me a little queasy.

A few days later I called Nick to tell him I'd be back diving again, because I was 'all better now'.

From that day, my motto about tiny white spiders invading abscesses on my body is the same as my motto about farts and projectile vomiting: 'Better out than in.'

I thought I'd share that nugget of information with you, in case any of you are wondering why after all this time on the island I *still* didn't have a girlfriend…

What I did have, was a use for the cash that had been miraculously restored to my bank account. Losing it had driven home a lesson I should have learned much earlier; I was never going to get richer in Thailand, only poorer. My diving wages were never going to keep me in the style to which I'd become accustomed; slowly but surely the money would trickle out, never to return. Were it not for the goodwill of the fraud squad, I'd already be stuck in a very tricky position – forced to live on the charity of others until I got so sick of it (or they did) that I begged money from my parents to buy a ticket home.

It wouldn't be the noblest end to my grand adventure.

But there was one other choice, and even though I shied away from making it, I knew that sooner or later I would run out of options.

While I was still solvent I emailed Gill, and asked her how she was doing in Australia.

And if there was a place there for me.

Even typing the words felt like a betrayal of all I'd experienced in Thailand. I was part of the expat crowd now, that handful of somewhat damaged individuals that no longer wanted to face life outside the island. All of us were looking for some way to stay there forever – from Ridvan with his t-shirts and websites to the English guys that married Thai girls and opened bars, or struggled to make a name for themselves as DJs on the party scene.

It worked for some of them – the ones who had skills perhaps, or just the right level of determination.

But Gill was right. I couldn't stay here forever. Sooner or later I'd become as jaded as the bitter old English guys that sat inside drinking right through *Songkran*. If I even lasted that long.

My money, alas, would not.

Gill's reply was jubilant. Without saying 'I told you so' in so many words, she explained that she'd been expecting the email and was looking forward to my arrival. She'd even predicted when I'd get in touch, based on my panicked messages when I first realized I'd been robbed. She told me there was room for me in Roo's family home in Perth, and that I should stop arsing around and get over there ASAP.

It made me feel better, knowing that I had *options*.

But then, who was I trying to kid? Unless I wanted to go home to England, I really had no options at all.

So I splashed the last of my cash on two rather expensive items, neither of which I really wanted; a working holiday visa for Australia, which would at least allow me to find some sort of work over there, and a one-way flight to Perth.

The decision was made.

Now all I had to do was tell Linda and Ridvan.

By way of an epilogue, many moons and many thousands of miles later, I was advising a friend to take advantage of the cheap diving gear available in Thailand, when something clicked in my head.

"I bought mine on credit from the dive school," I'd told him. "There was a random ATM about three doors down, so I took out as much as I could each day, and paid it off in instalments."

And that's when it hit me.

That tiny ATM wasn't even attached to a bank; its transactions must have been processed somewhere else – say, on the mainland for instance.

Those fraudulent transactions, evenly spaced, coincided directly with the days I'd been diving; that was one of the reasons I'd given to prove that I couldn't have been in Surat Thani to make the withdrawals.

Whereas in actual fact, on each of those days I'd been giving Nick a chunk of cash to pay for all the gear he'd ordered for me.

I'd defrauded myself, without even realising it.

And luckily enough, the bank never realised it either. So, just for now let's keep that between us, okay?

All Good Things...

...must come to an end.

And so it was with my time in Thailand.

I'd been on Koh Pha Ngan for over ten months; it felt more like home than any place I'd ever known.

Linda had taken the morning off to help me pack, and to drive me to the ferry – I was bike-less for the first time in as long as I could remember.

When I'd returned it (and settled my final repair bill), Yorik had offered to give me a lift to the pier himself. I'd told him thanks, but I'd be okay.

It wouldn't have been the most emotional of farewells.

I dug out the running shoes I hadn't worn since my arrival, and held them up for Linda's approval. "I'll have to wear these when I get to the airport, or they won't let me board the plane. Don't tell Ridvan though."

"Tone, I don't *care* what Ridvan thinks. Just please be careful."

"I'm always careful!"

"No, you're not."

She had a point. "Well, I'm lucky then."

She thought about this for a couple of seconds. "Not really, you're not."

"Ah. Well then. Hey, I'll survive!"

"Yes, you'll survive," she conceded. "But I don't know if I will."

"I know what you mean. Oh Linda, I'm going to miss you so much."

"I know. And you only came here for three months!" she shook her head sadly. "Oh, Tone. I can't believe you're going."

Ridvan had gone one step further; he refused to believe I was going. In fact he was so sure that I'd change my mind at the last minute and stay here for good, that he told me he wasn't coming to the pier to say good-bye at all.

He'd said he knew I could never leave.

Unfortunately… I was going to.

I had no choice, really, or I'd have stayed for sure. I had way too much to lose here. But I'd been eking out my cash for as long as humanly possible; there was no hiding from it now. I was completely and utterly broke. I had almost nothing to pack; my enormous rucksack was stuffed with diving gear. I'd divided my remaining clothes into two small piles – one to keep, and one to donate to the clinic. Then I'd looked hard at the clothes in both piles and decided to donate the lot. The clinic was always in need material to use as rags and cage-liners, and most of my wardrobe was fit for nothing else.

The rest of it – what I thought of as the good stuff – I was wearing.

The flight to Perth, and my Australian visa, had been partially paid for on my credit card.

I'd be arriving there penniless, in debt, with no friends and few prospects… well, Gill would be there. I'd be relying on her, and her friend Roo, and Roo's family – for everything.

At least until I got a real job.

I stood on the pier, rucksack at my feet, and scanned the circling traffic for Ridvan. He really wasn't coming. I should have known he'd be dramatic about this.

Linda embraced me one last time as a blast on the ferry whistle signalled its imminent departure. I'd put this off until the last possible moment, even to the point of nearly missing my boat, but I finally had to say good-bye.

The words stuck in my throat, so Linda said it for me; "Come back to us, Tone, when you can. It won't be the same without you."

"I'll try," I managed.

And suddenly there was Ridvan, hurtling down the pier at breakneck speed. He leapt off his bike almost before it stopped moving, sprinted towards me and threw himself bodily onto me. If he'd been a bigger man he might have knocked me down with the force of his hug, but Ridvan weighed less than my bag full of diving gear; I could have picked him up with one hand.

So I did.

"Don't go!" he wailed.

"I'll be back," I promised him, and the cheesiness of the moment nearly rescued me from tears.

Nearly. But not quite.

And then I really did have to go, calling out to the boat crew to replace the gang-plank they'd just removed. I carted my luggage across it and stood by the railing, tears streaming down my face, and watched as the people and the life I'd loved so much receded into memory.

I climbed up through the rusty decks of the boat and stared back at the magnificence of Koh Pha Ngan.

This view of the island, a ribbon of pristine sand wrapping the lush green jungle, was every bit as beautiful as the day I'd arrived – and it was sharpened now by a heart-breaking poignancy.

I turned my back on it, and wept some more.

My thoughts drifted back over all that had happened to me since my arrival. The parties – yeah, well they all kind of blended into each other after a while. Jumping through fire hoops, staggering around a beach crowded with drunken revellers from every corner of the globe – snapshots of memory, like pages from a photo album I only half remembered making.

What had really made me feel alive on Koh Pha Ngan was the sense of responsibility and identity. The warm, easy friendship of so many volunteers come and gone over the months. And the feeling of belonging – both to a group of close friends, and to something just slightly bigger than all of us.

I wasn't just leaving Linda and Ridvan, and Por and Avril; not just the bricks and mortar, and temperamental washing machines of the clinic, the kennels full of patients and the house full of puppies and kittens; somewhere back there amidst those gleaming strips of white sand I'd found something even harder to part with. I'd found a purpose.

The train to Bangkok – First Class this time – passed in a melancholy blur.

Eventually I found myself on the plane, accelerating through the night sky towards Australia.

I sat there, pondering my future, trying to feel hopeful.

I couldn't. I was bereft.

It was the lowest I'd felt since leaving Ecuador.

And even back then, I'd buoyed myself up with the thought of adventures to come.

But this time was different. *This* had been that adventure – a year in the planning, and the waiting, and the dreaming, and the setbacks, and then finally getting here – and now it was all over.

The real world was coming back with a vengeance.

I didn't have much in the way of work references; I was going to have to take any shitty job I could get. I couldn't imagine it would be pretty.

Good-bye hammock-time, hello to eight-to-six.

Manual labour…

I'd never see the sun again.

Okay. This was getting silly. It wasn't the end of the world. It might be the end of life as I'd known it, but that was no reason to get upset. *Change is always difficult,* I reminded myself, *and always much scarier to think about than to actually experience.*

Sure, I'd have the blues for a while – it was only to be expected.

I'd been borderline suicidal after Ecuador, but I'd gotten over it eventually.

It would work out. It would also be tough. But I'd survive.

And in all my time on Koh Pha Ngan, and as happy as I'd been, one thing had still eluded me: true love.

Maybe I'll get me some of that in Australia?

That thought made me smile for the first time since waking up in my bungalow over twenty-four hours ago.

I arrived in Perth, disconsolate and hollow.

Later on in the flight I'd turned to drink, which would have been my undoing were it not for the incredible tolerance for alcohol I'd built up over the last ten months.

Now I was dehydrated, sweating and clammy, stinking of booze that had hardly affected me, and wearing clothes that would earn a scarecrow some pity.

It didn't occur to me until I was stood in front of the Immigration desk that they might not like the look of me; that they might not let me in at all.

Especially since I was technically still AWOL from the British Army…

"G'day mate," said the Customs Officer, fulfilling a stereotype I'd been wondering about.

"Hiya. I mean, hello, sir."

"How long are you hoping to stay in Australia?"

"A year. I have this working holiday visa…"

I had a bad feeling. I'd been in this queue before. I had no money. I didn't even have a return flight. I braced myself for the inevitable barrage of questions.

"Working holiday eh? Great! Enjoy your stay, mate." And he stamped me through.

Just like that! Perhaps Australia really was as chilled out as people said.

Through the doors to the baggage claim, I dragged my dive gear off the carousel. There was a palpable air of excitement, as though the other people on my flight actually wanted to be here. I pushed my trolley down a corridor thronged with happy, hurrying people, and felt more alone than ever.

My great adventure, I said to myself, *and this is where it ends*.

The Arrivals hall was awash with sunlight. The front wall was entirely glass, the blue sky beyond it, spotless.

Even before my eyes adjusted, I heard Gill's shriek of joy.

She ran over and wrapped me in a bear-hug.

"Tony, you're HERE! At last! And you're wearing SHOES!"

"Well, it… seemed rude not to."

"You remember Roo, right?"

Roo also stepped in and gave me a big hug, which went a long way to restoring my spirits. She'd changed too, in the time since I'd last met her. She seemed… confident. Happier. More at peace.

I'd almost forgotten how pretty she was.

"I can't believe you're finally here," Gill said. Excitement shone in her eyes, her whole face was lit up with enthusiasm.

"Well, you know…" I didn't really have anything to say in the face of such an ecstatic welcome. Truth be told I felt a bit guilty now, that I'd been stringing her along all this time.

The girls led me outside to the car park, where my eyes beheld the most ridiculous vehicle I had ever seen.

It was a van – but a crappy old thing, that was clearly falling apart at the seams.

And it was completely covered in red, yellow, blue, green and purple splodges, artfully applied so that not an inch was left undecorated. And in the centre of every splodge, was a hand-print. "Those are ours," Gill said proudly.

"No shit."

"And on the roof is a life-size silhouette of Roo. We drew around her and spray-painted it onto the van!"

"It's for the traffic 'copters," Roo chipped in.

"That's… that's very creative."

"It's awesome, is what it is!"

You know what? I had to agree with her. It did look kind of awesome.

But I couldn't tell Gill that. Not straight away.

"It looks like a unicorn threw up all over it."

"Pah! You're just jealous."

"Jealous? Of you guys, riding around in that thing?"

"Hey, watch what you say about Rusty. You'll be riding in him too, you know."

"In *him?*"

"He's called Rusty. He's a boy."

I sighed. "So we're going home in that then, are we?"

"Not just home. We're going to travel all around Australia! We're going to go everywhere, and do everything! I'm so glad you're here, we've been waiting for you for weeks."

"Waiting for me?"

"Yes! Don't you see? This is *it!* The big one. We'll work as we go, whenever we need to, and camp out in the bush, and see Ayers Rock and Sydney and… and all the other cool places. Loads of them! We'll call it the Voyages of Rusty."

"No shit he's Rusty! I don't think you'll get very far in that thing… I can see daylight through the floor in at least three places."

"Hey! What did I say about dissing Rusty? Treat him with respect, because he's going to take us all over the country. You, me and Roo. What do you reckon? Are you up for it?"

They were both looking at me, both so eager, that I could feel my own excitement rising to match.

Gill and I had been best friends my entire life; there were worse things to do than take a road trip with her. And I was already starting to like the way Roo was looking at me. Yup, being penned up with her in a knackered old van for a couple of months didn't sound like too much of a hardship.

And anyway, I had a reputation to think about.

This was what I did.

"Yeah, alright then. Why not? Let's do it."

"Hell YES!" Gill was elated. She unlocked a sliding door in the side of the van. As she yanked it open it gave a squeal of protest, then fell off in her hands.

"Don't worry," she said, "he does that."

"Oh, goody. What else does he do?"

"I don't know, but we're going to find out! This is *it*, Tony. It's going to be epic, I can feel it. This is where it all starts! After all this time – the adventure is about to begin!"

THE END…?

Hi folks! Tony here...

Thank-you so much for buying and reading my book! I'm sorry it's not as good as the first one. But don't worry, it doesn't end there – the adventure continues in 'Kamikaze Kangaroos!'. If you have any questions, or feedback (or you're interested in dating my sister) please do get in touch. I love to hear from my readers, and I'm always on the lookout for suggestions and critique, so don't be shy!

Check out my website, which includes pictures than accompany this book:

www.TonyJamesSlater.com

And you can find me on Twitter:
> **http://twitter.com/TonyJamesSlater**

or catch me on Facebook:
> **http://facebook.com/TonyJamesSlater**

or you can always email me:
> **TonyJamesSlater@hotmail.com**

Also, please consider leaving a review on Amazon. It can be super-short – even just a line or two – but it might fool other people into buying my books. BWAH HA HA! Yes, word of mouth is vital to me. I always read my reviews (and sometimes dance around the room a bit afterwards) – and I really, *really* appreciate you writing them!

'Kamikaze Kangaroos!'

This is my third book, and it carries on directly from where 'Don't Need The Whole Dog' leaves off. It follows the misadventures of Gill, Roo and myself as we try to coax poor Rusty across the length and breadth of Australia. Suffice to say, we ran into a few snags here and there – not the least of which was the apparently suicidal wildlife!

'Kamikaze Kangaroos!' is a tale of fun, adventure, accidents and – dare I say it – romance. It is followed by a fourth book, but I can't tell you anything about that yet. It would spoil the surprise...

Here's the blurb:

Tony James Slater knew nothing about Australia.
Except for the fact that he'd just arrived there.

The stage is set for an outrageous adventure: three people, one van, on an epic, 20,000 mile road trip around Australia. What could possibly go wrong?

Of course, the van – nicknamed 'Rusty' – is a crumbling wreck, held together by the world's most garish paint job.

They're criss-crossing the continent through some of the most inhospitable land on the planet – the infamous Aussie Outback.

And isn't there something about Australian animals being... well, you know, kind of dangerous?

Unprepared, under-qualified and hopelessly inept, Tony battles gigantic pumpkins, mechanical mishaps and suicidal kangaroos, armed only with a thong and a sense of humour.

His companions struggle to keep him safe whilst climbing in drag, snowboarding off cliffs, and hiking hundreds of miles through the bush.

One thing's for sure; this 'adventure of a lifetime' – if they survive it – is something they're never going to forget.

So, scull those stubbies!
Grab your galahs!
And put down that platypus.
LOOK OUT, AUSTRALIA!
There's an idiot coming…

Find it by typing 'Kamikaze Kangaroos!' into Amazon now!

And check out the next page for a pair of books written by some close friends of mine – if you're enjoying my memoirs, you'll LOVE theirs!

'Free Country'
by George Mahood

The plan is simple. George and Ben have three weeks to cycle 1000 miles from the bottom of England to the top of Scotland. There is just one small problem... they have no bikes, no clothes, no food and no money. Setting off in just a pair of Union Jack boxer shorts, they attempt to rely on the generosity of the British public for everything from food to accommodation, clothes to shoes, and bikes to beer.

During the most hilarious adventure, George and Ben encounter some of Great Britain's most eccentric and extraordinary characters and find themselves in the most ridiculous situations. Free Country is guaranteed to make you laugh (you may even shed a tear). It will restore your faith in humanity and leave you with a big smile on your face and a warm feeling inside.

Find 'Free Country' on Amazon now!

'More Ketchup than Salsa'
by Joe Cawley

When Joe and his girlfriend Joy decide to trade in their life on a cold Lancashire fish market to run a bar in the Tenerife sunshine, they anticipate a paradise of sea, sand and siestas. Little did they expect their foreign fantasy to turn out to be about as exotic as Bolton on a wet Monday morning.

A hilarious insight into the wild and wacky characters of an expat community in a familiar holiday destination, More Ketchup than Salsa is a must-read for anybody who has ever dreamed about jetting off to sunnier climes, finding a job abroad, or momentarily flirted with the idea of 'doing a Shirley Valentine' in these trying economic times.

Check out 'More Ketchup' on Amazon!

About the Author

Tony James Slater is a very, very strange man. He believes himself to be indestructible, despite considerable evidence to the contrary. He is often to be found making strange faces whilst pretending to be attacked by inanimate objects. And sometimes – not always, but often enough to be of concern – his testicles hang out of the holes in his trousers.

It is for this reason (amongst others) that he chooses to spend his life far from mainstream civilization, tackling ridiculous challenges and subjecting himself to constant danger. He gets hurt quite a lot.

To see pictures from his adventures, read Tony's blog, or complain about his shameless self promotion, please visit:

www.TonyJamesSlater.com

But BE WARNED! Some of the writing is in red.